ANIMAL FACTORIES

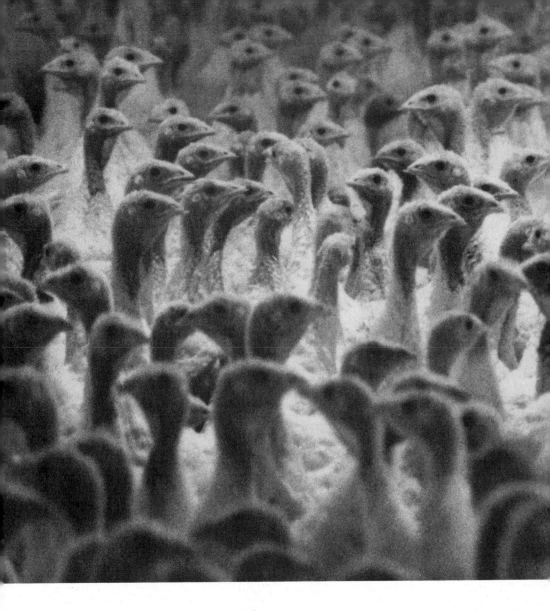

ANIMAL

Jim Mason

FACTORIES

and Peter Singer

HARMONY BOOKS/NEW YORK

Books by Jim Mason
Animal Factories

Books by Peter Singer
Animal Factories
Democracy and Disobedience
Animal Liberation
Practical Ethics
Animal Rights and Human Obligations
(edited with Tom Regan)

Copyright © 1980, 1990 by Jim Mason and Peter Singer

Published by Harmony Books, a division of Crown Publishers, Inc., 201 East 50th Street, New York, New York 10022. Member of the Crown Publishing Group.

HARMONY and colophon are trademarks of Crown Publishers, Inc.

Manufactured in the United States of America

Library of Congress Cataloging-in-Publication Data

Mason, Jim.
    Animal factories / Jim Mason and Peter Singer. — [Rev. and updated ed.]
        p.   cm.
    "A Herbert Michelman book."
    1. Livestock factories. 2. Livestock factories—United States.
3. Animal food. 4. Animal industry—United States. I. Singer, Peter. II. Title.
SF140.L58M37   1990
179'.3—dc20   89-26750
                                                               CIP

ISBN 0-517-57751-8
10 9 8 7 6 5 4 3 2 1
Revised Edition

CONTENTS

ACKNOWLEDGMENTS

AS WE LOOK BACK FIFTEEN YEARS to the beginning of our work on this book, we think of a great many people who helped. For those early years, we owe special thanks to Alice Herrington, who suggested that we get together and write a book about the brave new world of mechanized animal farming.

Among the other early contributors to this book are Peter Roberts, Thelma Knight, and Kim Stallwood of Compassion in World Farming and Joanne Bower of the Farm and Food Society. We owe special thanks to them for information on farm animal welfare issues and legislation in Europe. Many others helped collect information or point us to the right sources: Jim Behrenholtz, Connie Salamone, Tom Smith, Alex Hershaft, and Robin Hur, to name a few. We had some good help, too, with typing, photography, translations, and travel, so thank you again, Jennifer Killian, Esther Mechler, Ede Rothaus, Kristin Johnson, Heidi Lindy, Susan Markey, and Eileen Myerson.

We owe special recognition to Patricia Curtis for reviewing those early drafts and for her helpful suggestions. Finally, thanks again to our first editors at Crown Publishers, Herbert Michelman and Peter Burford, for helping us put together an important and lasting book.

Upon revising this book in 1989, we learned that that can be as big a chore as writing it the first time. We had an awful lot of work to do in a very short time, and we could not have done it without the help of these very good people:

Cheryl Freedman of *Farm Journal* made sure that we were informed and up to date on major agricultural issues, as did Louise Risk and Robert A. Brown of Food Animal Concerns Trust. Gene and Lorri Bauston of Farm Animal Sanctuary and Donald Barnes were helpful with relevant information as well as general encouragement. Special thanks, too, to George Cave and Dana Stuchell of Trans-Species Unlimited for updating us on the rabbit industry.

For details on regional issues and developments, we thank Margaret Asproyerakas, Eileen Liska, Alex Hershaft, Melinda Calleia, and Vicky Eide.

Special thanks to Dan Howell, Roger Blobaum, and Beth Kaufman of Americans for Safe Food for briefing us on the food safety legislative and regulatory front and for steering us to other good sources of information on agricultural issues.

For in-depth information on the European scene, thanks to Joyce D'Silva of Compassion in World Farming and Diane Halverson of the Animal Welfare Institute.

Special thanks to the unsung hero of this book, J. A. Keller, the photographer who trudged over, through, and under dozens of confinement facilities and endured weeks of solitary confinement in his darkroom to produce the photographs for this book.

Finally, Kathy Belden, our editor at Harmony Books of Crown Publishers, deserves special thanks and recognition for initiating this revised edition, and for her thoughtful advice and hard work on our manuscript.

To all of the above, we are grateful; the responsibility for errors and inaccuracies, however, is ours alone.

J. M.
P. S.

PREFACE

SINCE THIS BOOK FIRST APPEARED in 1980, the trends that we documented have worsened. Some would say they have reached the crisis stage. We think things reached the crisis stage for farm animals decades ago, as soon as growing them in narrow crates and crowded pens was made viable by antibiotics and powerful veterinary drugs.

But then people have a way of keeping animals out of their sphere of concern. In retrospect, it would have been wiser to have noted the diseases and suffering in the first factory animals, for they were a harbinger of what was to come for all who consume meat, milk, and eggs.

Few would deny that we are having a farm crisis, as we watch small-to-moderate, family-run farms going under at record rates. Their rural communities—local businesses, civic organizations, schools, and churches—are drying up with them. Yet right beside them, among the ruins of barns and farmhouses, agribusiness corporations are building larger and larger new megafactories where farm animals never see the light of day until they are herded into trucks for the ride to the slaughterhouse.

Only the foolish would deny that we are approaching an environmental crisis across the land, and much of it is occurring in the regions where our food is produced. For years, agricultural drugs and chemicals brought amazing productivity and profits for some. Lately, yields have been less than amazing and the long-deferred costs of chemical carelessness are coming due. Much of the land and its waters are polluted with agrichemicals. In some farming regions, farmers' wells cannot be used because the water table is contaminated. What are we to do for food when the nation's breadbasket is poisoned?

Fortunately, as you will learn toward the end of this book, many farmers and others are fed up with these trends and are beginning new directions in agriculture and animal production. There is so much to be changed, but there is much cause for hope.

Our only disappointment is that *Animal Factories'* message did not get through to farmers. What little of it that did was filtered through agribusiness channels and heavily colored with hostility. Many farmers and rural people have never read what we have to say about their situation because they have been taught to hate this book, these ideas. We humbly ask them to lay aside their prejudices and what they have heard and to see for themselves whether we understand the farmer's plight. To those who will do so, we suggest that they begin reading with chapters 7 and 9, the parts of most interest to farmers.

We want to emphasize, then, that this book does not intend to brand farmers as cruel or abusive to farm animals. Those terms denote deliberate, calculated acts, which are quite beside the point of this book. The main idea here is that through modern humanity's obsession with efficiency and productivity, a cruel, oppressive, costly, and dangerous *system* for managing farm animals has been created, and this system takes its toll on not only the animals, but the farmers as well.

Jim Mason

INTRODUCTION

by Jim Mason

THE REALITY OF A MODERN ANIMAL factory stands in sharp contrast to the farm of our fantasies. The farm in our mind's eye is a pleasant, peaceful place where calves nuzzle their mothers in shady fields, pigs loaf in mudholes, and chickens scratch and scramble about barnyards. The farm animals in our fantasy live tranquil, easy lives. So we like to believe—because if they have fresh air, good food, exercise, and rest, we have more wholesome and delicious meat, eggs, and milk.

I remember this kind of farm. I was raised on one in Missouri in the forties and fifties. The animals on farms then were truly domestic, that is, they were a part of the farm household. Families lived from and cared for their animals. Through natural growth and reproduction, the animals produced enough to supply the household and bring in a small but steady flow of cash from sales in nearby markets.

Farms like the one of my childhood are rapidly being replaced by animal factories. Animals are reared in huge buildings, crowded in cages stacked up like so many shipping crates. On the factory farms there are no pastures, no streams, no seasons, not even day and night. Animal-wise herdsmen and milkmaids have been replaced by automated feeders, computers, closed-circuit television, and vacuum pumps. Health and productivity come not from frolics in sunny meadows but from syringes and additive-laced feed.

I began learning about the trend to animal factories in the early 1970s. I knew that our routine uses of animals involved restrictions and manipulations that would be regarded as atrocities if practiced on humans. I began to realize that to make things easier on ourselves as we make use of animals, we also hide or deny the unpleasant reality of what we are doing.

The real nature of factory farming was indeed hard to believe. The contrast to my own farm experience was too strong; I assumed that there were only a few factories and that they were isolated examples. As I looked more deeply, I was overwhelmed by the awesome scale and pervasiveness of this new way of animal rearing. I was amazed how little the public knew about these drastic changes in the production of their food.

My efforts to find out more about factory farming were given a boost in 1974 when I met Peter Singer, who was then teaching philosophy at New York University and writing his book *Animal Liberation*. The book documents humans' tyranny over other animals and explains why it is wrong. Together we decided to look more closely at the trend to animal factories and to write this book. At first my view of factory methods went little further than the animal welfare problems that Peter exposed in *Animal Liberation*. Before long, I learned that "confinement," or "intensive" farming as it is called in agricultural circles, raises many other problems as well: health, waste, dislocation of rural communities, pollution, and an overemphasis on technological solutions to problems arising from animal nature.

Research into any major activity of this sort requires a firsthand look. I subscribed to farming magazines and wrote to agricultural schools and states for information. I traveled about fourteen thousand miles, visiting farms and agricultural research centers from Canada to Nebraska to Georgia. I spoke with farmers, scientists, and others involved in the trend toward factory farms. The methods described here and the photographs shown are not intended to be typical of all American agriculture. There are still many traditional, diversified farms. But these descriptions and photographs do illustrate the trend in animal production toward greater concentration of animals, large-scale production, labor-saving machinery, growth acceleration, and other factory methods.

It should be clear that this book is not intended to be an attack on farmers and the people who run factory farms. They are as much victims of factory technology, although in a different way, as are the animals. No stranger to the economics and other realities of farm life, I am familiar with farm people and the feelings they have about making a living from their land. They are buffeted by economic developments that force them to try to push their animals to greater and greater productivity. It is a double tragedy that many farmers wind up losing their farm livelihood because the present trend culminates in a way of farming beyond their financial reach.

This book, then, is about a dominant trend in perhaps our most basic economic activity. For the past nine thousand years, farm animals have relieved humans from much of the toil of production, allowing us to devote time to civilization. Today, animal agriculture is our largest food industry and one that affects our lives daily. We must not be blind to the changes it undergoes—not only for our own good but for the good of nature around us.

No light, but rather darkness visible
Served only to discover sights of woe,
Regions of sorrow, doleful shades, where peace
And rest can never dwell, hope never comes
That comes to all; but torture without end . . .

—John Milton, *Paradise Lost*

1 FACTORY

LIFE

What It's Like
to Be a Biomachine

The modern layer is, after all, only a very efficient converting machine, changing the raw material—feedstuffs—into the finished product—the egg—less, of course, maintenance requirements.
—*Farmer and Stockbreeder,* January 30, 1962

Forget the pig is an animal. Treat him just like a machine in a factory. Schedule treatments like you would lubrication. Breeding season like the first step in an assembly line. And marketing like the delivery of finished goods.
—J. Byrnes, "Raising Pigs by the Calendar at Maplewood Farm," *Hog Farm Management,* September 1976, p. 30

Broilers blooming to market size 40 percent quicker, miniature hens cranking out eggs in double time, a computer "cookbook" of recipes for custom-designed creatures—this could well be the face of animal production in the 21st century.
—"Farm Animals of the Future," *Agricultural Research* (Washington, D.C.: U.S. Department of Agriculture), April 1989, p. 4

THERE ARE TWO KINDS OF CHICKENS. In the realm of symbol, baby chicks are Life and Innocence; the broody, nesting hen is archetypal Mother; and the rooster, or cock, is Sentinel and Protector of the household. But the other chicken, the actual chicken, is something else—or so we believe. They are brainless, cowardly, mean-tempered, and filthy; chickens scratch in the dirt and eat disgusting things. All the more reason, then—since they are to end up on our dinner plates—to strictly confine and regiment them to a factory-style assembly line.

This makes the modern factory farm seem a wonderful necessity, as it cleans up the chicken's act for us. Put well beyond the range of our sympathies, the birds can be hatched, sorted, stocked, stacked, slashed, scalded, plucked, hacked, and packed by the billions each year. What was once a scrappy jungle fowl—ruler of its own roost in the rain forests of southeast Asia—now seems hardly an animal at all, but edible biomass, fungible goods, and a sort of living food processor.

There were some two thousand years of domestication, but the real plunge in

1

the demise of the chicken occurred in the twentieth century. It began in Delaware in 1923 when Mrs. Wilmer Steele succeeded in raising the first few flocks of broiler chickens indoors through the winter. The discovery of vitamins A and D had made this possible: When these vitamins were added to the birds' feed, sunlight and exercise were no longer necessary for adequate growth and bone development. Then in the years before World War II, farmers near large cities began to specialize in the year-round production of chickens to meet the demand of nearby markets for eggs and meat.

Large-scale production caught on. Farmers built bigger buildings for larger flocks and larger profits. But large flocks meant more labor, and the crowding produced a host of problems. In the poorly ventilated new buildings, contagious diseases were rampant, and losses multiplied throughout the budding poultry industry. Entire flocks were wiped out. Nightmarish scenes occurred in large, crowded flocks: some birds would peck others to death and eat their remains. Many farmers were ruined and gave up farming; but the more persistent looked for solutions to these self-induced problems.

During the war years, demand for poultry was high. The boom in the chicken business attracted the attention of the largest feed and pharmaceutical companies, and they put their experts to work on the new problems associated with large-scale production. The breakthroughs to commercial production by factory methods began to come thick and fast. Burning off the tips of birds' beaks was found to reduce losses from pecking and cannibalism. An automatic debeaking machine was patented, and its use became routine within a few years. Newly developed hybrid corn made chickens put on weight faster. Automatic, chain-driven feeders ended the chore of carrying feed to the birds. Automatic fans, lights, and other labor-saving equipment followed. A mechanical chicken-plucker with whirling, rubber-fingered drums increased processing capacity while lowering labor costs.

The chicken itself, however, was not quite ready for mass production. In 1946, the Great Atlantic & Pacific Tea Company (now A&P) launched the "Chicken of Tomorrow" contest to find a strain of bird that could produce a broad-breasted carcass at a low feed cost. Within a few years, the prototype for today's fast-flesh broiler was developed. In the late 1940s, sulfa drugs and antibiotics were introduced as additives in chicken feed, for they held down disease losses and stimulated the chicken's rate of growth.

Bigger money was now being attracted to mechanized broiler production while bankruptcies and takeovers of small farmers, feed companies, and processors eliminated the old ways. These "shakeouts" occurred because the small producers and operators could not muster the capital that the factory mode of broiler production now needed. The end of World War II brought chaos to the growing industry through the loss of its biggest customer, the United States government. Conditions were ripe for those who had the money to take over production from the shakeouts at bargain prices. In the fifties and sixties, the major feed companies bought up most of these broiler operations, and major pharmaceutical companies began buying up breeding companies that were producing commercial chicken strains.[1]

The Cage Arrives

News of the success on the meat side of factory chicken production had spread to egg producers, and they tried the same methods. But one major new problem literally piled up: the confined, egg-laying hens produced tons of manure each week. Broiler producers had had the manure problem in their large flocks too, but their birds were in and out within twelve weeks and accumulations could be cleaned out between "crops." Egg farmers, however, kept their birds indoors for a year or more. They had to find a means of manure removal that would not disturb the hens or interfere with production. Producers discovered that they could confine layer hens in wire-mesh cages suspended over a trench to collect droppings. The manure pile could be cleaned out without bothering the hens above. At first, producers placed their birds one to each cage. When they found that birds were cheaper than wire and buildings, crowded cages in crowded houses became the rule. Crowding did mean that more hens died, but this cost was slight compared to the increased total egg output. Ever since, the Egg has come before the Chicken, and eggs—and chickens—have never been the same.

Nor have chicken farms. Between 1955 and 1975, flock size in a typical egg factory rose from twenty thousand to eighty thousand birds per house as producers learned to stuff and stack the cages.[2] Just as the cage brought a Brave New World for laying chickens, it brought the end of an era for family egg farmers. The automation of feeding, collecting eggs, and removing wastes made human labor and thousands of family egg farms obsolete. And it did so quietly and quickly. In 1967, 44 percent of commercial layers were caged; by 1978, 90 percent were caged.[3] Today, 95 percent or more of all egg production comes from caged birds in automated factory buildings.[4]

It took some time before anyone attempted to extend the mechanization practices of the poultry industry to larger farm animals. But poultry industry successes were an irresistible model for livestock experts. During the 1960s, they designed and built systems for pigs, cattle, and sheep that incorporated the principles of confinement, mass production, and automated feeding, watering, and ventilation. Instead of wire cages, which could not hold these heavier animals (although young pigs are now kept in wire cages on some farms), indoor pens and stalls were built over manure pits and fitted with slatted floors of concrete or steel planks spaced a fraction of an inch apart. This signaled the end of hand labor with pitchfork or shovel; now the farmer merely pumped out the pit every month or so.

As in any other industry, the fine details in methods and systems vary, but the basic processes are fairly standard.

Sorting chicks. Discarding males.

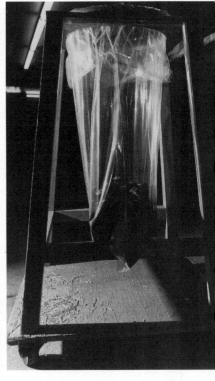

Manufacturing Egg-Laying Machines

The modern chicken is a business creation; it owes its existence to the sterile laboratories of a few "primary breeders." There are only about four of these companies, and their business is to engineer chickens into highly specialized makers of eggs and meat. They sell breeding males and females to some two hundred "multiplier" companies, which in turn produce the chicks that go to egg and broiler operations.

At the multipliers, the breeding birds are kept on open floors in long, low buildings. They are given ample space by poultry industry standards because uncrowded, unstressed birds turn out a greater stream of fertilized eggs. Their eggs are placed in an incubator for nineteen days and then transferred to a hatcher. When the chicks break out, they encounter the poultry industry's mass-handling techniques for the first time.

If the hatchery is turning out "egg-type" birds, the first order of business is to destroy half of the newly hatched chicks. Males don't lay eggs, and the flesh of these strains is of poor quality. So they are, literally, thrown away. We watched at one hatchery as "chick-pullers" weeded males from each tray and dropped them into heavy-duty plastic bags. Our guide explained: "We put them in a bag and let them suffocate. A mink farmer picks them up and feeds them to his mink."[5]

Now that the public has been made aware of the ongoing mass destruction of male egg-type chicks, the hatchery industry is making efforts to promote more humane methods, or at least methods that appear more humane. Some of these include killing by decapitation or by asphyxiation in a carbon dioxide chamber. Many hatcheries simply grind up the live, newly hatched chicks and their shells into a meal, which is dehydrated and used as a protein supplement in the feeds of other factory animals. The latest machine of destruction is a type of rapid-decompression chamber in which the chicks explode and die, one hopes, instantly. The new methods and machines for quick and easy mass chick elimination, however, add to the producer's expenses for capital and labor. Since they do not increase production and income, we can suppose that producers are reluctant to adopt them.

By whatever methods, the egg industry kills roughly half its birds every year. In 1987, some 214 million chicks were destroyed as soon as they crawled out of their shells and revealed their sex.[6] Ironically, this waste is the result of a constant quest for efficiency: industrial poultry science has genetically souped up the chicken so that it lays ten times the eggs its ancestors did, yet the bird is otherwise useless to agribusiness.

Factory-Made Eggs

The female chicks are sold to egg producers to begin their careers as "layers." Egg producers clip the beaks and, in some operations, the toes of new chicks and vaccinate them against a variety of poultry diseases. Producers house the pullets (young hens) in "grow-out" buildings for about twenty weeks until they are ready to begin laying eggs. To hold down excitement and fighting as growing birds crowd the pullet house floor, many producers keep the buildings dark except at feeding time.

◀ When the birds are mature, they are moved to the automated layer house where they are confined in cages that run the length of the building two, three, or four levels high. A watering system and two conveyor belts, one to bring feed and one to collect eggs, run along each level. The cage floor slants to allow eggs to roll through an opening onto a belt that carries them to a processing room for washing, grading, packing, and storage. Droppings from birds in the upper cages fall on sheet metal dropping boards mounted over lower cage rows. A power-driven winch and cable assembly moves a scraper along these boards, forcing the droppings into a pit below. When droppings accumulate in the pit, another power-driven scraper moves along under the row and pushes them out of the building.

In automated buildings such as these, some 285 million hens produce virtually all of the commercial eggs in the United States.[7] Under natural conditions, chickens can live as long as fifteen to twenty years; in the modern egg factory, however, hens last only about a year and a half. Their ability to produce eggs is diminished by the wear and tear of cage life until it becomes unprofitable to house and feed them. When this point is reached, they are made into soup and other processed foods.

Factory-Made Broilers

The early life of broiler chickens is similar to that of their cousins in the egg business. Here, however, males are kept and raised for market, although separately from females on many farms. Chicks are debeaked and toe-clipped at a day or two of age and taken to the broiler house. A partition restricts the young chicks under warm lights or gas heaters at one end of the floor. At first, bright lights are kept on most of the day to encourage the chicks to start feeding. After a week or two, the partition is removed and the young birds take over the entire floor. The floor is covered with wood shavings or other litter material, and two or three rows of heaters, automatic feeders, and waterers stretch the length of the building.

The birds reach a market weight of about four pounds in a little over six weeks. During the last few weeks in the broiler house, when crowding is most severe, dim lights or near-darkness are used on many farms to reduce fighting. When the flock is ready for the slaughterhouse, the birds are crowded toward one end of the building. Then, at night when the birds are drowsy, crews of "catchers" wade in, catch them, and load them in crates stacked on the trucks outside.

This reliance on human labor seems old-fashioned, and the broiler industry is trying to grow birds in cages similar to those used by egg producers. Birds could then be reared and shipped to market, cages and all. There are problems, though, in that caged broilers develop breast blisters, bruises, foot and leg injuries, and too much abdominal fat. Undaunted, the primary breeding companies are trying to perfect a strain that can withstand the cages. Once they succeed, the broiler industry will switch to these birds and retool for more thoroughly mechanized production. In the words of one poultry expert:

> Poultry growing units will become larger and larger. Cage production of broilers will gradually take over. The new "factories" will move the birds to larger equipment. . . . A push-button control system will move the belts supporting the cages. The housing units will be on a flow-through basis— chicks will enter at one end and the finished live broiler will come out at the other.[8]

Systems such as this will eliminate the labor of catching the birds; moreover, cages can be stacked so producers will be able to house three or four times as many birds in the same space. There are other possibilities for the elimination of labor in the broiler business: A mechanical "harvester," like a giant vacuum, sucks birds from the floor and sends them through a large hose into crates. An English equipment manufacturer has designed broiler cages with a drop-away floor that dumps birds onto a conveyor belt.

Over five billion chickens are factory-reared each year for American dinner tables.[9] If these birds were laid out beak to toe, the line would stretch to the moon and back twice. To bring that down to earth, they would form 338 rows between New York City and Los Angeles.[10] Over 240 million turkeys are mass produced each year in the United States by methods and in facilities similar to those of the broiler industry.[11]

Factory-Made Pigs

American farmers raise about eighty million pigs for slaughter each year. Their farms are concentrated in the Corn Belt close to the feed; 80 percent of U.S. pigs are raised in twelve midwestern states.[12] The structure and methods of pig farming are rapidly changing. Although most pig farms are still family owned and operated, about 90 percent of pigs are in some type of confinement system.[13] The degree of confinement varies considerably. On many farms, pigs are born in confinement but grow up outdoors in pens or on pasture. The trend, however, is toward larger farms, factorylike mass-production methods, and a greater degree of restriction for farm animals. If it continues, pig production may soon become as automated and monopolistic as broiler production. Ever since factory systems took hold in the late 1960s, small pig farms have been disappearing and more and more pigs have been produced by increasingly larger operations.[14] In 1982, 47 percent of all pigs were raised by farms selling more than one thousand pigs a year.[15] By 1986 these mid- to large-sized operations produced just over 70 percent of the nation's pigs.[16] These largest operations use

highly mechanized, "total confinement" systems] in which [the pigs never see daylight until they are put on the truck for the trip to the slaughterhouse. They are conceived, born, weaned, and "finished" (fed for market) in specialized buildings loaded with automatic feeding, watering, manure removal, and environmental control equipment [Two-thirds of all pigs produced in the United States, some fifty-three million animals a year, spend their lives in these total confinement operations.]

The total-confinement pig farm is specially designed for maximum exploitation of the pig's reproductive and growth cycles. Typically, the farmer maintains a breeding herd of about three hundred or more sows (females) and a few boars

A "flat-deck" egg factory.

(males). These animals produce the "crops" of pigs that are fed and sent to market; they are not sold as long as their reproductive performance is satisfactory. Because breeding animals in controlled-environment buildings tend to lose interest in sex, most farmers move them outside at breeding time. Some use artificial insemination to eliminate the repetitive, time-consuming labor involved in moving animals to and from pens during breeding.

After conception, sows are put in a "gestation" building for about sixteen weeks. In this building, a sow shares a small pen with a few other pregnant sows, or, in newer systems, she is confined to an individual stall. In either event, she remains in her pen or stall for the entire sixteen weeks—all, so the experts say, to give the producer "better control" over pregnant sows. In fact, the strict confinement creates a need for controls: to hold down stress and excitement, the rooms are kept dark except at feeding time; to hold down excessive weight gain (and feed bills) in the inactive sows, they are "limit fed" once every two or three days.

● About a week before her piglets are due, the pregnant sow is moved to a "farrowing" building to give her time to settle down and adjust to the change before the births. Here she is restricted to the tight quarters of a farrowing stall for two or three weeks until her piglets are born, nursing, and on their feet. The stall permits her to lie and stand, but she cannot walk or turn around; its purpose is to keep her in position only to eat, drink, and keep her teats exposed to the young pigs.

● The newborn pigs receive injections of iron and antibiotics, their "needle" teeth are clipped, their tails removed, and their ears notched for identification. The young males are usually castrated just before weaning. Two or three weeks after birth, the sow goes back to the breeding area and her pigs are taken to other buildings to start being fattened for market.

● In the "growing" buildings, the pigs encounter the usual factory equipment that removes manure and provides them with a steady supply of ground corn and other nutrients. They remain here for about twenty weeks until they are ready for market, at about 250 pounds. Farmers have now begun to stack pens and cages two and three decks high to expand production in the growing buildings while saving space and labor.

Confinement systems for pigs come in all shapes and sizes. A few producers use ingenuity and available materials to put up systems of their own design, but most choose from systems available from some sixty confinement manufacturers. The pages of farming magazines contain advertisements for "push-button farming," "plug-up-and-go systems," and "totally engineered" systems designed to tend the pigs while leaving the farmer only the job of checking on the equipment now and then. An Iowa pig producer and owner of a four-hundred-pig nursery and finishing building says, "It's just a matter of five minutes in the morning, and we try to check them every evening."[18] One manufacturer of the new systems advertises that with its systems "just a turn of the control dials in better pork profits."[19]

Factory-Made Milk

Both meat and dairy cattle are now being brought from pastures to mechanized confinement buildings as farmers turn to the new factory methods. On the factory dairy farm, cows live by the farmer's daily milk collection routine. For most of the day, a cow is confined to a holding area where feed and water are available. Twice each day—three times a day on the largest factory dairies—she goes into a milking parlor where a system of rubber cups, plastic tubes, and vacuum pumps extracts her milk and pumps it into a refrigerated tank. If a profitable operation is to be maintained, a dairy farmer must keep each cow in the herd producing milk

Cows awaiting milking.

for as many days as possible throughout the year. Since cows give milk only for about ten months after the birth of a calf, farmers rebreed each cow soon— usually about forty to sixty days—after each calf is born.

The calf is taken from its mother when a few days old, for otherwise it would drink the milk that is intended for sale and for human consumption. If female, the calf may be raised for the herd; if male, he will be sent to market as soon as possible. After a few years of routine calf and milk production, the cow's milk productivity wanes, and she is sent to the slaughterhouse. Because her carcass is not good enough to produce steaks, chops, and other cuts, she will probably end up in the hamburgers of one of the fast-food chains.

Factory systems and methods came gradually to dairying several years ago. As land values rose and farm labor became more and more scarce, some farmers began to install mechanical milking systems that could ensure speedy milk collection from larger herds. Dairy cows, like chickens, had been reliable producers of spending money for small, mixed-crop farms; now they have been converted to mass producers of profits for specialized dairy farms. About half of the nation's ten million milking cows and heifers are kept in some type of confinement system.[20] Most of these confined cows are in the traditional dairying areas in New York, Wisconsin, and other northern states.

A total-confinement dairy setup consists of only two buildings: the mechanized milking parlor and the holding barn. On a large dairy farm, where several hundred cows go through twice daily, these milking parlors are highly mechanized. Electronic sensors, automatic gates, automatic feeders, and vacuum-operated milking machines ensure a steady flow of cows and milk. About all the operator has to do is to wipe each cow's udder with disinfectant, apply suction cups to the cow's teats, and watch the machinery. To keep the herd conveniently near the milking parlor, most of the large farms have holding barns attached, equipped with the usual mechanized feeding, watering, and manure removal gear. In "free-stall" holding barns, cows are free to move from their stalls and walk about concrete or slatted floors when not at the milking parlor. Other farmers prefer to keep their cows stationary in "tie-stall" barns and move portable milking machinery to them. These cows remain in stalls for months, chained at their necks.

In a few southern and far western states, an industrial-scale type of dairying is taking over milk production. Some of these superfactories hold three thousand or more cows outdoors in crowded pens (similar to beef lots) rather than in confinement buildings. They buy all of their feed and hay and they hire teams of laborers to run the milking machines. Milking parlors are busy around the clock on these industrial dairies and the cows are milked three times daily.[21]

Factory-Made Veal

Veal factories are the harshest confinement systems. Newly born calves are taken from their mothers and turned into anemic, neurotic animals to produce the luxury "white," "milk-fed," or "prime" veal preferred by gourmet cooks and fancy restaurants. Compared with the production of other animal commodities, milk-fed veal production is a small industry. About 1.2 million calves go through these factories each year.[22]

Because they require an ample supply of newborn calves, veal factories tend to be located in dairying regions. The veal producer buys day-old calves and places them in individual stalls in the veal factory building. For fourteen to sixteen weeks the calf is confined to a space scarcely larger and wider than its own body, often tied at the neck to further restrict movement within the stall. Throughout this confinement the calf is fed on "milk replacer," a mixture of dried skim milk, dried whey, starch, fats, sugar, mold inhibitors, vitamins, and antibiotics. Commercially made replacers are high in fat to cause the immobile calves to gain weight rapidly.

A visit to a milk-fed veal factory in northern Connecticut gave us a feel for the business of veal production. Although it was broad daylight outside, the calves' rooms were pitch-dark; our guide explained that darkness helped keep the calves quieter.[23] At feeding time the lights were turned on as the producer made his rounds. In two rooms, more than a hundred calves were crated in rows of wooden stalls. Their eyes followed our movements; some appeared jittery, others

Veal factory.

lethargic. Many tried to stretch toward us from their stalls in an attempt to suckle a finger, a hand, or part of our clothing. The farmer explained: "They want their mothers, I guess."[24] The farmer mixed milk replacer in a barrel and rolled it along the rows of stalls. At each stall, he took a clean plastic pail, half-filled it with the mixture, and hung it on the stall. This liquid, twice daily, was the only "food" allowed to the calves. Buckets with nipples could relieve the young calves' urge to suckle, but are not used because they have more parts and recesses that might harbor bacteria. Moreover, the disassembly, cleaning, and sterilizing of two hundred buckets twice each day would be costly and time-consuming to the farmer. The stalls contained no straw or other bedding, for that could be eaten by the calves and the iron it contains would darken their flesh.

This goes on for fifteen weeks, by which time the calves weigh an average of 330 pounds and are ready for market. Producers would like them to gain more, but by this time the anemic condition is severe and the longer they are kept, the more will sicken and die in the stalls.

Factory-Made Beef

During the "beef crisis" in 1973, many Americans became critical of our wasteful and inefficient practice of feeding grain to cattle for the production of tender, fat-marbled steaks. Beef industry promotional organizations responded that cattle produce protein from grasses and roughage not edible by humans. They did not tell us, however, that more than fourteen million cattle and calves were then being fattened on soybeans and on corn, barley, and other grains.[25] Whatever industry propaganda says, most cattle marketed are still grain-fed in feedlots at some point before slaughter. Since the heyday of feedlot beef in the early 1970s, feedlots have become fewer and larger. In 1988, 1.4 percent of all U.S. feedlots confined enough cattle to produce 71 percent of the nation's beef.[26] Since the 1960s when the trend to large feedlots began, the number with over eight thousand animals has more than tripled; the number of lots with over thirty-two thousand animals has increased more than twelvefold.[27]

On conventional beef farms and ranches, producers maintain herds of "brood" cows and bulls. These "cow-calf" operations are more likely to be located in southern and western states where pastures and roughage are more available than corn and other feed grains. On these farms, calves are allowed to remain with the herd on pasture or rangeland until they are sent to market at one to two years of age. Some farmers round up yearling calves, confine them, and grain-feed them for three or four months before sending them to market; others sell "feeder calves" four to six months old to be fattened by their purchasers.

For many beef producers, however, these operations require too much land and labor and the calf "crops" come too slowly and too far apart. These are the cattle feeders whose speedier methods of beef production now dominate the beef industry. They buy feeder calves, put them in a feedlot, and finish them as quickly as possible to a market weight of about one thousand pounds. In combination with Ralgro, Synovex, Rumensin, or one of the other commercial growth promotants, the cattle are fed high-calorie feed consisting chiefly of ground or flaked corn and soy meal or another protein supplement. The feedlot itself is typically a fenced area with a concrete feed trough along one side. In regions where land is expensive and grain is cheap, cattle feeders use total-confinement buildings with automatic feeding and waste removal systems similar to those in other animal factories.

The Frontiers of Factory Farming

Other species of animals are now being reared in factory systems. Sheep experts at the University of Illinois have developed model confinement buildings in which growing lambs can be penned and fed to market weights. Sheep experts at Ohio State University have designed and built a model confinement unit that incorporates floors made of heavy-duty steel mesh, electrically powered manure removal, and automatic feeding by electric timer. All of this fits in with the American Sheep Producer Council's "National Blueprint for Expansion," designed to revive the sheep industry and bring it to eastern states.[28]

In cage systems similar to those used in egg factories, domestic rabbits are being raised for the meat and laboratory animal markets. Until recently, most rabbit producers were families with a few cages in the backyard and rabbit meat was a specialty food not sold in supermarkets. But the American Rabbit Breeders Association (ARBA) and a few animal scientists who specialize in rabbits are trying to build an industry modeled after the broiler business. Their sibling industry—the commercial rabbitries that raise animals for laboratory research and products testing—has shown that rabbits can be raised under intensive confinement conditions. So ARBA and its scientists are urging rabbit producers to follow the same route. One expert suggests that 160 rabbits can be raised in a four-by-twenty-foot (one-half square foot per animal) cage on wheels so that a breeding rabbit can "remain in the same cage for her entire reproductive life."[29] An additional advantage to this level of crowding, the scientist explains, is that the density keeps the animals from running and playing and otherwise expending energy that should go toward producing the maximum weight gain in the shortest possible time.

For these experts, the rabbit appears to have the potential to be the ultimate meat machine. Their industrial strategy, then, is to subject rabbits to the most efficient and mechanical regimen possible. Says another rabbit scientist:

> Unlike any other type of livestock, rabbits can be bred back on the day that they give birth. In an intensive production system it is theoretically possible to have one litter being raised from weaning to eight weeks, one litter with the doe, and one litter in the uterus. A litter can be weaned at four weeks and another litter kindled [born] three days later.[30]

Even the earth's waters are under invasion for more species to be converted into commodities by factory methods. Huge commercial fish factories are mass producing fish to meet rising demand as consumer tastes change from red meat to lighter foods. In the Pacific Northwest, the salmon are now running more in concrete tanks than in mountain streams. In southern states, the confined catfish is rivaling the confined chicken as most commercial animal. In the Bahamas, green sea turtles are being factory-farmed in concrete and fiberglass tanks to produce steaks, soup, leather, and jewelry. In Florida and Louisiana, alligators are mass produced in confinement for the handbag and shoe trade. And although the subject is beyond the scope of this book, millions of fur-bearing animals such as mink are confinement-reared each year to supply the ever-increasing demand for fur garments.

Regardless of the type of animal confined or the commodity purchased, all factory systems are designed to make more money from more animals. Instead of hired hands, the factory farmer employs pumps, fans, switches, slatted or wire floors, and automatic feeding and watering hardware. The factory farmer is a capital-intensive farmer whose greatest investment is in time- and labor-saving equipment. Success in farming is not achieved by direct care for the animals. It does not depend on the well-being of individual animals or even on individual productivity. Success comes from maximally efficient use of equipment. It is measured by year-end production records. Like managers of other factories, capital-intensive farmers are principally concerned with cost of input and volume

of output. A certain amount of wastage doesn't matter if the product wasted is cheap by comparison with overheads and if eliminating the wastage would raise costs or reduce output. All this is as true of animal factories as of any other factory; the difference is that in animal factories the product is a living creature capable of pain and fear, a creature worthy of moral consideration that inanimate objects neither require nor could benefit from.

Rabbit factory.

Estrus control will open the doors to factory hog production. Control of female cycles is the missing link to the assembly-line approach.
—Earl Ainsworth, "Revolution in Livestock Breeding on the Way," *Farm Journal,* January 1976, p. 36

HEALTH

Even Biomachines Get Sick and Die

Some have said that with our growing management sophistication and heavy concentration of animals in small areas, there's a danger of some entirely new disease popping up—not unlike the Andromeda Strain *in science fiction.*
—"Can We Keep Our Livestock Healthy?" *Farm Journal*, mid-March 1978, p. Beef-21

Necropsy surveys on market hogs at slaughter indicate that 10 to 30 percent have gastric ulcers, 30 to 80 percent have lesions typical of enzootic pneumonia, and up to 90 percent have osteochondrosis, which leads to synovitis and degenerative joint disease, the major cause of lameness in breeding-age swine.
—Vernon G. Pursel et al., "Genetic Engineering of Livestock," *Science*, June 16, 1989, p. 1285

In almost every country of the world livestock production is becoming increasingly intensive. The momentum of the change has been so great that it would not be untrue or unkind to say that it has been instrumental in presenting the veterinarian with problems that have outstripped his knowledge. The disease pattern has tended to change radically Instead 22 *of being presented largely with acute, specific, diagnosable and preventable or treatable diseases using vaccines, seras and antibiotics, the tendency has been for the occurrence of chronic, insidious, and complex groups of diseases.*
—David W. B. Sainsbury, "The Influence of Environmental Factors on the Health of Livestock," *Proceedings of the First International Livestock Environment Symposium* (St. Joseph, MI: American Society of Agricultural Engineers, 1974), p. 4.

ENVIRONMENTS FOR FACTORY ANIMALS are designed for efficiency, not comfort. Barren cages and stalls in darkened rooms do not satisfy even the stunted psyche of a factory animal. These animals are bored, frustrated, and fearful—as animal scientists say, "stressed." Until recently, no animal scientist would gamble his or her respectability by examining how animals *felt* about their living conditions. Such a study would imply anthropomorphism, a cardinal sin for a scientist, who is supposed to record only observable data. Lately, however, a few progressives have broken the taboo because, as they say, "A much more detailed understanding of the animals' psychological as well as physiological requirements (while also considering economic controls) would lead to greater returns."[1]

American animal scientists have been much slower to face the question of stress in the factory farm. When this book first appeared, our views on stress and its link to disease in closely confined animals were met with hoots and howls of derision by agribusiness animal experts. They argued to the public that we were anthropomorphists, as if this were some grave, new moral offense. Our suggestion that farm animals are living beings capable of fear, anxiety, boredom, frustration, and other feelings was received about as well as a bomb threat. Then, because the issue is so sensitive and so much money is at stake, they resorted to disingenuousness: they countered our charges with the plausible but spurious argument that even if farm animals could suffer, their sufferings in the factory farm would not be tolerated because it might push productivity down to unprofitable levels. (As we shall see in subsequent chapters, genetic and chemical manipulations are what keep animal productivity at profitable levels, even under conditions where overall animal well-being is poor.)

They still use these arguments before the public, but privately they are getting serious about the question of mental and emotional experiences in farm animals. At a recent conference at a Cornbelt university, an animal scientist who has long been an advocate of intensive and confinement husbandry told his audience that "animal mental activities are being seen as more important; stress is recognized. We must meet all of the animal's needs."[2] He added that, "Now we have to face what the critics are saying about the production systems. The public may support changes."[3]

After months of rubbing against the wire of their cages, hens lose their feathers.

"The longer sows are kept in confinement, the more problems occur. In general . . . sows kept under tethered conditions have done the poorest."—Neal Black, "Production Drops if Sows Confined," *National Hog Farmer,* November 1974.

Stress and Boredom

Factory animal experts are beginning, then, to look at stress, and for good reasons. In reacting to stress, animals burn up available energy and nutrients that would otherwise go toward growth, gestation, lactation, and disease resistance. The blood of a stressed animal carries increased levels of adrenal hormones that can break down muscle tissue into energy to meet the cause of stress. When an animal is stressed, its defenses are down and it is more prone to infectious diseases. Animals respond to stress in varying degrees; one particular animal may be stressed by a condition that produces no reaction in its penmate. But the stressed animal may catch a disease that spreads to the second animal.[4]

In the factory, animals are subjected to a variety of stresses. When birds are debeaked or when calves or pigs are weaned prematurely, some die from the shock. These causes of stress are occasional, however, and after a few days of adjustment most of the animals return to "normal." But other causes of stress on the factory farm are continuous: the animals have no relief from crowding and monotony. In a less restrictive environment they would relieve boredom by moving; confined animals cannot. Their instinctive drives are twisted into abnormal behavior.

● When animals are crowded and annoyed, the likelihood and frequency of aggressive encounters increases. When growing pigs are moved to larger pens, outbreaks of fighting can occur, leaving pigs dead or injured. In the restricted space of confinement pens, less aggressive animals cannot get away to make the show of submission dictated by instinct. Some animals may become so fearful that they dare not move, even to eat or drink. They become runts and die. Others remain in constant, panicked motion, a neurotic perversion of their instinct to escape.

● Cannibalism is common in swine and poultry operations. Cannibalism in poultry results from a distortion of the birds' instinct to establish a social hierarchy, or "pecking order." Birds that have evolved over millions of years, socializing in flocks of about a hundred members, cannot establish a pecking order among the thousands on the floor of a modern broiler or turkey house. In these superflocks, birds would peck each other relentlessly if controls were not used. Caged birds have the opposite problem: each cage contains a small "flock" and somebody has to fall at the bottom of the social ladder. This unfortunate bird cannot escape its tormentors.

● In pigs, cannibalism takes the form of tail biting, described by one expert as follows:

> Acute tail-biting is often called cannibalism and frequently results in crippling, mutilation and death. . . . Many times the tail is bitten first and then the attacking pig or pigs continue to eat further into the back. If the situation is not attended to, the pig will die and be eaten.[5]

Heightened levels of aggression and activity take their toll of stressed animals in a more direct way. Like any overworked machine, they simply wear out. Pigs in particular are prone to a reaction that we would probably call "shock" if it occurred in humans: the pig industry calls it PSS or the porcine stress syndrome. Pigs may literally drop dead from stress when they are weaned, moved to a new pen, mixed with strange pigs, or shipped to market.

Reproductive functions are not essential to survival at the moment of stress, and so are pushed into the background until the animal has escaped the stress-causing situation. Hence confined male pigs lose sex drive, females fail to become pregnant, and the daughters of these animals may have incompletely developed reproductive organs and may be slower to reach puberty.[6] Similar disorders of reproductive behavior occur in other confined animals.[7]

● Crowding and stress can disrupt normal patterns of behavior between parents and offspring. They may be unable to recognize each other because of the confusion of smells, sounds, and visual stimuli in the factory. In the farrowing house, for example, a bored, detached sow may not recognize the squeals of one of her own litter should she roll over or step on one. (On several occasions in the farrowing houses we visited, we saw young pigs trapped under their mothers' legs or rumps, squealing and struggling to free themselves. One farmer told us that he lost pigs this way even though his restrictive farrowing stalls were supposed to prevent sows from crushing their pigs.) Stress and stimulus confusion can also cause mothers to abandon their offspring and to refuse to accept their suckling, or the same conditions can make the young animals unable to seek out their mothers.

If you've been to a zoo and seen an animal repetitively rock back and forth or pace up and down its cage, you've seen another type of abnormal behavior, known as stereotypic behavior. It is a response to a boring environment. On the factory farm, sheep, calves, and pigs bite the bars of their stalls and caged chickens preen and pace. At one pig farm we visited, we watched one young pig methodically bite the large-gauge wire on the gate of her nursery pen. Starting at one side of the gate, she would bite at each square, work her way across, and then continue back and forth. Occasionally she would break this routine to run to the rear of her pen, then return and begin the pattern all over again.

Along with caged layer hens and crated veal calves, pregnant sows in total confinement suffer greatly. We described her living conditions in chapter 1: For the sixteen weeks of her pregnancy she is held, on most intensive farms, in a "gestation crate"—a steel stall scarcely larger than her body. On some farms she is "tethered," that is, chained at the neck for sixteen weeks. The severe restriction is mainly for producers' convenience. Crates and tethers make it easy to feed and control large numbers of animals for months at a time. At any rate, the crated sow cannot turn around, run, walk, or otherwise exercise during her pregnancy. These restricted sows would become obese if their feed rations were not drastically cut.

Victim of tail biting.

Anthropomorphism aside, these sows suffer demonstrably. (If a person were to confine a dog or cat or other favorite animal in this way, he or she could be prosecuted under the animal protection laws of most states. In those states, however, the strict confinement of sows is either specifically exempted from the law or regarded as exempt under a hazy theory of "agricultural necessity.") In Scotland, where the pork business is perhaps less important economically than it is in our midwestern states where most swine research is done, scientists have shown that "hunger, combined with restriction of movement which prevents foraging, is a major cause of stress" in strictly confined sows.[8] The same scientists have shown that repetitive bar biting, chewing, pawing, swaying, head waving, and other stereotypic movements are the result of frustration. They have found physiological evidence that stereotypic behavior is associated with stressful conditions.[9]

Diseases in the Factory

The "controlled environment" of the animal factory can be a hothouse of air pollution and airborne germs. Even with powerful ventilators working properly, the air of pig and poultry factories contains dust raised by mechanical feeders and excited animals. It is also full of ammonia and other irritating gases from the manure pits. Not surprisingly, respiratory diseases are very common in animal factories. In broilers avian influenza and infectious bronchitis plague production. In turkeys the respiratory diseases colibacillosis, fowl cholera, avian influenza, and turkey coryzasis are responsible for an estimated half of all death losses. We find the same high incidence of respiratory diseases in factory hog operations. A slaughterhouse check conducted by Elanco Products (a manufacturer of antibiotics) in cooperation with the National Pork Producers Council revealed that every one of 315 herds examined in twelve midwestern hog-producing states showed some sign of respiratory disease. According to an Elanco news release, "a substantial majority of the 9,500 hogs checked had some signs of respiratory disease, with 71 percent showing signs of atrophic rhinitis and 70 percent showing signs of pneumonia."[10]

Dust, irritating fumes, and toxic gases are so bad that even farmers and workers are being affected. According to *Feedstuffs,* an agribusiness newspaper, "Seventy to 90 percent of workers in swine confinement structures experience acute respiratory symptoms. Fifty-five percent experience chronic bronchitis and at least 14 workers have died suddenly from acute respiratory distress and systemic toxicosis."[11] An Iowa agricultural engineer said of the dust problem in the hog factory, "If I have to clean my nose after I leave a building, can you imagine what it's doing to an animal living there 24 hours a day?"[12]

It is killing them, apparently. According to one pork industry expert, "Pig death losses between birth and marketing average 20 to 40 percent."[13]

Because factory buildings are usually in use year-round and isolated from the cleansing effects of sunlight and rain, they develop what producers call "bacteria buildup." A producer may have relatively few health problems in a new factory building during the first year or two, but eventually the interior can become infested with a variety of disease-causing organisms.]Farming magazines indicate that both pig and dairy factories, for example, are plagued with diseases, some of which are aggravated by factory conditions.[14]

Confined calves suffer perhaps the worst disease problems of all factory animals. According to *Successful Farming*, "Calf losses are 15–20% on the average dairy farm. In some cases they zoom up to 40–50%."[15] In both veal and dairy operations, all of the conditions are right for disease: the animals are very young and highly stressed by separation from their mothers, their diet is inadequate, and they are concentrated indoors and unable to exercise. Veal calves' iron-deficient diet results in progressive anemia and marked stress; consequently they are more vulnerable to infections. The most common causes of death in veal factories are pneumonia and acute diarrhea.

Losses from disease and stress run high in the caged layer house, too. Some producers told us with pride that their ["cull rate"—the percentage of dead and dying birds removed from the cages each day]—was quite low, that it ran between 1 and 1.5 percent per month. That seemed quite low until we realized it added up to a loss of 12 to 18 percent of the original flock by the end of the first year in the cages. In most cases, layer hens are kept in the cages for eighteen to twenty months or more. The cull rate generally increases as the birds age, but let's assume that it remains constant at 1.25 percent per month. We find that the egg industry is accustomed to losing about one-quarter of its birds by the time their short egg-productive lives are over.[16]

Factory farmers' attempts to control some diseases often aggravate others. In more traditional systems of poultry farming, flocks picked up immunities from gradual exposure to germs harbored by their parents and older birds, and from the housing. Many modern flocks, however, have been bred to be "specific-pathogen free" (SPF), that is, certain disease-causing agents have been eliminated from the flock by breeding and raising birds under sterile conditions. The isolation necessary to successfully produce SPF chicks causes them to be isolated from other pathogens as well, and as a result they lack immunity to even ordinary microorganisms. When these birds are placed in the poultry buildings, they may develop unexpected diseases.

The factory operator, if a good manager, tries to control temperature, humidity, light, ventilation, drafts, dust, odors, noise, fighting, diseases, waste removal, the supply of food and water, and everything else that makes up an animal's environment. But when hundreds or thousands of animals are confined in a single room, it is unlikely that every element of the environment is satisfactory to every individual animal. Health then suffers, and the causes are so diffuse that they are difficult to trace.

Some producers attempt to maintain near-hospital conditions in an effort to reduce disease problems. Many factory farms do not allow visitors. At one of the large pig factories we visited, we were required to scrub, shower, put on white

coveralls, and spray our photographic gear with disinfectant. On many farms, we waded through disinfectant footbaths or pulled thin polyethylene coverings over our shoes and pants.

As mentioned briefly earlier, the anemic condition deliberately induced in calves to produce high-priced, pale veal is one of the most severe of the conditions suffered by factory animals. The relevance of anemia control to white flesh production is explained in an excerpt from a pamphlet, *Raising Veal Calves*, published by the University of Massachusetts.

The anemic condition resulting from milk-only feeding gives the desired lack of pigmentation to muscle tissues in the carcass. Milk is deficient in iron and thus a food source that will give the desired end product. Other

Barbed-wire and chain link fences: not to keep animals in but to keep germ-bearing visitors out.

feeds must be avoided, as they do contain iron. Trace mineral salts, hay, bedding are excellent sources of iron and must be avoided. Grains should also be avoided in the feeding program.]

Physiologically, this type of nutrition program results in marked stresses to the animals, especially as they approach ten weeks of age. . . . The calf does have stores of iron in the body at birth, primarily in the form of extra hemoglobin in the blood, with lesser added amounts stored in the liver, spleen and bone marrow . . . [that] can carry the calf pretty well through 8 to 10 weeks. However, by this time the calf is anemic, and with a longer growing period, there is a decreased energy utilization, decreased resistance to disease, decreased growth rate, and eventually death.[17]

Stressed and bored by confinement, this pig neurotically chews the wire-mesh front of its pen. Animal scientists call this "stereotypic behavior."

Now that it is the target of criticism from consumer and animal advocacy groups, the veal industry hotly denies that its calves are deliberately made anemic. Nevertheless, it acknowledged and openly discussed the calves' anemic condition before 1980, when the criticism began. It is rather hard to believe that the same feeding and husbandry systems no longer produce anemic calves; it is rather hard to believe that the pallid flesh could come from anything but anemic calves.

One producer explained to us that restriction to stalls assists the development of pale flesh by keeping the calves from "running around a little bit too much." He added that "keeping them confined does not allow muscle development and it keeps the meat tender."[8] When they are a few weeks old, the calves develop an urge to ruminate, that is, to eat roughage such as hay, which is regurgitated and chewed as the "cud." In their craving for iron and roughage, veal calves attempt to chew their stalls and will lick at nails or any metal about them. Not surprisingly, digestive disorders, including ulcers and chronic watery bowel movements, are common in these calves.

The health of the veal calf can best be described as anemic, weak and susceptible to disease.
—Stanley N. Gaunt and Roger M. Harrington, eds., *Raising Veal Calves* (n.p.: The Massachusetts Cooperative Extension Service, n.d.), no. 1066, p. 4

Factory Diets

Even when not deliberately deficient in an essential nutrient like iron, the factory farm animals' feeds are designed primarily for cheap weight gain and consequently nutritional deficiencies do occur. Even if feed is properly formulated (mixing errors do happen), some animals get inadequate diets. At the feed mill, nutrients are added in amounts according to what the "average" animal needs. Because of stress or individual differences, some animals need more of an essential nutrient than they get. But if prices are right, a large factory still makes money even if large numbers of animals die or suffer from dietary deficiencies. Vitamin deficiencies common in poultry factories, for example, result in a variety of conditions, including retarded growth, eye damage, blindness, lethargy, kidney damage, disturbed sexual development, bone and muscle weakness, brain damage, paralysis, internal bleeding, anemia, and deformed beaks and joints.[19]

Dietary deficiencies and other factory conditions can cause a variety of bodily deformities. In poultry, fragile bones, slipped tendons, twisted lower legs, and swollen joints are among the symptoms of mineral-deficient diets. Birds raised on wire-mesh floors tend to develop crooked breast bones. Some poultry diseases can leave birds with malformed backbones, twisted necks, and inflamed joints. In broiler chickens, bruised and swollen hocks are common because the industry has produced a sluggish, top-heavy bird that spends most of its time "down on its haunches."

Digestive disorders, nutritional deficiencies, and other health problems in cattle are on the rise now that more and more of these animals have been moved from pasture to feedlots and factory dairy systems where they are fed primarily grain. Cattle have a digestive system equipped to handle a diet of grasses, stalks, stems, and other roughage. The first of the cow's four stomachs, the rumen, contains populations of one-celled plants and animals that help break down the tough plant stalks and fibers. A diet of high-energy grain disturbs the proper environment for these microorganisms and several side effects occur: the lining of the rumen may become damaged, protozoa are destroyed, and the types of bacteria change. Certain abscess-producing bacteria proliferate, penetrate the rumen, enter the bloodstream, and settle in the liver. This condition, said to occur in most every feedlot, is termed "acidosis-ruminitis-laminitis-liver-abscess syndrome." It is responsible for 90 percent of all the rejections of beef liver by meat inspectors at slaughterhouses.[20] Despite this maldigestion, beef producers continue to feed grain because it produces a heavier animal more quickly and consumers prefer tender, grain-fed flesh to that of less intensively fed animals.

In factory dairy systems, new health problems are traceable, in part, to deficiencies of vitamins A, D, and E, which are available in forage and pasture diets but are not adequate in the premixed feed of the confinement barn. Predictably, these vitamin deficiencies are corrected not by turning the cows out to pasture but by resorting to injectable vitamins and feed additives.

Factory Feet and Legs

31

The feet of birds and mammals contain complex joints composed of numerous small bones, ligaments, cartilage pads, tendons, and muscles. This complexity of design is not gratuitous; it equips the animals to scratch for food, kick or claw for defense, and stand or move on different types of terrain. About the only kinds of surfaces for which these feet and legs are not designed are the wire-mesh, concrete-slab, and metal-slat floors of confinement buildings. On these alien surfaces, some joints, muscles, and tendons are overworked, others are underworked, and consequently the complex structure of the animals' feet breaks down. Pigs are cloven-hoofed animals and in most the outer half of the hoof ("claw") is longer than the inner half. Outdoors, this extra length is absorbed by the natural softness of soil. On the concrete or metal floors of the factory pen, however, only the tissue in the foot can "give." As a result, many confined pigs develop painful lesions in their feet, which can open and become infected. Pigs with these foot sores usually develop an abnormal gait and posture in an attempt to relieve the pain. Eventually the crippling may worsen when this abnormal movement and weight distribution overworks joints and muscles in the legs, back, and other parts of the pig.[21]

"Unquestionably, modern housing-management systems result in more severe stress to feet and legs than preconfinement production."—Robert D. Fritschen, "Floors and Their Effects on Feet and Leg Problems in Swine," *Confinement*, June 1976, p. 12.

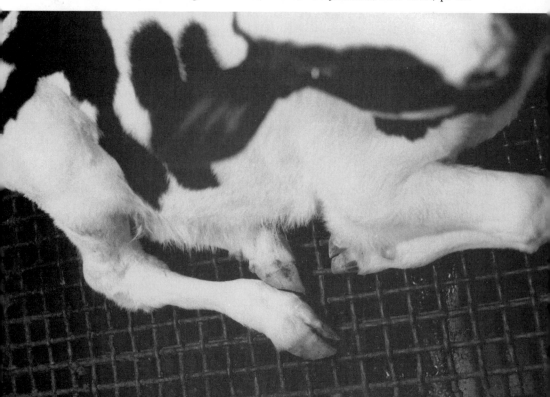

• Foot and leg weakness has been accidentally bred into modern animals as breeders have turned out heavier-bodied, "meat-type" animals; their old-fashioned feet and legs can't take the extra strain. Lameness, however, affects only the living animal, not its flesh. Afflicted animals are valuable meat whether or not they can walk, and they usually go to the slaughterhouse before they can become a liability to the farmer.

• Caged birds often develop foot and leg problems as a result of months of standing on a wire-mesh surface. To allow droppings to pass through the cage floor with the least interference, cages are manufactured with a rather large-gauge mesh—usually about an inch square; thus the bird must stand on only a few fine wires, which is an unsuitable perch for a heavy bird.

Worn-Out, Flipped-Out Biomachines

Factory experts are puzzled by some health problems in factory animals for which they are unable to find precise causes. One condition common in layer operations is termed CLF, or caged layer fatigue. According to *Poultry Digest, 32* birds with CLF withdraw minerals from their bones and muscles and eventually are unable to stand.[22] These fatigued birds have brittle or broken bones and a pale, washed-out appearance in their eyes, combs, beaks, and feet. Another mystery is the "flip-over syndrome" observed in bigger, faster-growing broiler birds. This condition "is characterized by birds jumping into the air, sometimes emitting a loud squawk and then falling over dead."[23] Upon postmortem examination, the bird's heart is full of blood clots, though these are believed to be a result rather than a cause of death. At one of the broiler operations we visited in North Carolina, the operator had been losing several birds each day from this condition, which he called "heart attack." He told us that the problem is "in the birds—they grow too fast these days."[24]

Factory Hazards

Under natural conditions an animal's instincts, conditioning, and senses guide it to food, steer it from danger, and generally promote survival. Factory production strips away the animal's freedom and ability to take care of itself. Control of life-support activities passes from the animal to machines and managers. In this vulnerable situation a power failure, a slight maladjustment, or a minor mistake can quickly cause the death of a very large number of animals.

Factory-farmed animals are vulnerable to less obvious hazards as well. Young birds die of thirst because they do not learn to drink from nipple-type watering devices; after debeaking, they can starve to death within inches of an adequate supply of feed. Because of the large concentrations of animals in factory systems, lack of adequate ventilation can be critical, especially in hot weather. Metabolic activities produce heat and a "hot-air envelope" develops around the body of each animal. If the temperature becomes too high, the animals may just

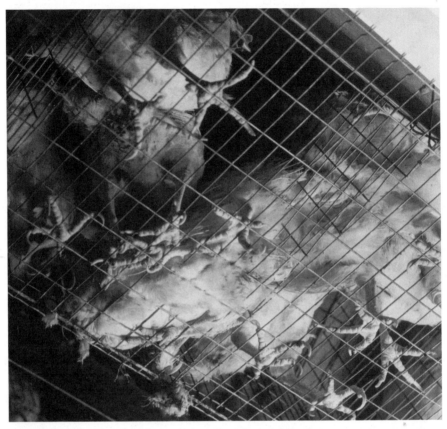

"Birds get their legs caught in the wire floor of the cage and die because they cannot get to feed and water."—C. I. Angstrom, "Mechanical Failures Plague Cage-Layers," *Onondaga County Farm News,* Syracuse, N.Y., December 1970, p. 13.

plop over and die. And this can happen rather quickly, as USDA scientists in Mississippi found out. They monitored temperature and humidity in a broiler house when the fans went out on an eighty-eight-degree day. In just twenty minutes, the temperature inside the building climbed from eighty-six to ninety-nine degrees and the relative humidity rose from 56 to 81 percent.[25]

Factory advocates often defend total confinement with the argument that the controlled environment protects animals from weather extremes. Perhaps it does. But doesn't this avoid the question as to what is a suitable climate for a species of farm animal? Animals of tropical origin (pigs or chickens) ought not be raised in northern regions where confinement is "necessary" to shelter them from winter blizzards. And the confinement building does not always protect the animals inside from winter storms. During the winter of 1988–89, heavy snows hit the

Ozark region of Oklahoma, Missouri, and northern Arkansas crushing hundreds of poultry sheds and killing an estimated four million birds.

At the other extreme of the weather scale, confinement does not appear to protect, but rather, as we have seen, to endanger animals. Nearly every summer now we see news accounts of the deaths of millions of chickens and turkeys across the country as power failures stop the ventilating fans and birds smother, trapped in their own body heat.

The wave of health problems associated with the industrialization of animal agriculture is not abating. Industry leaders speak glowingly of eliminating diseases, but they succeed only in making disease control more complicated. The solution is to abandon the new methods of concentrating and confining animals; but economic pressures on farmers, together with a proconfinement bias on the part of many of the industries that sell drugs, equipment, and other products to farmers, are hastening the conversion of animal agriculture to factory systems.

And what do we hear from the veterinary profession about the health problems of animals in factory systems? A recommendation that large-scale confinement systems be eliminated?

No. At present, factory farming pays and it pays handsomely. It pays for drugs, medicines, feed additives, and veterinary services. In any profession, when ethics and economics collide, ethics has a hard time of it. Nowhere is the collision more head-on than in factory farming, where the animals are the patients but the farmers pay the bills. Some veterinarians may boldly criticize factory farming, but the majority will go on trying Band-Aid solutions: more drugs, stricter isolation from the natural environment, better equipment, and a reformulated diet. We cannot look to the veterinary profession for the fundamentally different approach that is needed.

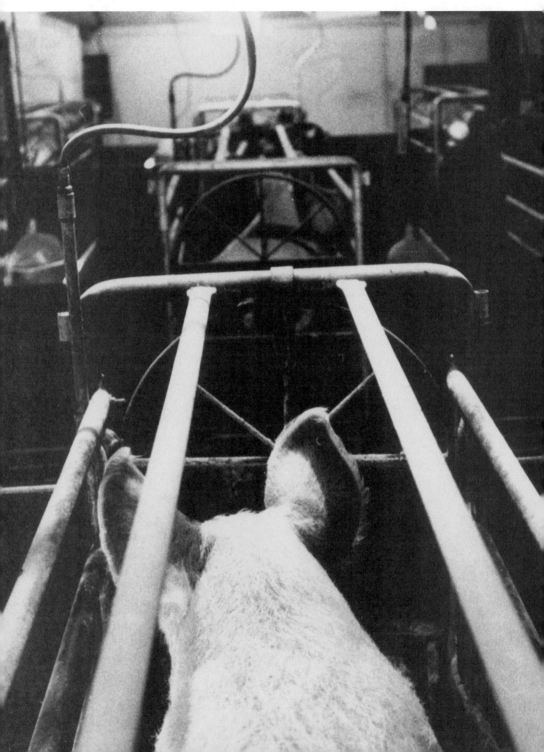

MANAGEMENT

The Biomachine
Designed, Assembled,
Modified, Tuned In,
and Turned Up

The breeding sow should be thought of, and treated as, a valuable piece of machinery whose function is to pump out baby pigs like a sausage machine.
—L. J. Taylor, export development manager for The Wall's Meat Company, Ltd., in *National Hog Farmer*, March 1978, p. 27

We know what goes into the animal (feed) and what comes out (milk), but we know very little about what happens inside the animal which represents a sort of black box.
—Dr. Dale E. Bauman, developer of bovine growth hormone, in a press release, "Growth Hormone Triggers Dramatic Increases in Milk Yield in Cows," *News and Feature Service*, Cornell University, Ithaca, N.Y., October 16, 1981

At the Animal Research Institute (Agriculture Canada) we are trying to breed animals without legs and chickens without feathers.
—R. S. Gowe, Director of the Animal Research Institute, Agriculture Canada, speaking at "Livestock-Intensive Methods of Production," a conference in Ottawa, December 6 and 7, 1978

THE COMPOUNDING PROBLEMS OF FACTORY FARMING are seen as "challenges" for an ever-growing army of experts who churn out increasingly elaborate management schemes to keep the factory profitable. Despite the claims of equipment manufacturers advertising "push-button farming," the new systems need careful management. Constant manipulations of animals' anatomy, physiology, heredity, and environment are required to keep health problems and other costs down so that commodity production can proceed at a profitable level.

Farmers know that crowding, diet, air pollution, and other environmental conditions aggravate their animals' health problems, but because elimination of these adverse conditions would require elimination of factory techniques, farmers turn to those few manipulations that can be carried out within the factory system. Stress and related health problems can be reduced by keeping animals in darkness or under very-low-intensity lights. The total-confinement veal and pig operations we visited kept animals in total darkness around the clock except for brief inspection and feeding periods. Egg factories cannot be kept dark around the clock as the illusion of day is necessary to stimulate egg production. Poultry scientists have been trying to change that. Their theory is that hens need only brief exposures to light at critical moments during their ovulation cycle. Once these moments are mapped out, layers may lay eggs as usual on only two or three hours of light each day.

Chemistry, of course, has been explored as a means of controlling stress. Poultry scientists at Southern Illinois University found that an antibiotic feed additive "apparently relieved the stress of crowding" in layer chickens.[1] At Virginia Polytechnic Institute and State University and elsewhere, poultry researchers have tried to find steroid drugs that could be used to "block stress factors that interfere with optimum performance."[2] Various researchers have tried to find a feed additive that could be used to control tail biting in pigs.

Such lines of research prevail in the animal sciences these days, as the financial and political influence of chemical and pharmaceutical industries steers research away from *systemic* changes and instead toward additives, injections, devices, and other kinds of husbandry shortcuts that can be packaged as commercial products. Every company—and practically every university—is looking for a "magic bullet," a technological quick fix, which will eliminate any problem at hand. From an agribusiness point of view then, the rise of animal factories is a godsend because it has created a whole new universe of husbandry problems that call for new research, new engineering, and so many new magic bullets.

The question of stress in factory animals is the latest constellation in this universe. Publicly, animal scientists downplay stress in the animal factory; privately and within the walls of agricultural academia, it is one of the hottest topics around, and researchers are climbing over each other in a headlong rush to get grant money for round after round of stress studies. The irony here is not to be missed: The animal science community—apparently short on the objectivity required for science—heatedly contests the claims of animal protectionists that there is stress and psychological suffering in the animal factory. All the while, however, scientists are enthusiastic about the huge, new frontier of research opportunities opened up by those claims.

Which gives us reason to be watchful and critical as the results of all the stress studies come pouring out. We know from fifteen years of experience that the animal science community generally fails to be truly objective and open about the questions of stress and psychological suffering in animals. This has not made us antiscience; rather, it has made us more perceptive and critical of the ways in which science professionals are able to maneuver and misguide science according to the interests of those who pay the bills for research. The scientific *method* is objective and value free, but scientific professional groups are not always, and they are often as loaded with politics, ideologies, and money concerns as are other biased groups. This is especially so when a new technology offers vast realms of career opportunities to a scientific field.

It is reasonable, then, to be skeptical of the sort of information about stress that will be coming from a profession that has denied and resisted the subject for so long. We can expect well-designed attempts to minimize the existence of stress and suffering in the animal factory. And we can expect efforts to accommodate or alleviate stress and suffering so that the factory system can pass as being humane. Swine experts are already suggesting introducing bowling balls, tires, paper sacks, and other "toys" into crowded pens as a means of reducing boredom and tail biting.[3] We can even expect to be exposed to data suggesting that animals "prefer" the "protection" of their cages and crates to normal freedom of movement and social interaction.

The new biotechnologies, however, offer the most powerful tools for dealing with the problems of animal stress and suffering. Much of the work on stress at the moment is devoted to mapping out its neural, chemical, and genetic dynamics. Once scientists know these mechanisms, they can reach into a biotechnological toolkit for a way to make adjustments. Most likely, they will identify the genes that control key mechanisms for stress and suffering. The next step is to modify those genes somehow, probably by gene insertion.

Let's suppose a researcher at one of the chicken-breeding firms wants to create a stress-proof layer hen. The researcher finds a gene in another species that drives the animal's stress mechanisms in a desirable way, removes it, and installs it in the nucleus of some reproductive cells from layer hens. After fertilization, these cells begin dividing, multiplying, and carrying the newly introduced gene all the way through development into layer chicks. Now the researcher—rather, the breeding company—has a new breed of *transgenic* layer hens that can be patented for their special ability to pass on stress resistance.

Another method for creating stress-proof animals might use similar biotechnological tools to adjust other mechanisms of the stress reaction. For example, it might be found that a particular enzyme inhibits stress by neutralizing one of the hormones key to the stress response. The next step is to invent ways to raise the levels of this enzyme in, say, factory pigs. This could be done by creating transgenic pigs who carry the genes that raise levels of the enzyme. Or perhaps the stress-reducing enzyme could be kept at high levels through injections or feed additives.

Such is the current direction of research on stress and what most of us call animal suffering. If it is successful, agribusiness will have the perfect factory animal: a dull, oblivious food machine. It will grow and produce eggs or milk at a profitable rate even though its living conditions might be harsh enough to cause stress or inhibit production in a normal animal. Factory animal engineers will then have us believe that they have eliminated suffering. We will discuss what is wrong with their approach in chapter 8.

Stressful situations can be greatly reduced by feeding chemicals such as metyrapone or DDD (rhothane) which reduce the production of corticosterone by the adrenals.
—Paul Siegel and Bernie Gross, "We're Learning How to Let Bird Defend Itself," *Broiler Industry,* August 1977, p. 42

A chick being debeaked.

Cutting Off the Offending Part

Manipulations of environment, chemistry, and genetics may lower stress to some extent, but in pig and poultry operations additional steps must still be taken to hold down losses from cannibalism. Management of factory farms calls for deliberate animal engineering: if the factory cannot be modified to suit the animal, the animal is modified to suit the factory. To ensure that stressed pigs cannot tail bite, farmers routinely cut off ("dock") the tails of young pigs a few days after birth. In poultry, cannibalism is controlled by routine debeaking. This began around 1940, when a San Diego poultry farmer found that if he burned away the upper beaks of his chickens with a blowtorch, they were unable to pick and pull at each others' feathers. His neighbor caught on to the idea, but used a modified soldering iron instead. A couple of years later a local company began to manufacture the "Debeaker," a machine that sliced off the tips of birds' beaks with a hot blade. With various modifications, this machine still debeaks most factory birds. Broiler chicks require only one debeaking because they are sent to market before their beaks grow back. Most egg producers debeak their birds twice, once at about one week of age and again during the growing period when the birds are between twelve and twenty weeks of age.

Sometimes the irregular growth of beaks on debeaked birds makes it difficult or impossible to drink where a normal bird would have no trouble.
—C. I. Angstrom, "Mechanical Failures Plague Cage-Layers," *Onondaga County Farm News* (Syracuse, N.Y.), December 1970, p. 13

In view of the size of flocks and the cost of labor, the debeaking procedure must be carried out as quickly as possible, with experts recommending a speed of about fifteen birds a minute. But patience and precision tend to give way in monotonous work, and the beaks of many birds are sloppily cut.

An excessively hot blade causes blisters in the mouth. A cold and or dull blade may cause the development of a fleshy, bulb-like growth on the end of the mandible. Such growths are very sensitive and will cause below average performance. . . . Incomplete severance causes torn tissue in the roof of the mouth. The bird's tongue must be held away from the blade. Burned or severed tongues result in cull [worthless] hens.[4]

Even if debeaking is "properly" done, it is painful and can affect birds' health later. Some debeaked birds do poorly during the production cycle and do not grow to full size because "beak tenderness" makes it difficult for them to eat and drink.[5] Of course, the poultry industry insists that debeaking is painless, that it is comparable to trimming one's fingernails. This issue was thoroughly explored twenty-five years ago by the Brambell Committee, a group of veterinarians and other experts appointed by Parliament to investigate animal welfare concerns that had arisen as factory farming became visible in Great Britain. On the question of debeaking, the Brambell Committee said:

> Irrespective of whether the operation is performed competently, and in the way that meets with the general approval of the poultry industry, we are convinced that it causes considerable pain lasting for much longer than the second or so that the operation takes to perform. It has been frequently represented to us . . . that the operation is similar to the clipping of finger nails . . . of humans. There is no physiological basis for this assertion. The upper mandible of the bird consists of a thin layer of horn covering a bony structure of the same profile which extends to within a millimetre or so of the tip of the beak. Between the horn and the bone is a thin layer of highly sensitive soft tissue, resembling the quick of the human nail. The hot knife blade used in debeaking cuts through this complex of horn, bone and sensitive tissue causing severe pain.[6]

At the same time the birds are debeaked, on some farms their toes are clipped just behind the claw using the same hot-knife machine. This operation is said to keep the birds quieter as it prevents "back-ripping" and fighting. To hold down pecking and fighting among males on breeding farms, producers usually cut off their wattles and combs. As these "dubbed" males are not able to recognize each other easily, there is less competition for social position.

Getting Rid of Bugs

The battle against disease calls for strict measures throughout the factory. Everyone—animals, managers, and visitors—must follow a one-way route from building to building to avoid bringing germs back to younger animals. Between "crops" of animals, farmers sterilize practically everything inside with an arsenal of hot water, high-pressure hoses, acids, cleansers, and disinfectant chemicals. Animal disease experts recommend "health programs"—routine doses of sulfa, antibiotics, vitamins, and other medication at regular intervals throughout the production cycle—to help hold down disease losses. In addition to routine medication, factory animals receive other doses of antibiotics, drugs, and medicines when specific health problems occur. The mass-production schedule does not allow for precise, individualized treatment and so many producers use a "shotgun" approach to symptoms of disease. According to one veterinarian: "Often the wrong antibiotic is used, a high enough level is not used, or the correct level is not used long enough."[7]

In all, government officials estimate that there are between twenty thousand and thirty thousand drugs on the market for use in animals.[8] "The present technique of raising animals makes it dependent on an array of drugs," according to a senior staff scientist at the Natural Resources Defense Council, an environmental group that has been critical of the routine use of antibiotics in animal feeds to control disease and promote rapid growth.[9]

```
Arrival:
  1. physical exam of each calf
  2. rectal temperature of each calf
  3. nasal and fecal swabs of five selected calves
  4. selenium (Mu-se)® ½ cc IM once
  5. vitamins A, D, and E (Injacom)® 2 cc IM once
  6. injectable iron (Ferrextran)® 5 cc IM once
  7. injectable B-complex vitamins (Betaplex V)®
     3 cc IM per day for 4 days
  8. injectable antibiotics as indicated
  9. bicarb and dextrose in milk as prescribed with
     antibiotics, if needed, on basis of cultures
 10. close observation of calves 4 to 5 times a day for
     first 2 weeks
 11. delouse using Korlan II, observe closely
```

A schedule of drugs and chemicals administered on the first day of a typical factory "health program."

Keeping the Biomachines at Work

At the core of factory farming are those controls or manipulations that are intended to push up production while holding down costs. The business of animal farming is being brought squarely into the late twentieth century by experts who scorn traditional methods as they explore every scientific nook and technological cranny for ways to "improve" it. With neither exaggeration nor political bias, it is accurate to say that "improvement" is measured solely by profitability. In the literature of factory farming, traditional animal management practices are deemed to require too much labor; natural animal reproductive and physiological cycles are too slow and unpredictable; and much of animal behavior is just plain unbusinesslike. Animals had it easy on traditional farms; now they must be made to pay more dearly for their brief keep.

Restricting animal mobility is a fundamental tenet of factory management. It is both an unintentional consequence of the economic pressure to crowd factory animals and a deliberate means of manipulating them toward greater productivity. Chickens, if not confined, would doubtless prefer to lay their eggs in nests of their own making rather than on wire-mesh floors crowded with a half dozen other birds. But the costs of nest materials, space, and the labor required to track down and collect eggs from nests would not permit large-scale factory production. Layer hens must be put in cages designed to permit mechanical egg collection. Similarly, narrow stalls confine calves to ensure that flesh of the right color and texture develops rapidly. Farrowing stalls and tethers hold sows in place to allow a maximum number of piglets to suckle and grow to meaty maturity.

Together with other manipulations, restriction of movement contributes to the illusion of greater productivity in factory animals. The "high feed efficiency"

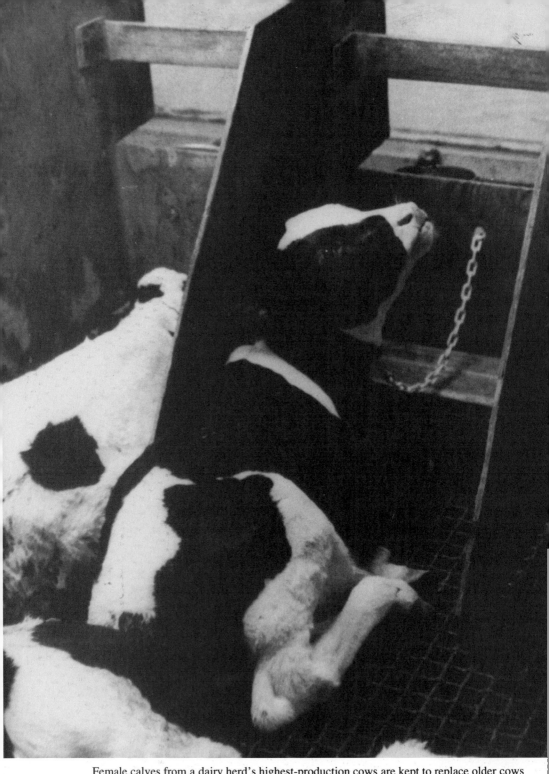

Female calves from a dairy herd's highest-production cows are kept to replace older cows when their milk productivity declines.

boasted of by factory experts is achieved by feeding high-calorie mixtures of ground corn, soy meal, and other nutrients to animals virtually immobilized in warm buildings. During cold weather, pig and broiler producers heat their buildings because growing animals put on weight more quickly if they don't have to burn food energy to keep warm. Nor can factory animals "waste" food energy on exercise in their cramped quarters; all activities must defer to cheap, rapid production of tissue.

Building a Better Biomachine

Genetics is the factory farmer's most effective tool. For thousands of years, farmers have selected the "best" animals of each generation to be the breeders of the next. The criteria for selection once ranged broadly over a great number of factors because earlier animals had multiple uses and, without modern drugs and medicines, their health had to be reliable. In those days, the all-around animal was the best animal. But over the years, especially after market economies arose and animal products became commodities, farmers began to select primarily for productivity.

Through breeding, animals have now been split up into subspecies according to what they produce: we have "beef" cattle and "dairy" cattle, "egg-type" chickens and "meat-type" chickens. Lately, this emphasis on productivity has intensified. In dairy cattle, for example, awards and championships are awarded to farmers whose cows produce the most pounds of milk annually. Layer hens of the 1930s produced an average of 121 eggs a year. Through genetics, today's hens nearly double that figure. But apparently this is not productive enough, for poultry scientists keep trying to develop a "superchicken" that will lay an egg a day.

Such superproductivity has been the goal of factory animal science for decades. But the speed and precision with which animals could be manipulated into egg, milk, and meat machines was always limited by animal behavior and reproductive cycles. Animals mate, breed, and rear offspring only so fast. Conventional genetics had to rely on selective breeding, that is, choosing breeding pairs from only those animals with the most desirable traits. Generally, the parents passed on their desirable characteristics to the offspring. By constantly selecting for a favored trait generation after generation, eventually the breeder produced a specialized *breed* of animals known to express the chosen characteristic reliably. In the broiler industry, the chosen trait was rapid growth; in the egg industry, it was a high number of eggs per lay cycle. In each case, it has taken poultry geneticists many years and many generations of breeding flocks to achieve their goals.

Now molecular biology and the biotechnology revolution promise ways to deliver these desirable production traits with greater speed and precision. Selective breeding is a thing of the past now that the chosen trait can be produced in the laboratory. Generally biotechnology refers to *in vitro* (literally, in the glass;

in the laboratory) techniques for altering genetic material. These techniques include:

Recombinant DNA Technology. Often called gene cloning, it is used to manufacture synthetic hormones, for example. The genes that control formation of a desired hormone are removed from cells of a cow and inserted in the nuclei of bacteria suspended in a growing medium. As the bacteria divide and proliferate, they produce quantities of the cow's hormone.

Gene Engineering. One can change the genetic makeup of an animal by inserting, splicing, or removing genes in cells of reproductive tissue. Once altered, the new genetic makeup is repeated throughout all cell divisions and expressed in the animal as it develops to maturity.

Cloning. Creating identical chips off the genetic block. All of the cells of an animal are the products of one original, fertilized cell. As such, every cell at every stage of development has the same genetic makeup. By manipulating some of these early embryonic cells, a geneticist can separate them and artificially produce identical twins, triplets, or a large number of individuals with identical genetic makeup.

Embryo and Ova Transfer. Removing a fertilized egg or a developing embryo from a mother and placing it in the reproductive organs of another female for gestation to birth.

Using combinations of these techniques animal scientists are already producing custom-made life-forms and animal characteristics. Much of this work so far is limited to altering single-cell organisms or production-related processes in animals, such as egg, milk, or muscle formation. But there are inevitable tendencies to stretch the limits. At the University of California, Davis, animal scientists have created chimeras—animals that have the faces and horns of goats but the bodies of sheep. These "geeps" are made by combining the genetic materials of sheep and goats and implanting the embryos in either sheep or goats.

Among the first new biotech products about to become commercially available to factory producers are synthetic growth hormones, or somatotropins, made by recombinant DNA technology. These hormones occur naturally in animals, so it is claimed that their recombinant DNA substitutes will cause no harm to human consumers of treated animals. In dairy cattle, daily injections of bovine growth hormone (BGH; also called bovine somatotropin, BST) have caused cows to give up to 25 percent more milk. In pigs, porcine growth hormone (PGH; also called porcine somatotropin, PST) has sped up growth by 16 percent. The pork industry is most excited about PGH's ability to produce a pig that has as much as 70 percent less fat. Because it is believed that these synthetic hormones will cause no harm to humans, the U.S. Food and Drug Administration (FDA) has already approved them. Producers are waiting for drug manufacturers to perfect a more convenient means of administering these hormones to dairy cows and pigs than by daily injections.

Under development also are biotech products that will have the same growth-promoting effect as BGH and PGH without the delivery problems. A Canadian firm has developed a product that reduces levels of somatostatin in animals. Normally, somatostatin holds down levels of an animal's naturally occurring growth hormone. When the product is used, the animal produces higher levels of its own growth hormones. Animal scientists are also experimenting with beta agonists, synthetic hormones similar to adrenaline, which have effects similar to growth hormones. These have advantages in that they need not be injected, but can be administered as a feed additive.

"Bugs" in the New Models

Emphasis on speed and volume of production has brought unexpected problems in factory animals. When humans attempt to take over the entire process of mate selection (a complex process that has been millions of years in the making) for their own profit, many important traits get ignored and eventually the genetically modified animals can go haywire. High-producing dairy cows are tense, nervous, hyperactive animals. Fleshy bodies of broiler chickens and pigs grow heavy so quickly that development of their bones and joints can't keep up. Skeletal disorders are common. Many of these animals crouch or hobble about in pain on flawed feet and legs. The pig breeder's emphasis on larger litters and heavier bodies, coupled with a lack of attention to reproductive traits, has produced poor mothering traits in sows and high birth mortality in their pigs. These new, improved females produce such large litters that they can't take care of every piglet. To cure this problem, producers began to select sows with a greater number of nipples—only to discover that the extra nipples don't work because there's not enough mammary tissue to go around.

Some of the genetic manipulations for higher productivity seem to work against factory farmers. In beef cattle, for example, the fastest gainers are not the most efficient converters of feed to flesh; slower gainers are more efficient because they eat less and waste less. Although chickens are laying more eggs than ever before, the eggs are different. Factory eggs now are smaller, with more white and less yolk than eggs produced a decade ago; they are also paler and more watery than eggs from barnyard chickens.[19]

We are finding that the power of biotechnology can produce problems in animals just as easily as it can produce production benefits. The "geeps" at the University of California are frail, sickly, and incapable of reproducing themselves. And transgenic pigs—bearing genes from cows to make them grow fast and lean—showed "a high incidence of gastric ulcers, arthritis, cardiomegaly, dermatitis, and renal disease."[1] The same study notes that the pigs and other transgenic animals have various infirmities, are infertile, and die prematurely. The authors summarize the problems:

The most common clinical signs of disease associated with transgenic expression included lethargy, lameness, uncoordinated gait, exophthalmos [bulging eyes], and thickened skin. The following gross and histopathologic changes were noted in some of the transgenic pigs: gastric ulceration, severe synovitis [inflamed joints], degenerative joint disease, pericarditis and endocarditis, cardiomegaly, parakeratosis, nephritis, and pneumonia.[12]

They noted also that the females could not come into estrus and the males "lacked libido."

Advocates of the new BGH and PGH products have been very vocal in claiming that these will be harmless to humans, but they have offered little information about what they might do to animals. If the studies on high PGH levels in transgenic pigs are any indication, it seems likely the other means of raising hormone levels—through injections or implants, or by somatostatin antibodies—may cause similar health problems. Synthetic growth hormone experts already know that treated animals have increased needs for the feed and food energy needed to supply the faster growing tissues. If the producer does not supply these increased needs and tries to cut corners on feed, the animals will become debilitated, stressed, and more susceptible to disease.

Whether by traditional selective breeding or by the latest genetic engineering techniques, the quest for high productivity seems to produce animals with reproductive problems. The agribusiness turkey is a case in point. The bird has been made heavy and big-chested so that it will look plump and meaty on the carving platter. As a result, male turkeys are top-heavy, weak-legged, and physically unable to mount breeding females. Now it takes assembly-line artificial insemination to fertilize the millions of eggs that grow into the turkeys for holiday dining tables.

Engineering Animals for the Factory

Animal engineers are bent on making custom creatures for the factory production line. "Minihens" about two-thirds the size of ordinary hens enable egg producers to house more birds per cage. Because machines for beheading and defeathering chickens often leave a ring of neck feathers that must be removed by hand, scientists at the University of Georgia tried to develop a "naked-neck" chicken. And to have a truly global industrial chicken, the poultry industry needs a bird that can flourish in hot climates. Therefore, at least six universities in the United States and Canada have tried to produce a model of commercial chicken with no feathers.[13] Apparently feather research captures the scientific imagination, for there have been attempts to produce a commercial chicken with "bangs"—head feathers long enough to fall over the eyes.[14] These built-in blinders, it was hypothesized, would screen out distractions, leaving serene, calm birds that would gain weight more quickly and would have fewer bruises at the time of slaughter.

Pigs, too, are being modified to fit the factory. Breeding experts are trying to create pigs that have flat rumps, level backs, even toes, and other features that will hold up better under factory conditions. Pigs' natural physiological reactions to stress are seen by factory experts as abnormalities that must be eliminated; to them, normal pigs are "stress prone." Current efforts to build the better hog include searching for animals that release the lowest levels of ACTH, cortisol, and the other hormones related to the stress reaction.[15] Like its broiler prototype, the stress-resistant pig is the perfect factory animal—a lethargic creature whose only abilities are eating and gaining weight.

Although, as we shall see in more detail in chapter 5, animals destroy far more protein and energy than they contribute to the human food chain, animal science is determined to use every means to add another point or two to their efficiency of conversion. Just when it seemed that they had exhausted the possibilities, biotechnologists have come along and offered a new order of means. Researchers at the U.S. Department of Agriculture (USDA), as well as at other public and private institutions, are using these means to make today's superproductive factory animals even more superproductive. Some are already boasting of efforts to create a biotech broiler chicken that will grow nearly twice as fast as the present commercial bird.[16] They also predict hens producing twice as many eggs, cows producing twice the tonnage of milk, and cattle and sheep that can grow up on sawdust and wood by-products.[17] Dairy cows are already producing twenty-five thousand pounds of milk per year. At double that, a cow would produce twenty-five tons of milk—almost fifty times her body weight—each year.

The Joy of Sex, Factory Style

Control over genetic traits requires strict control of the bodies and sexual behavior of both male and female animals. [Artificial insemination offers producers much greater control over genetic selection and the timing of births; it also eliminates the burden and expense of keeping quality breeding males.] The technique is widely used on turkeys and dairy cattle; it is used less extensively on beef cattle and pigs. It is successful, however, only if the female receives semen at the right time during her estrous cycle. And timing is critical. In pigs, for example, the right moment may last for only a few minutes. If the artificial inseminator misses, the farmer must bear the expense of maintaining the "useless" female until her next heat period and, of course, the "crop" is delayed.

[Under natural conditions the breeding animals themselves determine the right moment by sounds, smells, and other signals. To make artificial insemination more reliable then, it helps to have a few good, old-fashioned males around to take care of this business—up to a point. These males are supposed to detect, not copulate with or fertilize, females in heat. To ensure that their inferior sperm does not get ahead of the artificial inseminator's vials and tubes, their penises must be neutralized. On some cattle operations, farmers block the penis with a removable plastic tube and a stainless steel pin through the bull's sheath.

Because this device holds the penis inside the animal, soreness and infection may set in and the bull may lose his desire to mount. Other producers, then, prefer the permanent solution of penectomy, surgical removal of the penis (these males are called "gomer bulls"). At some animal factories, males' penises are surgically rerouted to exit their bodies at the flank. These males are called "sidewinders."[18]

Most factory farmers who use artificial insemination, however, would rather eliminate boars entirely. They consume feed and take up space. After all, the whole boar is unnecessary; all that is needed is his "essence." Not surprisingly, someone came up with an aphrodisiac for pigs handily packaged in an aerosol spray can. The product, called "Boar Mate" and marketed by a British firm, contains a synthetic hormone similar to the sex-odor pheromones that boars emanate when they are in the presence of a sow in estrus. At breeding time, a few spurts from the can of "instant boar" directed around the sow's snout are supposed to accelerate her heat period and improve the chances of fertilization by artificial insemination.

Supersex and Reproduction

Research on the biochemistry of animal reproduction has recently begun to get much more attention in animal science because it is turning out new techniques for increasing "crops." This is one of the few remaining new frontiers for factory animal science in its quest for production efficiencies, for little else of animals' life and life cycles remains uncontrolled. Under one new technique, called *superovulation,* producers inject hormones into females to stimulate their ovaries into producing a large number of eggs instead of the usual one or two. Another technique, called *synchronization,* uses hormones to synchronize the estrous cycles of two or more females. These biotech tools are used by animal scientists and producers to make reproduction of high-producing animals cheap and fast.

Essentially, profit drives this intensified exploitation of the cow's reproductive organs. If we have a cow whose annual tonnage of milk is breaking all records, her calves will bring high prices because they, too, will have her milk-productive genes. Before biotechnology we could get only one calf per year from our supercow. Using biotech tools, we can make her produce a dozen or more calves each year. Then, of course, we make a dozen or more times as much money each year. Here is how it is done: Our pedigreed cow is dosed with hormones to cause superovulation and her eggs are fertilized by artificial insemination. After a few days they (now embryos) are removed, sorted by sex (by microscopic examination of chromosomes), and implanted into the wombs of ordinary cows. This procedure, called ova or embryo transfer, is catching on with producers of pigs and dairy cattle. In cattle, the high-producing cow's eggs are flushed out by sterile water and then implanted in recipient cows through a small incision in the flank. In pigs, under present methods, the eggs are removed through an incision in the donor sow's abdomen. If her genes are in demand, she may be cut open and sewn up six or more times in a year.

Although the procedures can cause shock or death, hormone control of estrus, ovulation, gestation, and birth gives greater control over the entire factory operation. Estrus control decreases time between pregnancies, aids assembly-line artificial inseminations, increases the chances of conception, and makes planning and record keeping easier. Use of prostaglandins to induce labor contractions makes calving and farrowing more convenient for the farmer. Injections of progestins or steroids bring on twin calves, larger litters of pigs, and bigger lamb "crobs." As soon as they give birth, females can be dosed again with hormones to tune in their cycles for rapid rebreeding.

Speeding Up the Assembly Line

Even without the use of drugs, farmers speed up reproductive cycles by separating calves, lambs, and pigs from their mothers much earlier than nature would. In nature, a calf might nurse and run with its mother for about a year; on a dairy farm, a calf is lucky to spend more than a day with its mother. Although most factory pig farmers leave their sows and pigs together for about three weeks before separation and weaning, a few are trying to wean only a few days after birth in order to rebreed sooner.

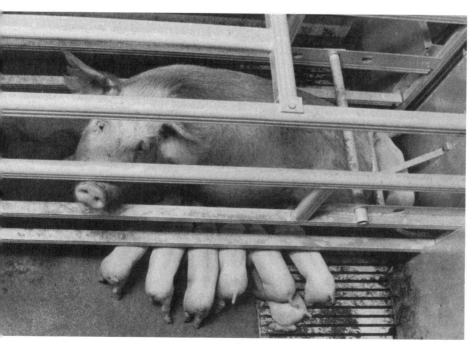

"It would not be unusual to perform enough [ova transplant] surgeries on an individual [sow] in a year to equal the number of offspring that she would produce in a lifetime of normal farrowings."—Jason James, D.V.M., Sullivan Veterinary Clinic, Sullivan, Ill., quoted in *National Hog Farmer,* December 1975, p. 28.

In addition to manipulations of sex and reproduction, factory experts control growth rates to increase production. The poultry industry has known for some time that birds' rates of growth and egg laying depend on the daily change in the ratio of light to dark. In the spring, when days grow longer and nights become shorter, birds' body cycles pick up and their rates of egg laying increase. It didn't take poultry producers long to figure out that control over light meant control over production. They began to experiment with various light schedules. Some broiler producers have total control over light in their windowless houses; others take advantage of sunlight during the day and use artificial lights after dark. Egg producers try to create the illusion of eternal spring by keeping the lights on a little longer each day. After about a year of this, the flock's productivity drops, and many producers use "force molting" to revive it. This technique shocks and disorients the birds by leaving them in the dark for a few days without food or water. A few birds die in the process, but most come through and begin producing all over again on a renewed pseudospring light routine.

"It is obvious that the light supplied by sunshine during the day and normal darkness at night is the most inferior of any lighting program."—Mack O. North, "A Case Can Be Made for Continuous Lighting," *Broiler Industry*, September 1976, p. 48.

Other attempts to boost productivity involve the substances fed to animals. Not the least of these is the high-calorie feed itself; but feed additives are the mainstay of factory productivity. Antibiotics are the most widely used. Each year, about fifteen million pounds of antibiotics go into animal feeds.[19] Exactly how antibiotics help animals put on pounds is not known, but some experts believe they provide a shortcut around good animal care. According to one expert, "the 'growth promoting' effect of antibiotics is seen only when animals are raised under suboptimal conditions—that is, in crowded, dirty, and heavily contaminated pens and feedlots."[20] To get rapid gains in feedlot cattle, many operators also implant in their animals' ears pellets containing synthetic hormones and other growth-promoting compounds. The most commonly used hormones in these implants are estradiol, testosterone, progesterone, and two synthetic compounds, zeranol and trenbolone acetate.[21]

Cheaper Raw Materials

Every so often new gadgets and ideas come out that are claimed to boost production. There is a nylon device with extending prongs like an umbrella that is implanted in the vaginas of young feedlot cows. The device is believed to enhance growth by stimulating nerve endings in the vaginal tract, creating biochemical changes like those of pregnancy. But no one really knows for sure how it works; all they know is that it produces an average increase in profits of twelve to fourteen dollars per head—and more if used with chemical growth stimulants.

Scientists want to know about the body chemistry that curbs appetite when a beef animal eats its fill: "Obviously, if the thing that turns a beef animal away from the feed bunk were found and could be overcome, it would mean a lot. . . . It could even mean an added supply of beef at a cheaper price."[22] Even ordinary cement dust has been used as an additive in cattle feed because, according to the USDA, it produces weight gains 30 percent faster than cattle on regular feed.

Controls over appetite and feed consumption are much sought after now that animal scientists see their relationship to productivity. Researchers in Europe and Australia have bred animals that eat, chew, and digest faster as these traits indicate high productivity. These experimenters have also tried depriving cattle of sleep to make them hungrier, heavier eaters that produce more meat and milk. They also have tried destroying sheeps' sense of smell to make them heartier, less-finicky eaters of cheap commercial feeds.[23]

In their efforts to cut costs, factory experts try almost anything cheap and disposable as feed for animals. Ground-up cardboard has been promoted by a Chicago firm as "an exciting development" in animal feeds. "The cost savings would be tremendous," the firm claimed, because some ten million tons of cardboard would be saved from the dump and channeled through dairy cattle to be converted into milk for humans.[24] Old newspapers have also been suggested for recycling through cattle. A farming magazine featured a Missouri farmer who

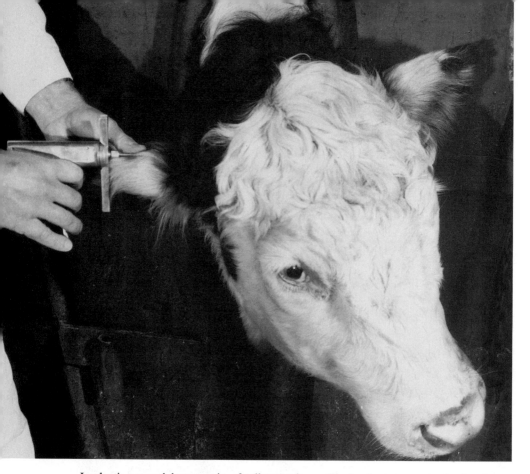

Implanting growth hormone in a feedlot steer's ear. The implanted capsule slowly releases the hormone over the feeding period.

fattens his cattle on feed composed mostly of sawdust laced with ammonia. In many animals' feeds, the protein supplement is a meal made from feathers, feet, intestines, chicken heads, and other animal parts discarded at slaughterhouses. Our meat and milk, as Orville Schell documented in his gripping 1984 book, *Modern Meat,* is made by animals fed on plastic hay, newspaper, cardboard boxes, by-products from the manufacture of corn and potato chips, municipal garbage, and animal manure.[25]

Manufacturers of feeds for animals appear to know no bounds to their search for cheap ingredients. Peanut hulls, corn cobs, rice hulls, sugar beet tops, cottonseed hulls, citrus pulp, and other crop leftovers regularly go into animal feeds. Leftovers from breweries and distilleries go into feeds. Dried blood, meat, condemned carcasses, and other parts left over at the slaughterhouse go into feeds. The rendering industry, which picks up dead and diseased animals that do not make it to the slaughterhouse, supplies materials to animal feed manufacturers. Although the recycling of these materials appears to be economically and ecologically sound, it increases the flow of pollutants and contaminants in the human food chain and we shall see in the next chapter how it may be harmful to human health.

"There are no waste products from industrial or agricultural processing that some entrepreneur does not try to salvage," according to Dr. Gerald Guest, head of the FDA's Center for Veterinary Medicine, the agency responsible for keeping dangerous chemicals out of food animals.[26] The FDA has to be constantly on guard for imaginative new attempts to find cheap ingredients for animal feeds. Fats and oils, for example, are a major ingredient in animal feeds to supply energy and to increase palatability. Usually these are animal fats left over at the slaughterhouse or vegetable fats left over from food processing. These may come from a variety of sources and for economic reasons or for convenience the feed manufacturer may blend them freely. This has opened up the door to "unprincipled brokers [who] have taken the opportunity to buy and sell nonfeed oils, such as waste industrial by-products, and label them for animal feed use."[27] In one case, FDA field investigators traced polychlorinated biphenyl (PCB) residues in turkeys to waste oils from a chemical plant's scum pond. FDA investigators have discovered that "brokers buy and sell railcars and tankers of oils and invoice the products to feed manufacturers as feed grade regardless of source. The manufacturer may be aware that the product is suspect but, since the price is right, blends it with other fats and oils to [sic] its original identity and any contaminants are greatly diluted."[28] FDA investigators have also found feed manufacturers using "tall oils," by-products of paper mills, in making animal feeds.

Recycling of animal wastes back into feed has caught on as a means of dietary cost cutting. In about a dozen states, mostly in the broiler country of the Southeast, recycled animal wastes have been approved for shipment and sale intrastate as a feed material. In other states, producers can recycle waste on their own farms without violating any laws. One factory expert admits that the motivation behind waste recycling is "raw and simple economics."[29] It cuts feed bills and reduces disposal problems.

According to farming magazines, factory operators have tried various ways to recycle their animal wastes—some of them most simple and direct: In Pennsylvania, a factory egg producer ran pigs in the manure pits under his caged birds. In Kansas, a farmer confined his pregnant sows in the manure pits under his finishing pens. He boasted that he did not have to feed them for ninety days, which saved him $9,300 a year on feed costs.[30]

On some factory farms, dirty litter from broiler houses is scraped up, hauled away, and added directly to cattle feed. Raw poultry and pig manure is mixed with ground corn or shredded stalks and fed to pigs and cattle. Animal waste is also processed and sold as a cheap feed supplement by agribusiness companies. Animal scientists have developed the "oxidation ditch" to channel liquid wastes from factory manure pits back to the animals; they have to drink it because it's the only "water" offered to them. Even ways of processing human sewage into animal feed are being studied.

Spreading the Cost of the Factory

The quest for higher profits can cause severe crowding of animals in factories. Animal studies show that the animal death rate increases as crowding increases. They show also that these losses are insignificant compared to the much greater yield of meat or eggs per unit of space, labor, and overhead. In the earliest days of the broiler industry, when birds began to be raised indoors, "Scientists went to work to determine the optimum amount of floor space needed per bird."[31] The study of the economics of crowding had begun.

Dozens of experiments were reported over the next several years. They showed that reducing the floor space below one square foot per bird also reduced growth and feed conversion. But conflicting evidence showed that more pounds of chicken could be produced in a house when the birds were "crowded."[32]

The table below shows how "more pounds of live broiler can be produced per square foot if floor space per bird is reduced."[33]

Effect of Floor Space on Weight, Mortality, and Pounds of Birds Produced Per Square Foot

Floor space per bird (square feet)	Average live weight (pounds)	Mortality (percent)	Weight of birds raised per square foot of floor space
1.0	4.12	2.1	4.12
0.9	4.09	2.3	4.53
0.8	4.05	2.6	5.03
0.7	4.00	3.0	5.66
0.6	3.94	3.6	6.40
0.5	3.86	4.5	7.54
0.4	3.75	5.8	9.03

Source: Mack O. North, "Some Tips on Floor Space and Profits," *Broiler Industry,* December 1975, p. 24.

Economics determines the limits of crowding in other factories as well. When two Iowa cattle producers tried to put eighty animals per pen in their new confinement building, the cattle started having arthritis and joint problems. The producers realized that the animals weren't getting enough sunlight and exercise, so they reduced the number per pen from eighty to seventy and started feeding mineral supplements. According to one producer, "After we did this, we stopped our leg and feet problems."[34] But this change increased the investment cost per animal by $17.86 and lowered the building's overall capacity and profitability.[35]

The trick is to find the maximum number of animals that can be crowded into the factory without stress and disease taking such a high toll that profits go down. Up to that point, stress and disease do not matter. One study on the "Effects of Density on Caged Layers" showed that a higher degree of crowding in cages, even though it pushed up mortality, produced better profits if the price of eggs was above a given point. According to the authors, "When the farm price of all eggs is 40¢ or more . . . five layers per [12-by-18-inch] cage make a greater profit."[36]

In other words, when eggs are expensive hens are cheap.

This simple economic fact gives the lie to claims that since animals in factory farms are productive, they must live happy, contented lives. Even if it were true that putting on weight is a sign of well-being—which it is not—productivity of individual animals is not what counts in factory farm economics. As the studies above illustrate, individual animals' well-being and productivity can suffer as long as more pounds of meat or dozens of eggs can be squeezed from a factory building. This view is supported by Dr. Michael W. Fox, veterinarian, ethologist, and a leading critic of intensive animal husbandry systems, who writes in the preface to *Farm Animals: Husbandry, Behavior, and Veterinary Practice*:

> Animal "productivity" and feed-conversion "efficiency" figures are no direct indicator of animal well-being, even though they are often touted as being so. This book dispels this agribusiness myth by showing that productivity is only one of several indices of animal well-being (all of which must be used to assess the validity of animal welfare concerns and the humaneness of husbandry practices). Productivity can be boosted with drugs, special diets, and by environmental, genetic and surgical manipulations, any of which can adversely affect the animals' well-being.[37]

Agribusiness and animal science show no signs of giving up their search for further manipulations to increase efficiency and cut costs in the animal factory. Too much has been invested to think of turning back. Even though animals' efficiency in converting plant protein and energy into commodities has biological limits, no factory advocate will acknowledge it. They push at these limits with a religious fervor and faith, for they act from our oldest and most sacred belief that man (meaning human beings) must conquer nature. That conquest is all the more urgent now that it has been made so profitable.

Factory-farming managers have not yet learned the lesson that Rachel Carson tried to teach those who would attempt to manage the natural environment: biological mechanisms are more complicated than we realize, and our attempts to manipulate them in our own interests are likely to have unexpected costs.

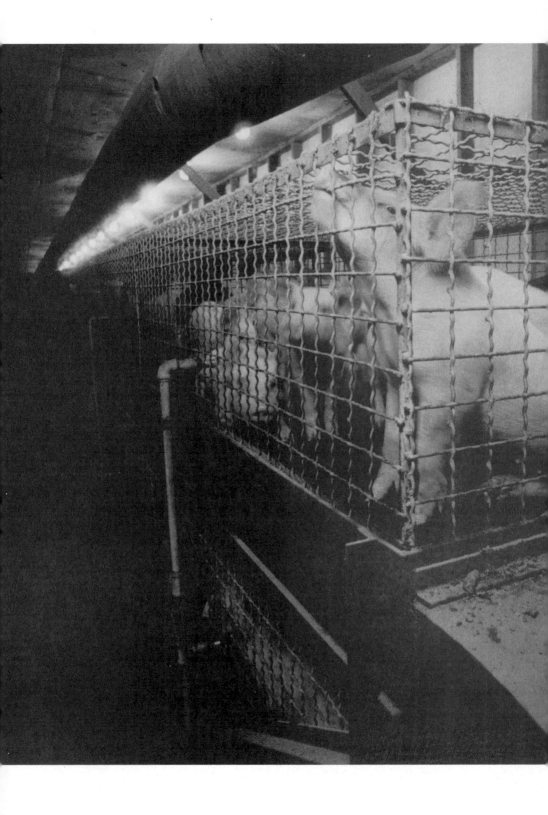

"There's too much wasted space in a typical controlled-environment single-deck nursery. The cost of the building is just too big a cost factor. Stacking the decks spreads that building cost out over more pigs."—John Byrnes, "Stacking 3 Decks of Pigs." *Hog Farm Management,* January 1978, p. 16.

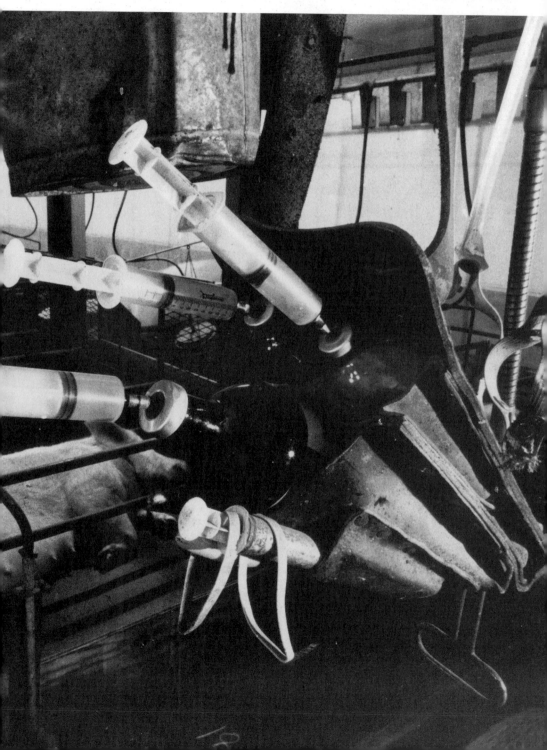

THE FACTORY

Are Biomachines
Good to Eat?

We've been accused of selling a chicken with less flavor than the "old-time" chicken. . . . Attempts are being made at overcoming the flavor problem by injection or marinating.
—W. J. Stadelman, "Old-Time Flavor: New Injectables Possible,"
Broiler Industry, April 1975, p. 79

The majority of pesticide-contaminated human food incidents of the last decade were the result of human exposure through consumption of contaminated animal products.
—Remarks by Gerald B. Guest, D.V.M., Director of FDA's Center for Veterinary Medicine, at the FDA Pesticide Coordination Team Conference held February 1989, excerpts reported in "CVM Looks at Pesticide Residues," *FDA Veterinarian*, May/June 1989, p. 8

Adequate regulatory methods are currently not available for over 70 percent of the animal drug residues in meat, milk and eggs that the United States Department of Agriculture has responsibility for monitoring. The Food and Drug Administration has no timetable for ensuring that all approved new animal drugs are supported by adequate methods for detecting their residues in milk and edible animal tissues.
—Committee on Government Operations, U.S. House of Representatives, *Human Food Safety and the Regulation of Animal Drugs* (Washington, D.C.: U.S. Government Printing Office, 1985), p. 4

SINCE THE MAIN END PRODUCT of animal factories is food for humans, we should take a close look at the relationship between current farming methods and food quality. Reflect for a moment on the farms of yesterday—when rates of animal growth and reproduction were determined by nature rather than by mortgages, and animal health came from sunlight and exercise rather than from injections and additives. Typical farms kept a few milk cows to provide fresh milk and butter for the family and sold the small surplus to markets nearby. Nearly every farm had a flock of chickens that roamed barnyards, fields, and pens looking for seeds, worms, and insects. Freedom of movement was allowed not out of any humanitarian motives but simply because farmers needed not to waste grain on scavenger chickens. A few hogs nourished on table scraps and food rooted from the earth could provide the family with lard, sausage, hams,

59

and bacon. These animals, though valuable to the farm family, were not regarded merely as cash on the hoof; because they were comparatively few in number, the health and well-being of individual animals was important to the family's survival and not just a matter of profits. These animals were "domestic" in the precise sense: they were part of the rural household.

Though closely watched, yesterday's farm animals were not completely under the farmer's control. Many, of course, were in pens or enclosures and some were subject to abuse and neglect. But for the most part they had space, daylight, seasons, social interaction, free range about the fields for choice of forage, resting areas—in other words, some degree of what humans might call freedom. The farmer expected no more from them than they could naturally produce if provided with food, water, and shelter.

Freedom for animals within their environment had advantages for people, too. The health of animals was not so precarious and expensive to maintain as it is now. Contact with the soil gradually exposed animals to a range of microorganisms, allowing their natural immunity systems to work and combat disease effectively. Roving animals ate a variety of foods as their appetites dictated, and this diversity in nutrients and exercise produced a quality in foods not found today. (Compare the taste, appearance, and nutritional content of an egg from a "free-range" hen with one from the supermarket.) And because they sustained themselves on insects and plants inedible to humans, free-ranging animals did not compete with humans for food to the degree that most farm animals do today. Unconfined and dispersed over the land, these animals distributed their wastes to enrich the soil without pollution.

Agribusiness denigrates this vision of farming as old-fashioned, obsolete, a "thing of the past." Pure nostalgia, they say, and those who carry this vision are said to be out of touch with reality. Agribusiness, please understand, is terrified of ways of producing food that do not depend on expensive inputs of technology and expertise. Agribusiness, after all, is a conglomeration of industries that make their profits from sales of chemical fertilizers, feed additives, pesticides, and other "magic bullets" to the people who farm. And the former make more money in the process than do the latter.

Fortunately, more than a few farmers and others in agriculture are realizing that these magic bullets are coming back at us and killing us. Day by day, the low-input, diversified farming of preagribusiness days is making more sense to more people at all levels of the food chain—from fields to dinner tables. The tide of public demand is turning away from cheap, bland food mass-produced by risky, ruthless farming methods. Owing to the recent waves of concern for diet, health, and environment, people want food of quality and they want certainty that it is safe and wholesome. They are learning that this kind of food can come only from an agriculture with some basic, humane values, with some respect for living beings and natural cycles.

And before long the agriculture that attempts to strip-mine soil, plants, and animals, the one that operates from arrogant, nature-busting ideals, will become the "thing of the past."

Fast Food, Fatty Food

Today's animal-rearing methods are geared to mass production. Animals' environment now consists of cages, steel bars, fluorescent lights, dusty air, and total darkness except at feeding times. Animals' health and vitality—mental and physical—suffer. The quality of the flesh, milk, and eggs they produce also suffers. Chemically dosed and genetically hyped up to meet industrial standards of profitability, today's animals are artificial to the marrow.

An egg assembly line—three levels high.

The poultry industry, the trendsetter in factory ways, has known for some time that the factory's impact on animals depresses food quality. It uses chemistry to impart flavor, color, and other characteristics lost or distorted in the factory process. Food from the industrial chicken is bland, pale, and washed-out compared with that from free chickens—birds with their feet on the ground. The factory diet, environment, and single-minded genetics are partly to blame, but much of it is because the birds are slaughtered younger than ever. They have been made to swell up to adult weight in about seven weeks, but their flesh is still immature. And the layer hen, machined to crank out a biologically absurd number of eggs, produces them accordingly.

Most commercial poultry operations therefore use feed additives containing xanthophyll or beta-carotene to enhance the yellow color of skin and egg yolks. The brighter color may be attractive to the shopper's eye, but there is evidence that color additives actually lower the quality of eggs.[1] More important, eggs from caged layers may be lower in some nutrients—particularly vitamin B_{12} and folic acid—than eggs from free-ranging hens.[2]

Nutritional quality suffers, too, because of the factory's emphasis on fast weight gain from high-energy feeds, which increases production of storage-type (concentrated, saturated) fats but not of protein, "structural" fat, and other nutritious material. A grain-fed feedlot steer, for example, produces a carcass that is about 30 percent storage-type fat and 50 percent "lean." The "lean" portion contains from 7 to 20 percent of its fresh weight as saturated, storage-type, triglyceride fats—the "marbling" in your steak. Unlike structural fat, which is highly unsaturated and contains essential fatty acids, storage-type fat is waistline fat—nutritionally nonessential and a contributor to various health problems for its consumer. At best, then, only about 45 percent of the feedlot animal's carcass is actual muscle cell and if muscle water is excluded, only about 9 percent of the entire carcass is nutritious material. In the factory-farmed steer, there is about three times as much nonessential, storage-type fat as there is nutrient material; by way of contrast, in free-living animals there is between five and ten times as much nutrient material as there is storage fat.[3] According to an expert on nutrition:

> The extreme end product to modern intensive husbandry, "the heavy hog" is a method of fat production; this system seems pointless in terms of satisfying nutrient requirements of the human population the animal industry is meant to serve.[4]

As anyone who buys chicken knows, today's broiler contains too much fat, which must be cut out and thrown away, either at the slaughterhouse or at the kitchen sink. We are, in effect, throwing out some grain, soy meal, and other feed ingredients along with some of the fossil fuels used in growing these feedstuffs, and transporting them to the automated feed troughs of the broiler shed. Aside from wasting animal lives, we are using up a considerable amount of topsoil, land, energy, and labor to produce this throwaway fat. As we shall see in chapter 8, this misuse of our resources is indefensible in a world where an estimated one billion people subsist on an inadequate diet, where thirteen million die each year from hunger-related causes.[5]

Calves separated at birth, drug residues in milk, and now BGH (bovine growth hormone). . . . Milk is a natural?

How did the chicken come to be so fatty? This account from a report on animal foods by the National Research Council best sums it up:

> The onset of the problem has been developing over several generations of selection. Poultry breeders produced broilers in 1950 that were marketed at 4.0 pounds live body weight at 12 weeks of age. . . . Intense genetic selection by poultry breeders for increased body weight at younger ages resulted in broilers being marketed in 1986 at 4.0 pounds live body weight at 6 weeks and 5 days of age. . . .[Genetic selection for body weight caused chickens with above average appetites to be chosen as breeders.] As a result, broilers were produced that ate more feed at a given age and became unable to synthesize protein and lean meat fast enough to keep pace with increased intake of food energy. The excess food energy was deposited as lipids, and broilers became fatter.[6]

All told,[the industrial broiler chicken is 15 to 20 percent fat, by weight.[7]

Similar factory genetics and feeding practices work in combination with the USDA's meat-grading system to produce fatty feedlot cattle. Oddly, in this era when health-conscious people are reducing the level of fat—especially animal fat—in their diets, the red-meat-grading system puts a premium on carcasses "marbled" with fat. The amount of marbling, or intramuscular fat, is "the main determinant used in the quality grading of carcasses of red meat animals" by USDA meat inspectors.[8] If the intramuscular fat is abundant, the carcass is graded Prime or Choice and the meat fetches the highest prices. To get carcasses rated so, cattle feeders keep their cattle on high-calorie feeds longer than is sensible. Now, the clincher is that excess fat is stored all over the rest of the body before an overfed animal begins to deposit it in the muscles as marbling. Excess fat goes first under the skin, between the muscles, and around the internal organs; when these sites fill up, fat begins to go into the muscle tissues. By the time the highly rated marbling is achieved, the entire carcass is from 25 to 40 percent fat.[9]

In chapter 9 we will outline a new system for grading animal products that will promote sane farming methods and safe food.

Chemical Feast

Of all the forces behind factory farming, the prime mover is chemistry. Animal husbandry has manipulated animals from the start, but twentieth-century chemistry has made possible an entirely new order of manipulations.[The identification of vitamins A and D made it possible for the broiler industry to crowd large numbers of animals indoors as early as the 1920s. Then in the early 1940s another great wave of change came out of a California chemical plant where the American Cyanamid company made antibiotics. One of the company scientists, Dr. Thomas Jukes, found that chickens grew faster when fed the mash left over from the antibiotic manufacturing process. To this day, no one knows for sure precisely why antibiotics speed growth, but within years after Jukes's discovery they became standard feed additives for poultry, cattle, calves, and pigs.

The third wave came in the fifties and sixties as animal scientists mapped out the roles of hormones in growth and reproduction. In this era, feed and pharmaceutical companies packaged hormones and hormonelike substitutes into implants, feed additives, and other commercial products geared to farmers. The feedlot cattle industry is the main buyer of these, but some are used by pork producers to manage the new reproductive problems brought on by factory systems.

Chemistry changed farming, all right, and it surely changed the food we eat. We are used to hearing about the tasteless, juiceless tomato engineered by University of California scientists so that it could be more easily harvested and packaged by machine. Without chemical fertilizers, herbicides, and pesticides it probably would not grow at all. For some odd reason we readily accept that fruits and vegetables are contaminated with pesticides and assorted carcinogens, but we balk at believing animal products are. Meat, milk, and eggs are thought to be somehow "natural" and not susceptible to chemical pollution and manipulation.

So we think and believe. In doing so, we deceive ourselves. Why do you suppose we deceive ourselves so frequently, so consistently, when it comes to foods from animals? Denial and self-deception aside, food from animals today is markedly more altered by chemistry and invasive manipulations than is any food from plants. If you think this is a sweeping statement, remember that factory animals grow up on agribusiness grain and other plant materials. Whatever "bad" toxins there are on these plant materials are generally compounded and concentrated as they accumulate in the fat and tissues of growing animals. Thus animal agriculture repeats and multiplies all of the chemical excesses of plant agriculture.

In addition, industrial animal agriculture uses whole families of potent chemicals, drugs, and pesticides not even used in horticulture. It uses these in various ways:

"Quality" Control. You think the agribusiness tomato is "plastic"? How about the agribusiness egg? The agribusiness turkey? For some time now the turkey industry has used injections containing flavorings and phosphates to improve the taste and texture of turkey meat.[10] Manipulation of chicken flavor through chemistry is touted as a way for the biggest packagers to establish a "unique identity" for their products.[11] Says one expert, "It should be possible to uncover a material or materials that could impart that 'old barnyard' flavor in chickens."[12] Xanthophyll, zeaxanthin, marigold petals or extracts of them, and caroteneic acid are some of the feed additives used to give that golden glow to factory chicken skins and egg yolks.

Appetite Boosters. Factory feed of cardboard, dried poultry manure, and crop by-products may be nutritionally balanced with feather meal, synthetic vitamins, mineral supplements, and other additives. Then it may be medicated with antibiotics, wormers, and growth stimulants and laced with a fly larvicide. After all this "scientific formulation," the feed mixture tastes so bad that factory animals need some coaxing to eat it. The coaxing comes in the form of flavor enhancers—or palatability agents, as the budding seventy-million-dollars-a-year industry prefers to call them. They make an imitation milk flavor that gets weaned calves and pigs on feed more quickly. One company makes a product called "Hog-Krave" that stimulates the appetites of slow-eating stressed pigs.

Pest Control. Obviously flies, mites, rodents, and other creatures tend to grow in number around factory farms where there is a plentiful supply of feeds, animals, and manure. Since they may spread disease and otherwise hamper production, they are, by definition, "pests" and must be eliminated. Some egg producers use power sprayers that roll along the aisles shooting mists of insecticides up through the cage floors onto the birds. For cattle, organophosphate insecticides may be applied as sprays, dust bags, backrubbers, pour-ons, or feed additives. Some producers affix eartags carrying pyrethroid insectides to their animals. In factory dairies, some operators use blowers that mist their facilities with Vapona, whose active ingredient is dichlorvos, a highly toxic organophosphate of the nerve gas family used also in household No-Pest strips. Factory pig farmers spray or dip their animals in Lindane or Permethrin to get rid of mange and lice. For fly control, a larvicide is added to the feed that stays active in the animals' manure (Larvadex in poultry, Rabon in cattle). Dozens of rodenticides and insecticides are used around feed mills and factory farms. Gentian Violet, a known carcinogen, is used to prevent molds in animal feeds.

Disease Control. The main weapon in the factory farmer's arsenal against diseases is the class of agents known as antibiotics. These kill bacteria, so they are helpful tools against a variety of diseases caused by bacteria. About half of the thirty million pounds of antibiotics produced in the United States each year are fed to food-producing animals.[13] Penicillin and tetracyclines are the most extensively used. Nearly all poultry, 90 percent of veal calves and pigs, and a debatable number of cattle get antibacterial additives in their feed. (Cattle producers claim that they have eliminated antibiotic feed additives, but we suspect many do continue to use them. Unfortunately, there is no way to establish the truth because antibiotics manufacturers do not keep records to show which industry buys their products.) According to the National Research Council, about 90 percent of antibiotics used in animal agriculture are given to animals in low, "subtherapeutic" levels, usually in the form of feed additives. Of this 90 percent, about 70 percent is used to prevent diseases, the rest for growth promotion.[14]

In pigs, antibiotics are used to treat or prevent erysipelas, leptospirosis, respiratory infections and pneumonia, mastitis, atrophic rhinitis, and enteritis. In cattle, they are used against mastitis, liver abscesses, calf scours, shipping fever, lump jaw, salmonellosis, listeriosis, blackleg, pinkeye, leptospirosis, and footrot. In poultry, antibiotics are used to prevent or treat chronic respiratory disease, colibacillosis, synovitis, and other bacterial disease.

In addition to antibiotics, factory farmers use a number of families of drugs against a wide variety of diseases:

- **Sulfonamides**—include sulfathiazole, sulfamethazine, sulfanitran, sulfadimethoxine, and sulfaquinoxaline. Sulfamethazine, or SMZ, is used against atrophic rhinitis and pneumonia in pigs, against mastitis in dairy cows, and against fowl cholera in poultry.

- **Nitrogen heterocyclics**—include carbadox, ipronidazole, and dimetridazole. The latter two have been used against blackhead in turkeys. Carbadox is used against swine dysentery and bacterial swine enteritis.

- **Nitrofurans**—include furazolidone and nitrofurazone. These are used primarily in poultry and pigs to control diseases caused by bacteria and protozoa.

- **Benzimidazoles**—include albendazole, fenbendazole, and thiabendazole, drugs used to control parasites in cattle.

Productivity Boosters. In pig and poultry operations, the principal growth promotants are antibiotics. Some 30 percent of antibiotics in feed are added for their growth-promoting effect.

Cattle feedlot operators claim that they do not use antibiotics, but they do use hormones and hormone substitutes as growth promotants. These are the same anabolic steroids used by athletes and bodybuilders. They are sold in the form of a pellet that slowly releases the hormones after it is implanted in a feedlot animal's ear. The implant raises the animal's hormone levels two to five times the normal amount, which changes metabolism and stimulates muscle growth. Thus two desirable goals are obtained: the animal puts on weight more quickly and fat formation is reduced somewhat.

Hormones may be used to enhance growth through other mechanisms if experiments at the USDA's Meat Animal Research Center in Clay, Nebraska, work out. An animal scientist there has treated pregnant sheep with the male sex hormone testosterone. The female lambs born were chromosomally female with uteri and ovaries, but they also had penises, scrota, and other male characteristics. These artificially created hermaphrodites gained weight 10 to 30 percent faster than regular females and their meat was 13 percent leaner. According to *Omni* magazine, this work "will sooner or later spell good news for supermarket shoppers [and] we'll eventually see cheaper, leaner lamb."[15]

As we saw in chapter 3, pigs may soon be made to grow faster on PST (or PGH) and dairy cows made to give more milk on BST (or BGH), both synthetic growth hormones made by recombinant DNA technology. Beta agonists, immune system regulators, and other products of biotechnology promise more powerful tools to make animals produce more, faster.

In the meantime, animal agribusiness has quite an array of chemicals to boost animal productivity. Some examples:

- Shell Oil Company has sold a feed additive to boost the number of pigs born to a sow. "We don't know 'why' it works," said a company official. Nevertheless, Shell had advised that every dollar spent on the chemical brings seven to eleven dollars in returns.[16]
- Feedlot operators use probiotics to aid the development of types of bacteria in the animals' stomachs that improve digestion. They also use a class of antibiotics called ionophores to speed weight gain. One of these, monensis sodium, is one of the five best-selling drugs. The ionophores are deadly to horses, however, and every year a few horses die because of feed mix-ups.
- The egg industry adds antioxidants to chicken feed to lengthen hens' laying cycles. These chemicals inhibit the formation of peroxides during the birds' metabolic activities, which can damage and age hens' egg-producing cells and tissues.
- Poultry and pig producers use arsenical compounds to speed growth, feed efficiency, and boost egg production.
- Sulfamethazine, carbadox, and the nitrofurans are often used as feed additives to boost growth or milk production.

Thanks to modern animal science and its agribusiness cohorts, the factory farm uses, according to FDA estimates, between twenty thousand and thirty thousand drugs to control diseases and boost productivity.[17] In the words of a letter writer to the agribusiness weekly *Agweek,* "To the average livestock owner drugs may be profitable; for the factory farmer they've become essential."[18]

Changing the "art" of growing chickens from a backyard enterprise to a "science" has involved chemistry in many ways.
—Milton L. Sunde, "The 'Chemical Feast' That Helped Us Grow," *Broiler Industry,* March 1977, p. 54

Deceiving Consumers

Reliance on chemistry, along with other factory practices, deceives consumers into thinking animal products have better quality than they really have. What other purpose would skin and yolk yellowers serve? Agribusiness tries to dodge the issue by saying that the purpose is to enhance "eye appeal," which is only another way of saying that its products sell better if they have the look that consumers believe to be associated with quality.

Purveyors for animal factories know what chords to strike to move their products. In spite of the extensive use of chemistry in egg production, one poultry industry leader advised his colleagues: "Slant egg carton copy along this line. 'Eggs are a health food. A natural human food. No additives, no preservatives.' "[19] "Milk is a natural," the dairy industry tells us in slick, upscale television commercials in which cows loll in lush, green fields. The TV cows are hardly typical of factory milk cows with their chronic ketosis and mastitis, their artificial insemination, superovulation, and embryo transfer. One wonders if the dairy industry will continue the milk-is-a-natural theme once the nation's cows are running on implants of recombinant-DNA-synthesized BGH.

In the meantime, milk is often not as pure and natural as dairy industry hype would have us believe. In Wisconsin, "America's Dairyland," USDA has found that more than 13 percent of commingled Grade A and Grade B milk had more bacteria than federal standards allow. "It's about time that [the dairy] industry produces a product that is at least as good as the one they advertise," a USDA official told a meeting of milk company representatives.[20] And, as we shall see, more and more milk contains residues of antibiotics.

As we saw in the last chapter, factory genetics has diluted egg quality over the years. When manufacturers of vaccines need high-quality eggs, they don't buy them from factory farms but from Amish farms with smaller flocks and manual labor methods. Big broiler companies are rich enough to afford slick advertising campaigns that allege the superiority of their brand of chicken, but according to Consumers Union, the ad claims don't hold up. In tests, a Consumers Union panel found that the heavily advertised brand-name broilers were no plumper or better tasting than the unbranded supermarket ones, although they were priced 9 to 14 percent higher per pound.[21]

Our canned hams are fattier and flabbier than European brands, and an American meat-packer believes it is due to corn-feeding and controlled-environment housing in the U.S.[22] The flesh of these cramped, corn-fed pigs turns to fat and the bacon produced nearly disappears in the skillet. Slaughtered, factory-stressed pigs yield flesh that inspectors and packers call PSE (pale, soft, exudative) because of its appearance and the watery ooze it gives off. The pork industry, like the dairy industry, is fond of slick ad campaigns that appeal to the diet-and-health conscious consumer. "America Is Leaning on Pork," the ad slogan goes, implying that we will be slim if we eat more pork. Throughout the 1980s the pork industry told us that the new, improved factory pig was lean and low in fat. Privately, however, the industry is concerned that its pigs are still too fat. There are reports of thick backfat and wide variations in hog carcass quality. The reason, according to a Purdue University animal scientist, is essentially because of the economics of factory farming: "[W]ith the high facilities cost and interest rates, industry [has] put emphasis on sow productivity—pigs per sow per year—just moving more pigs into the facility and out of the facility. It's a kind of a 'Rawhide,' move-'em-in, move-'em-out attitude toward swine production, with very little emphasis on the quality of the pigs that [are] being produced."[23]

More and more cattle these days end up as hamburger probably because that's the only way industry can get rid of culled dairy cows and the fatty meat produced by feedlot methods. The beef industry was not completely up front with us when the European Economic Community banned imports of U.S. meat raised on hormones. Fearful that the public might see the ban as a sign that hormone-fed beef is unsafe, the National Cattlemen's Association (NCA) warned its members not to overreact to the ban and create a lot of bad press about drugs and growth promotants. NCA tried to persuade its members to downplay hormones and emphasize the trade, business, and competition motives behind the ban. "If consumers are led to doubt the safety of U.S. beef [raised on hormones], then a more severe market reaction could result," NCA warned.[24] "Our whole strategy when we talk to the popular press is to make sure this stays on a trade-issue level," said an NCA spokesperson.[25]

The latest deceit, practiced at all levels of each of the animal agribusiness industries, is the claim that producers are reducing and eliminating antibiotics in feed. Agribusiness says that the practice does no harm, yet it is aware that the public perception is otherwise. So they tell us, "We are not doing that anymore." Apparently someone is lying, because the figures indicate that the use of antibiotics in animal agriculture has risen from nine million pounds in 1978 to about fifteen million pounds in 1988.[26]

Let Them Eat Carcinogens

Factory methods do worse than rob consumers of quality: they also expose them to greater risks than ever before. Mechanization, chemistry, and greater centralization may reduce the costs of feeding animals, but they multiply the risk of harm from what might otherwise be a simple accident. In June 1973 several hundred pounds of a flame retardant containing cancer-causing polybrominated biphenyls (PBBs) were accidentally dumped into animal feed at one of the Michigan Farm Bureau's feed mills. As a result, more than thirty thousand cattle, two million chickens, and thousands of sheep and pigs died or had to be killed by farmers. Through bureaucratic inertia or incompetence, state authorities did not withdraw the feed or trace its source until ten months later when the poison was identified by a USDA chemist. By that time, the PBB-poisoned meat, milk, and eggs had gone out to consumers. By the summer of 1976, 96 percent of nursing mothers tested in Michigan had PBB in their milk. PBB in the manure of contaminated animals ended up in the soil, lakes, and rivers. Michigan vegetables began to show residues of the carcinogenic chemical. According to testimony before Michigan's Senate Commerce Subcommittee hearings on March 29, 1977, nearly all Michigan residents had intolerable levels of PBB.[27]

An isolated incident? One authority on toxic substances believes that "PBB represents the kind of problem we're beginning to see not only in Michigan but in the United States and many parts of the world."[28]

Similar episodes have occurred since then, but thanks to alert authorities the damage has not been as great as in Michigan. In 1988, for example, residues of chlordane showed up in several flocks of broilers in Maryland. Chlordane, an organochlorine pesticide known to cause cancer in humans, is banned for all uses by the Environmental Protection Agency. An investigation traced the pesticide to corn grown for the broilers' feed. A corn farmer had illegally applied chlordane to the inside of his grain storage bin which contained 4,500 bushels of corn. The contaminated corn became contaminated feed, which contaminated the chickens. USDA officials caught this problem before the chickens reached the consumer.[29]

Burying mistakes: disposal of poisoned cattle after the 1973 PBB incident in Michigan.

In another case, the pesticide heptachlor was found in broilers in Arkansas in early 1989. Heptachlor, a carcinogen, is used to treat seed grains and grains not intended for use in the human food chain. Once again, fortunately, USDA officials intervened and put nearly two million pounds of poultry meat on hold in warehouses until testing could be completed.[30] It sometimes happens, as it did in this incident, that pesticide-treated grain ends up in animal feeds. This may happen because of an accident or a mix-up at the feedmill. In some cases it happens because unscrupulous grain farmers, feedmill operators, or factory farmers trade in pesticide-treated grain and wink at the risks to human health.

Can we depend on state and federal agencies to catch every one of these incidents and to remove contaminated animal products from the food chain? No matter how well state and federal agencies may police animal products, they are trying to regulate an agriculture that is drug and chemically dependent from top to bottom, and it is probably inevitable that some dangerous residues will creep through the official safety nets from time to time. Ten years ago the General Accounting Office reviewed USDA's efforts to protect consumers from illegal and potentially harmful residues of animal drugs, pesticides, and environmental contaminants in meat and poultry. At the time, USDA claimed that only 2 percent contained illegal residues. From the same data, GAO estimated that 14 percent of meat and poultry contained illegally high levels of drugs and pesticides. GAO noted that many of these were known to be dangerous:

> Of the 143 drugs and pesticides GAO identified as likely to leave residues in raw meat and poultry, 42 are known to cause or are suspected of causing cancer; 20 of causing birth defects; and 6 of causing mutations.[31]

We contacted GAO in the hope that it had continued to check up on USDA's meat inspection and drug monitoring efforts. It seemed to us that GAO had enough justification for an ongoing review of these vital programs. For no apparent reason, GAO has not followed up on this shocking 1979 report. Could it be because of the antiregulatory and cost-cutting policies that took over in the 1980s?

The factory's search for cheaper feedstuffs may cause additional health problems for consumers. According to a veterinarian who became a meat inspector after twenty years of farm animal practice, "There are a number of major human diseases, namely, cancer, heart disease, and gallstones, that . . . originate in the meat-packing plants of this country." He believes that animal feed manufacturing practices contribute to a high incidence of cancer in factory animals because cancerous tissue is recycled.

What happens to the 15 million pounds of animal tissues which are too severely affected with cancer to be used? They are processed into hog and chicken feed. The result is a recycling of potential cancer substances repeatedly through the human and animal food chain.[32]

Cancerous tissues are not the only risky materials recycled through animal feeds, as we noted in chapter 3. Manure and dried poultry litter often contain increased levels of cadmium, lead, arsenic, or other heavy metals. These metals build up in bones, kidneys, or livers, which are discarded at the slaughterhouse, ground up, and recycled back through animal feed. Since all of the wastes and by-products contain heavy metals and they are constantly recycled, they surely accumulate in the factory-farmed animal. Don't worry, the proagribusiness American Veterinary Medical Association's journal tells us, the toxic metals accumulate in the parts we don't eat.[33]

Hormones, too, are safe in animal products, the agribusiness experts say. This was declared again recently by U.S. officials when the European Economic Community banned American meat from hormone-treated cattle. As discussed, USDA and U.S. trade officials decided to treat the move as a trade barrier and "not a decision based on legitimate health or safety grounds."[34] They usually qualify the declaration with the proviso "if properly used." But hormones are sometimes improperly used, that is, implanted in the wrong place or injected deep into muscle tissue where they cannot be detected. Diethylstilbestrol (DES), for example, was being improperly implanted by cattlemen after it had been banned in 1979. Or the properly placed implants (in the animals' ears) end up in the wrong place at the processing plant. In either case, hormones end up in the human food chain.

Pesticides, which we have learned to fear on our apples and tomatoes, are now prevalent in beef, pork, and chicken. All three meats are in the top fifteen foods with the greatest risk of causing cancer, as estimated by the National Research Council. Of the ten foods most likely to cause cancer from herbicide residues, beef is number 1 and pork is number 3.[35] Of the ten foods most likely to cause cancer from insecticide residues, chicken is number 2, beef is number 3, and pork is number 7.[36]

We have seen how animal products can be contaminated with dangerous pesticides through accidents, mistakes, or unscrupulous practices. Aside from these means, there are chemicals in animal foods because of ordinary feed industry practices. According to an FDA official:

Many ingredients used in animal feeds are waste products from food processing, where pesticide residues concentrate in excess of the permitted tolerance for the raw agricultural commodity from which the by-products were derived. And, chaff and fines, common waste products from agricultural and ornamental commodity harvesting, are pelleted for feed use. These products often contain residues of pesticides for which no tolerance has been established and for which no analytical method has been developed to detect residues in meat, milk and eggs.[37]

Remember that last sentence, for you will hear agribusiness claim that only 1 or 2 percent of all animal products *tested* show illegal residues of chemicals.

(With five billion broilers consumed each year, that is still a lot of carcinogenic birds—over fifty million by our calculations.) One or two percent sounds pretty safe, but our actual exposure to pesticides and other toxins may be much greater once we figure in those we cannot detect in animal products and those whose dangers we have not yet assessed. In fact, these may be the most dangerous of all, because they are the most likely to be abused, leaving very high levels of potentially dangerous residues. Dibutyltin dilaurate is such an animal drug. FDA's Cancer Assessment Committee has put it on the list of drugs for priority review because its structure is very much like other cancer-causing compounds. It is on the market even though there isn't a good method for detecting residues of the drug in animal products. USDA has an experimental method, however, and inspectors have tested it on turkey meat. They found a 20 percent violation rate—a much higher incidence than for any other drug.

And to what extent are pesticides a human health problem in animal products? According to an FDA official, "The majority of pesticide-contaminated human food incidents of the last decade were the result of human exposure through consumption of contaminated animal products."[38]

We are not talking yet about illegal drugs and abuse of legal drugs; we will discuss that under **Drug Abuse** in this chapter. For the moment we are concerned with risks to human health created by *proper* use of approved drugs and chemicals in animal agriculture. One would assume that such use would be safe, that it would not add carcinogens and toxins to our supply of animal products. The problem with that assumption is that some so-called safe drugs and safe uses turn out to be unsafe. After a drug product has been on the market for years and is widely relied on by factory farmers, information comes out that it is unsafe and then industry and FDA begin a tussle over controlling it or pulling it off the market. In the fifteen years since we began investigating animal agribusiness, we have seen this drama played out again and again with drug after drug. In our opinion, the play will continue because, no matter how many high-powered drugs are pulled off the market, agribusiness will still need high-powered drugs. One insider with a federal government regulatory agency advised us to be watchful for the drug that industry turns to when one of its favorite products is taken off the market as unsafe. In many cases, the insider told us, the replacement drug is just as bad—or worse. At such times, residues of the replacement drug may appear in meat and go undetected. This occurs because it takes authorities a while to get to know what the replacement drug is and to begin monitoring for it. And if a potent replacement is not on the market at the time, the pharmaceutical industry will come up with one—or many. Then, after FDA approval, the drug or drugs enter the market and are used for years until information comes in that they leave dangerous residues.

Our prediction is not from pure pessimism, but from an understanding of the kind of need for medicine on the factory farm. Ordinary, moderate drugs will not control disease problems of the intensity found in high-tech animal factories. Killer medicines and drugs are needed. Unfortunately their broad-spectrum power often kills or damages more than was originally intended. Agribusiness is locked into an arms race of industrial-strength drugs against industrial-strength diseases. So it will continue to develop new magic bullets to replace those found unsafe. FDA is well aware of this cycle and of the need for constant vigilance. In the words of an FDA environmental scientist:

> Organophosphates, organic arsenicals, hormones and very bioactive chemicals that are often also used as pesticides are approved as new animal drugs. . . . The general tendency in the animal drug industry has been to seek approval for more and more bioactive products, often with broad spectra of activity.[39]

FDA and USDA have been trying to keep up the safety nets as best they can, we suppose, considering the financial and political clout of the chemical and pharmaceutical industries. In 1985, however, FDA was found to be doing a pretty poor job of it. A congressional committee headed by New York Congressman Ted Weiss found evidence of years of neglect of the animal drug problem:

- As many as 90 percent or more of the twenty thousand to thirty thousand new animal drugs estimated to be on the market have not been approved by FDA as safe and effective and, therefore, are being marketed in violation of the new animal drug approval requirements of the Food, Drug and Cosmetic Act.
- As many as four thousand of these new animal drugs may have "potentially significant adverse effects on animals or humans."
- FDA failed to remove several potentially unsafe animal drugs from the market, including dimetridazole, ipronidazole and Carbadox, known to cause cancer and mutations.
- FDA failed to require drug manufacturers to develop methods to detect residues of the drugs for which they sought approval, as provided by law.
- Adequate regulatory methods are currently not available for over 70 percent of the animal drug residues in meat, milk, and eggs that USDA has responsibility for monitoring. FDA has no timetable for ensuring that all approved new animal drugs are supported by adequate methods for detecting their residues in milk and edible animal tissue. Nor has FDA advised corporate sponsors of the deadlines they must meet for developing such methods.
- Most approved animal drugs were cleared for marketing years ago on the basis of safety evaluations now considered inadequate.[40]

In the brouhaha that ensued as a result of the Weiss report, FDA and industry scurried to cover their tracks. Several dangerous drugs were either restricted or taken off the market:

Sulfamethazine (SMZ). This is one of the most widely used of the sulfa drugs, especially in pigs, calves, and dairy cattle. An estimated 70 percent of pigs in the United States receive some sulfa medication and SMZ is the drug of choice. It is a popular drug because it has unusually long "staying power"— that is, its medicinal effects last longer in the animal. This persistence and medicinal power, however, make for persistent major residue problems. SMZ has long been known to cause severe allergic reactions and anemia in some people. More recently it has been found to cause cancer in test animals. In the late 1970s, illegally high residues of the drug were found in 12 to 15 percent of pigs. Pressure from government and industry brought the violation rate down to 4.5 percent; then it rose again. Since 1980, the national average violation rate has been about 4 to 6 percent.[41] In recent times, illegal levels of SMZ have been found in milk nationwide. It should be noted that this detective work was done by concerned university scientists, not by the government officials who should have done it. At the time, FDA milk tests did not detect SMZ. In 1988, FDA developed a method and conducted a survey to check up on reports in scientific journals that SMZ residues were getting out of hand. Officials collected forty-nine samples of retail milk in ten of the largest cities. Of these, almost three-fourths bore residues of SMZ. Most were not high enough to be considered dangerous, but 14 percent were.[42]

FDA has since asked manufacturers to put this statement on the labels of the SMZ products: "Not for use in dairy cattle."[43] FDA is working with pork industry leaders in a plan to hold down the SMZ violation rate in pigs.

Dimetridazole and Ipronidazole. These were originally approved only for use in turkeys for the treatment of a disease called blackhead. Both drugs were widely used by pig producers and others against different diseases. Both of these powerful antibiotics have been shown to cause cancer and mutations. FDA has had information about dimetridazole's carcinogenicity since 1971. Ipronidazole's own manufacturer presented FDA with evidence of carcinogenicity in 1978. Neither drug's manufacturer ever gave the government an adequate means of detecting residues of the drug in edible animal tissues. Nevertheless, dimetridazole remained on the market until 1987, ipronidazole until 1988. At the Weiss committee hearings, this discussion of the time lag occurred:

> **Mr. Weiss:** Since FDA has no way to assure that the public is not being exposed to unsafe levels of [dimetridazole] in its food supply, on what basis has FDA permitted its continued marketing?
>
> **Dr. [Lester] Crawford** [then head of FDA's Center for Veterinary Medicine (CVM), the department responsible for animal drug regulation]: It does appear that these substances must be considered for administrative action, and so we are not getting around to it. As you correctly point out, there are questions about the continued approvability of these [drugs].
>
> . . . It is a long, involved process to get drugs off the market once they're on, and much less of a process is involved in approving them to go on the market.[44]

Carbadox. This drug is approved for use in pigs for growth promotion and improved feed efficiency. It is used also for control of swine dysentery and bacterial enteritis. Its residues are so dangerous that FDA directs farmers to stop using it seventy days before slaughter. In the words of an FDA scientist: "Carbadox was approved in 1972 for growth promotion and to control dysentery in swine despite the fact that we know the compound was a genotoxic carcinogen and that the most sensitive method of analysis available for residues in pork failed, by a wide margin, to permit monitoring of the drug's label-recommended withdrawal period."[45] Then in 1979, FDA found "strong evidence" of its cancer-causing power. FDA also found that carbadox breaks down in the animal to desoxycarbadox (called a "metabolite" of the drug), which is an even more potent carcinogen than the drug itself. To this date, FDA still has not required the manufacturer to develop a means for the detection of "safe" levels of residues of carbadox in animal tissues. As of this writing, the drug remains on the market and is widely advertised and used.

Gentian Violet. This drug is used to treat chickens and turkeys for a fungus infection that develops in the animals' throats. It is used also as a feed additive to inhibit molds and fungi. Gentian Violet is known to cause mutations and cancer, was never approved, and FDA has consistently contested industry's claims that it is GRAS (generally recognized as safe). FDA's own National Center for Toxicological Research (NCTR) advised CVM officials in 1982 that it was a cancer-causer. After years of paper-shuffling among FDA staff members, false starts, and foot-dragging by agency higher-ups, Gentian Violet is still on the market. This is all the more disturbing because the drug has never been approved; its marketers have simply said it is safe (GRAS). FDA would not have to go through a long hearing process as it does when it wants to withdraw an approved drug. Sales could be stopped simply by publishing a notice in the Federal Register, and sixty days later officials could seize it where they find it.

Now that the heat is on, thanks to the Weiss committee and the press, FDA is trying to get on top of the animal drug regulatory mess. But years of neglect have left a tremendous backlog and we cannot expect immediate results. The agency has renewed action begun back in 1973 to remove the nitrofurans, a family of cancer-causers. FDA officials say they will begin reviews of eight other dangerous drugs, including thiabendazole, fenbendazole, clorsulon, fenthion, dibutyltin dilaurate, and ronnel. Assuming this housecleaning goes ahead as planned, we have to wonder—given the agency's record and the antiregulatory mood that seems to be so in vogue these days: What sort of drugs will fill the void? What will the manufacturers come up with to meet the needs of factory farm diseases? As we shall see below, these needs are so strong that the most potent drugs will still move in commerce—illegally—and the risks to human and animal health will continue.

Farm industry and profarming government officials downplay these risks, arguing that drugs and chemicals are rigorously tested before they go into commercial use. The animal "health products" (read: drug and chemical) industry points to the government's long testing procedures through which new products must go before they can be marketed. But these procedures seem more and more inadequate as safeguards against the kinds of risks posed by today's agrochemistry. DES, DDT, and some of our other drugs and pesticides did not reveal their dangers until years after they had been approved as safe by the government.

I am one of the many practicing veterinarians who witness misuse or misapplication of millions of dollars of drugs on the farm, on a day-to-day basis.
—Letter from F. B. Lederman, D.V.M., Blue Earth, MN, in "Reader Speak Up," *National Hog Farmer,* November 1976, p. 42

"One reason large confinement systems have worked is because of antibiotics. Without antibiotics it would be hard to have these larger systems and crowd the pigs as we do in some cases."—John Armes, pig producer, McQuady, Ky., quoted in "Is Absolute Safety Impossible?" *Hog Farm Management,* March 1978, p. 98.

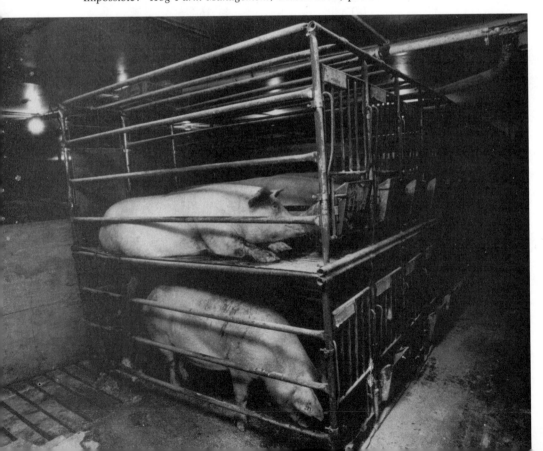

Let Them Eat Germs

Animal agribusiness is worried stiff about the animal rights movement and its efforts to bring the wrongs of factory farming to light. Industry leaders are afraid people will continue to lose their appetites for meat, milk, and eggs. Concerned people may, in fact, push that trend ahead, but we think the greatest incentive for people to eliminate meat from their diets will be *Salmonella enteriditis.* This single-celled plant causes food poisoning and is turning the livestock and poultry—especially the poultry—businesses upside down on both sides of the Atlantic. In England, in the wake of an outbreak of food poisonings just before Christmas in 1988, investigations revealed that two-thirds of all broilers and turkeys were infected with the disease. In the United States, according to *The New York Times:*

> Epidemiologists at the Federal Centers for Disease Control believe that roughly 2.5 million salmonella cases a year are food-borne, that most of these can be traced to poultry, meat and eggs and that both the incidence and the severity of such cases appears to be increasing.[46]

Thirty-seven percent of broilers are contaminated with Salmonella, according to a 1987 USDA study. Another USDA study showed that as many as 76 percent of chickens had Salmonella. An estimated one in every 200 eggs is contaminated with the disease.[47] In most cases, salmonellosis takes the form of moderate to severe diarrhea, but the National Research Council's Institute of Medicine estimates that it causes as many as five hundred deaths each year; others estimate nine thousand deaths a year.[48]

Salmonellosis, or Salmonella food poisoning, from contaminated eggs has been a problem primarily in the northeastern states. In 1988, there were two outbreaks in Connecticut nursing homes, an outbreak in New York City, and one in Maryland—all traceable to eggs.[49] Authorities report a sixfold jump in the disease in nine northeastern states during the decade ending in 1986.[50] According to the Centers for Disease Control (CDC), there were sixty-five outbreaks of salmonellosis in the Northeast between January 1985 and May 1987; these resulted in 2,119 food poisoning cases. Eleven of these people died, most of them elderly persons in nursing homes.[51] Another twenty-six outbreaks have occurred since May 1987, most in the Northeast, but egg-related outbreaks are also turning up in Texas and Virginia.

Why do you suppose salmonellosis (and, as we shall see, other food-borne diseases) caused by animal products is on the rise? By all accounts, it is because of factory methods—on the farm and at the feedmill. According to a study done by USDA scientists, Salmonella is increasing among beef cattle because of "transport, confinement and intensive management associated with the farm and sales barn-feedlot marketing system."[52] Apparently the crowded, manure-soaked pens provide a fertile medium for the bacteria.

The practice of recycling manure, dead chickens, feathers, and condemned animal parts back into animals' feeds is believed to be spreading germs. After the Christmas 1988 Salmonella uproar in the United Kingdom, experts criticized the practice and the public called for a ban. Said an article in *Feedstuffs*:

> Even among poultrymen and animal feed manufacturers there are now fears that the diets fed to poultry lie at the root of the current crisis. There is somewhat limited scientific evidence that producers may have been playing with fire by feeding cheap protein—feedstuffs containing the remains of dead chickens—which may have helped perpetuate salmonella in British poultry.
>
> As a spokesman of the Grain and Feed Trade Association pointed out: Efforts to eradicate Salmonella have not been helped by the practice of including the processed remains of dead chickens in poultry feeds.[53]

FDA officials also believe that Salmonella and possibly other food-borne diseases are being spread to meat-, milk-, and egg-producing animals "through consumption of contaminated feeds."[54]

Other germs appear to be joining *Salmonella eneriditis* in the single-celled-plant plot to overthrow animal agribusiness. Meat- and poultry-borne food poisonings number in the millions each year in the United States. Experts estimate that about five million cases of disease and over nine thousand deaths yearly are attributable to a few disease-causing germs carried by meat, milk, or eggs. These are Salmonella, Campylobacter, *Clostridium perfringens, Yersinia enterocolitica, Escherichia coli, Toxoplasma gondii,* and *Listeria monocytogenes.* Experts believe that the first two bacteria listed are responsible for 1.8 million cases of food poisoning each year.[55]

Listeria, which causes flulike symptoms and fever, is responsible for some sixteen hundred deaths each year in the United States. In 1987, USDA investigators found that 5 percent of beef was contaminated with Listeria. With a fatality rate of about 30 percent, the disease is much more dangerous than Salmonella. A large outbreak of Listeria occurred in Los Angeles in April 1985, killing more than three dozen people, mostly infants.[56] USDA recently found that "Listeria may be present in hot dogs" because temperatures are not hot enough to kill the bacteria during processing.[57]

The latest germ to cause food poisoning in consumers and headaches in the meat industry is *Escherichia coli*. An outbreak of bloody diarrhea and hemolytic uremic syndrome (a kidney disorder) in Minnesota schoolchildren was traced to *E. coli* in undercooked beef patties. A USDA official considered "special measures" because, he said, "we have something now that is more serious than Salmonella has been and more serious than we thought Listeria was going to be."[58] According to a news account in the *Journal of the American Veterinary Medical Association,* meat industry leaders met with USDA officals in an effort to contain "an overreaction" to the incident.[59]

So now if we consume factory-farmed products we face the risk of a relatively quick death from a food-borne disease as well as the risk of a long drawn-out death from cancer-causing residues. Well, USDA and the meat industry tell us, at least you can try to prevent the quick death from bacteria; you can just cook everything until well-done. This "solution" brought outrage from the editors of Tucson's *Arizona Daily Star*: "Consumers are requested to treat chicken like a loaded gun—armed with bacteria and considered dangerous." The editors noted that chickens are germy because of conditions on factory farms and in slaughter-houses. "Why is the buyer the one who has to worry? Why can't animals be raised and slaughtered with enough care that they reach market in a healthful condition?"[60]

A good question indeed.

Drug Abuse

Animal drug sales in 1988 came to $2.5 billion, up 6 percent over 1987. Feed additive sales went up 9 percent during the same year. 1988's sales were up 50 percent over all animal drug sales in 1979. Clearly, animal drug use grows year by year because the trend toward factory animal production grows year by year. Natural growth and reproduction: too slow. Natural disease resistance: in-effective in crowded masses of animals. Natural husbandry methods: unprofit-able against competitors, all of whom use factory methods with all the shortcuts and magic bullets. Indeed, the modern agribusinessman carries a deep contempt for nature and a great worship of biomanipulative technology. As a result, we have drug-addicted farm animals and drug-dependent animal industries.

This is America's Other Drug Problem. It is the more dangerous one in a sense, because it harms the health of vast numbers of people other than those who are the real traffickers and users. We cannot "just say no" to drugs when they are in the food chain.

Government and industry officials are finally beginning to recognize that a problem exists and take long-overdue action. When they speak to the public and press in the wake of a scare over drug residues or food poisonings, they calmly tell us all is well, all the safety nets are in place. The most often recited statement is: *Americans enjoy the safest, most wholesome food supply in the world.* When they talk among themselves at symposia, conferences, and trade shows, howev-er, discussion of animal drug and disease problems is anything but calm. Of course this is no great surprise; it is the posturing of merchants fearful of losing sales. It also devastates their credibility and that of scientists who—more and more like lawyers—advocate and represent agribusiness' interests.] 80

Animal agribusiness has good reason to be anxious about the drug situation. The public is hearing about it and beginning to react while at meat and dairy cases in the supermarket. Agribusiness must fear the crackdown that lies ahead, which will bring more rules, regulations, red tape, and meddlesome bureaucrats. Or quite possibly agribusiness is afraid that something terrible will happen before it can control the negative effects of its drugs and germs.

The situation is out of control primarily because of attitudes about animal drugs that are fostered by the drug manufacturers. Rampant competition and commercialism have created a climate wherein drugs are portrayed as problem-fixers, money-savers, and profit-boosters. No doubt they can be all these things, but they can also cause undesirable effects in people and animals. These effects are downplayed—or ignored altogether—by the pharmaceutical companies. Farmers, feedmill operators, county agents, milk company field representatives, and people working throughout animal production tend to hear far more about the wonders than the hazards of animal drugs. In this climate, the prevailing evaluation of drugs is anything but cool, dispassionate, and strictly rational. More often than not, a drug's wondrous effects are highly exaggerated in both advertising and speech. Possible dangers or risks are rarely mentioned in drug advertisements and warnings are in fine print on drug labels. Any mention of a drug's possible dangers is often scoffed at by agribusiness experts. In his landmark book, *Modern Meat,* author Orville Schell observed this prodrug attitude in pure form in western cattlemen:

> Many cattlemen seem almost to cultivate a disregard for caution around potentially dangerous drugs and chemicals, as if prudence might be mis-interpreted as timidity or unmanliness. A corollary of this kind of machis-mo is the cattleman's often-haughty disregard for government inspectors, who are viewed not as protectors of the public health but as bothersome fuddy-duddies, sent forth from the disdained, and possibly socialistic, world of "big government" to spy and intrude on private enterprise.[61]

Pharmaceutical agribusiness's control over popular opinion on drugs used for animal production has obvious advantages: it keeps critics under foot, the feds at bay, the farm press in its pocket, and farmers knocking at the door with money for more and more wonder drugs. Some of the advantages are not so obvious. One is that it keeps as *many* drugs as possible as *available* as possible, the justification being that farmers need these to save animal lives and the family farm. Few critics can stand up to that, so the animal drug delivery system goes unfettered. Drugs are sold like cigarettes or chewing gum. According to CVM, 92 percent of the food animal drugs in the United States are sold over the counter (OTC).[62] This means anyone can buy them without any prescription or supervision from a veterinarian. This also means there is very little accountability in the food animal drug delivery system, and as history has shown in a variety of human endeavors, low accountability usually leads to shortcuts and abuses. These lax attitudes and low standards trickle down to the factory farm where dangerous drugs and chemicals are administered to animals. These drugs in turn trickle down into our food chain.

[Farmers feeding drugs to animals are supposed to "withdraw" the drugs (that is, stop feeding them) a specified number of days before the animal is sent for slaughter] The idea is that the drugs should not be present in the animal's flesh by the time it is killed; but farmers aren't always careful enough. Some don't follow directions; some don't stop feeding drugs before sending their animals to slaughter; and then, of course, there are mistakes. Mistakes are much more likely in a factory where various types of feed and additives are used. According to one expert, "It's incredible how many people don't know what additive is in their feed."[63] They aren't helped by the feed and drug manufacturers, who don't always state on their labels what drugs and additives are mixed in. Withdrawal schedules are supposed to help farmers decide when to remove additives before sending the animals to market, but the schedules can be confusing and hard to follow.[64]

As well as the farmers' failure, or inability, to withdraw drugs before shipment properly, the factory machinery appears to contribute to residues in animal products. Large feed-storage bins and long, mechanized tubes and troughs hold quantities of drug-laced feed for several days after the drugs and additives have been withdrawn. According to an FDA study, drug carryover in feeders was responsible for 57 percent of illegally high residues in pigs during the last half of 1977.[65] This is one reason why sulfamethazine (SMZ) residues have been an intractable problem in hogs for over a decade. Factory pig farmers continue to add it to feed to increase weight gain, and even when they stop it continues to contaminate feed mixers, bins, water lines, manure, and, finally, feed. This persistence of SMZ, incidentally, is contributing to the evolution of drug-resistant types of bacteria, reducing the drug's ability to control disease. In just eight years, pig herds in Iowa went from 90 percent sensitive to 90 percent resistant to SMZ as a therapeutic agent against the disease rhinitis.[66] This, in turn, contributes to more residues in pork because producers give higher and higher doses to try to get results.

Another big contributor to drug residues in meat and milk is the practice of extra-label use, that is, using a drug in a way not prescribed by the manufacturer's directions. Extra-label use has been the main cause of residues in milk, veal, and hamburger beef, much of which comes from cull dairy cows. A 1988 study of U.S. and Canadian milk showed that 150 of 174 samples contained residues of SMZ or tetracycline.[67] SMZ is not approved for use in lactating dairy cattle, so it is being used extra-labelly, illegally. Producers resort to these potent drugs most often to treat mastitis—an infection of the milk-producing organs that occurs in about one-third of today's stressed, high-performance factory milk cows. When FDA looked at the SMZ problem in milk it found that just one producer misusing the drug could contaminate quantities of milk:

It was very apparent that if sulfamethazine products (oblets, sustained-release boluses, intravenous infusions, etc.) are used in an extra-label fashion or illegally in dairy cattle, very high concentrations of sulfamethazine in milk will occur. For example, milk from one animal containing a sulfamethazine concentration of 80 milligrams per kilogram would require an equal quantity of milk from approximately 60,000 animals to reduce the sulfamethazine to a nondetectable level.[68]

Residues of antibiotic drugs, including SMZ, neomycin, and gentamicin, have been showing up in one in thirty "milk-fed" veal calves also because of extralabel (or illegal) use. (This is considered a very high level by authorities.) According to FDA, "no drug, not a single drug . . . is specifically approved at this time for use in fancy veal."[69] Veal producers are using drugs approved for cattle. Even if they observe prescribed withdrawal times, residues appear because the young calves receive no solid food and are nonruminating, hence they metabolize drugs differently than do other calves and cattle.

Hamburger beef has shown drug residues because of a combination of extralabel use and failure to observe withdrawal times. Much of this beef comes from cull dairy cows that are weeded out of the herd usually because of chronic mastitis or another disease. In many cases, the farmer has been unsuccessful in trying to cure a disease with SMZ or other antibiotics not approved for use in lactating cows. Rather than continue to feed a nonproductive, deteriorating animal, some farmers cull the sick cow from the herd and send her to market immediately, drugs still coursing through her flesh and blood.

These and other extra-label uses have traditionally been permitted by FDA, a policy that brought criticism from the Weiss committee:

> Although Section 512(a)(1)(A) of the Food, Drug and Cosmetic Act prohibits *any* unapproved use of a new animal drug, CVM has traditionally permitted veterinarians to prescribe and use new animal drugs for unapproved purposes. CVM permits a veterinarian under certain circumstances to prescribe or use a new animal drug "extra-labelly"; that is, not in accordance with its approved labeling. . . .
>
> In acquiescing to the use of animal drugs in unapproved species, the extra-label use policy also increases consumers' exposure to animal drug residues that are likely to go undetected by USDA's national monitoring program.[70]

Years of lax enforcement of drug laws by the FDA are haunting the agency now. Lately, officials have been concerned with the residues of gentamicin in cull dairy cows: "Since gentamicin is not approved for use in dairy cattle, it is obviously being used in an extra-label manner."[71] The FDA official quoted points out that this is "particularly inappropriate" in dairy cattle because gentamicin, like SMZ, is eliminated very slowly and is likely to leave persistent residues. The misuse occurs because gentamicin is the drug of choice for mastitis caused by gram-negative bacteria, a type of mastitis against which penicillin is largely ineffective. And because gentamicin is not approved for use in lactating dairy cows, the government has no method to detect residues of the drug in milk. Knowing this, many producers go ahead and use gentamicin and do not discard the milk of treated cows.

Bureaucratic inertia and industry lobbying efforts prevent government protective procedures from keeping up with new problems in factory methods. Waste recycling, for example, aids factory farmers' search for cheaper feedstuffs and solutions to their monumental waste disposal problems. But because the wastes may contain drug residues, the practice adds to the factory farm's problems with its products. According to one expert, "A producer refeeding waste almost has to assume those sows are getting some drugs."[72] But recycled waste is not as uniform in content as a commercial drug; its elements vary widely from farm to farm and from species to species. This means that a withdrawal period or dosage in feed that is safe for one batch might not be safe for one from another farm or from other animals. Another factory trend, that toward "flush-floor" systems for waste removal, can cause residue problems when that flush water is recycled. Water-soluble sulfa drugs can build up in the water and be taken in by pigs as they drink from the floors.

In addition to these mistakes and negligences there are the out and out illegal drug sales and uses. In the 1980s, FDA reports, there was "an alarming and widespread increase in the sale and use of illegal animal drugs."[73] This trend, and FDA's inability to control it, alarmed the Weiss committee:

> FDA field investigators have found widespread disregard of the use restrictions imposed by the prescription legend. Highly toxic veterinary prescription drugs are frequently being sold to laymen who do not have a prescription. . . .
>
> Illegal veterinary prescription drug sales are of such magnitude and pervasiveness that they threaten the "credibility of the veterinary drug approval and regulatory process." On one two-week road trip in Iowa, for example, an FDA investigator was able to make 40 illegal buys out of 43 attempts. Agency witnesses testified that the illegal sales problem appears nationwide in scope.[74]

In the wake of the Weiss committee's report, FDA officials are, according to *FDA Veterinarian*, apparently trying to curb illegal drug sales and uses. Some of FDA's recent investigations and drug busts, many of which have made nationwide news, should illustrate the pervasiveness of illegal animal drug use:

- In the first six months of 1985, officials surveyed 95 percent of Colorado's dairy producers "in response to concerns voiced at the national level regarding the illegal distribution and use of prescription drugs and pertaining to residues of toxic drugs such as chloramphenicol in food products derived from animals."[75] (Chloramphenicol has never been approved for use in food-producing animals because of its toxicity, even at trace levels. It has been linked to several fatal diseases in humans, including aplastic anemia, gray syndrome in premature and newborn infants, and various neurotoxic disorders.) The Colorado dairy survey revealed:
  —the presence or use of chloramphenicol on 20 to 50 percent of farms, depending on region;
  —frequent presence or use of unlabeled or mislabeled prescription and OTC drugs;

—frequent presence or use of expired, outdated, and otherwise potentially adulterated prescription and OTC drugs;

—presence or use of veterinary prescription drugs without a licensed veterinarian's prescription.

FDA concluded that "these survey results clearly [indicate] a potential risk for consumers" and the agency immediately initiated a new statewide veterinary drug control program. After two and a half years, FDA went back to assess its program. The second survey went out to the seventy-eight dairy farms surveyed in 1985. Here's what FDA found:

—all seventy-eight farms had expired, out-of-date drugs on hand;

—thirty-three farms had drugs with no labels or illegible labels;

—forty-one instances of potential or apparent extralabel uses of drugs;

—seventeen farms stored drugs inconsistent with directions, e.g., without refrigeration;

—chloramphenicol was found on five farms.[76]

• Illegal use of cloramphenicol shows up from time to time in veal calves and other food animals. USDA field tests in 1987 turned up a number of suspect violations in calves.[77] "Chloramphenicol has been used widely and illegally in food-producing animals," FDA stated.[78] Because of this persistent misuse and failure of efforts to stop it, FDA declared even the oral solution dosage form of the drug (for use in dogs and cats and other nonfood animals) an unapproved new drug and empowered its agents to seize the drug under certain conditions.[79] After a 1988 survey, FDA pronounced its ban "successful in deterring the use of this drug in lactating dairy cows."[80] In the same year, however, an independent survey found chloramphenicol in two of sixteen Colorado milk samples (see note 67). Tightening up regulations on chloramphenicol apparently forced drug-dependent factory farmers to turn to other drugs because FDA found extralabel use of Terramycin solution and triple sulfa boluses. This, FDA said, "raises concern that other drugs may be misused."[81] Chloramphenicol is not entirely out of the picture, because FDA has approved a 2.5 gram bolus of the drug for use in large dogs. The bolus is a perfect size for use in young calves, so it creates an easy setup for illegal use. Actions such as this make one wonder if FDA is in touch with the reality of illegal animal drug use.

• In July 1987, FDA agents seized 9.5 tons of illegal bulk animal drugs valued at approximately four hundred thousand dollars from an Omaha, Nebraska, warehouse. Authorities eventually charged three men, one a veterinarian, with illegal import and distribution of a variety of toxic drugs, including amprolium, carbadox, chloramphenicol, dimetridazole, ipronidazole, levamasole, nitrofurazone, oxybendazole, oxytetracycline, potassium penicillin, rifampin, spectinomycin, tetracyline HC1, trimethoprim, and tylosin. Several of the drugs are known carcinogens and have severely restricted uses. The three men had conspired to smuggle the drugs in from Canada and then to distribute them illegally to veterinarians and feed mills all over the

Midwest. Two of the men pleaded guilty to charges in April 1989, and agreed to cooperate with FDA's ongoing investigation into illegal animal drug traffic.[82]

- In May 1988, a veterinarian in Diamond, Missouri, pleaded guilty to repacking and selling chloramphenicol oral solution in unlabeled bottles for use in food animals. The good doctor was fined five thousand dollars.

- In August 1988, New Jersey veterinarian Robert Blease was enjoined from distributing adulterated and misbranded veterinary drugs. A similar injunction in 1981 had not prevented him from manufacturing and selling drugs illegally. Dr. Blease owned and operated a company, Vet Med, "a business dedicated to the raising of milk-fed veal calves," according to an FDA report.[83] Apparently Vet Med was dedicated as well to the selling of illegal drugs to over five hundred veal farmers in the region, as an FDA report explains:

  Dr. Blease did not deny that he distributed a variety of drugs which are antibiotics, anti-inflammatory agents, or combinations of them. These drugs included: CDC Plus (chloramphenicol, oxytetracycline and dexamethasone); A&S with furazolidone (tetracycline, sulfamethazine and furazolidone); A&S with neomycin; ALS 500 (lincomycin, spectinomycin, amino acid solution); sulfamethoxazole and trimethoprim tablets; gentamicin sulfate injection; "Stress Pills" (phenylbutazone tablets); chloramphenicol capsules and chloramphenicol oral solution; dexamethasone injection; and amoxicillin injection. With the exception of amoxicillin injection, these drugs had not been approved by FDA in any cattle, including veal calves.[84]

  The FDA report does not say whether Dr. Blease was fined or sentenced to serve time for these violations.

- DES was banned worldwide a decade ago after scientific opinion settled that it caused vaginal cancer in humans. Because it is such a powerful growth stimulant, it continues, however, to be used by some producers in both Europe and the United States. More on the battle against DES at the end of this chapter.

If the newest animal drug battle is over BST-boosted milk, the oldest is over the practice of mixing small amounts of antibiotics with animals' feed so that they receive low levels of the drugs every day. As we noted above in **Chemical Feast,** 90 percent of all antibiotics used in animal agriculture are used in this way. This is the "subtherapeutic" use of antibiotics that has received so much debate in scientific circles and so much coverage in the media over the past decade or so.

This practice, more than any other single factor, revolutionized the livestock and poultry industries. It took the place of old-fashioned animal husbandry; it warded off low levels of disease and accelerated animal growth without additional manual labor. As soon as farmers began adding antibiotics to feed in the early 1950s, the trend toward confinement, intensive management, large concentrations of animals, and huge corporate-owned "farms" took off. Animal production became a whole new ball game; it became factory farming. Antibiotics are central to its success, for without them it would probably not be possible to raise animals under such conditions. No wonder, then, that agribusiness leaders become apoplectic when antibiotics are challenged.

Nevertheless, subtherapeutic feeding of antibiotics has been challenged for over a decade. Opponents of the practice include members of the medical, consumer, and environmental communities who say the practice is rendering the "wonder drugs" useless in treating serious human illnesses. They believe farm use increases exposure of antibiotics to disease-causing bacteria. Just as weeds and insects develop resistance to herbicides and insecticides, bacteria develop immunity to antibiotics. If you become infected with bacteria from one of these strains and get sick, your physician will not be able to cure the disease simply by giving you a shot of antibiotics. To make matters worse, antibiotic therapy for one infection can actually induce a second, antibiotic-resistant infection if resistant bacteria are around. This happens because the injection of an antibiotic destroys most of the normal bacteria in your body, leaving it wide open to the rapidly growing resistant bacteria.

With evidence in hand, many have tried to persuade the proper authorities to see this view. The FDA itself tried to ban subtherapeutic feeding of penicillin and tetracycline in 1977, but strong congressional lobbying by agribusiness blocked the attempt. The wrangle brought out a call for more studies, more data. Meanwhile, European governments grew concerned about the health consequences and banned subtherapeutic feeding. The National Academy of Sciences reviewed evidence from both sides of the controversy in 1980 and concluded that the purported hazards could be neither proven nor disproven; again, the need for more scientific data.

Opponents of the practice thought they had "smoking gun" proof in 1984 when a landmark scientific article was published in the prestigious *New England Journal of Medicine*. Its authors, scientists at the U.S. government's CDC in Atlanta, traced hamburger eaten by a number of Salmonella victims in Minnesota back to the beef herd it came from—cattle that had been receiving subtherapeutic tetracycline in their feed.[85] On the strength of this, the Natural Resources Defense Council (NRDC), a New York-based environmental group, petitioned the Department of Health and Human Services in November 1984 to invoke federal law and to remove antibiotics as an "imminent hazard."[86] Agribusiness summoned its scientists and experts to the hearings and ultimately NRDC's petition was rejected; again, the evidence was considered inconclusive.

Since then, there have been several large outbreaks of drug-resistant Salmonella associated with dairy cattle. One in April 1985 affected some three thousand people in five states in the Midwest after they drank milk containing an antibiotic-resistant strain of Salmonella; two people died.[87] Another outbreak of Salmonella in May 1985 in California caused two more deaths and a number of hospitalizations. Researchers for CDC tracked the illnesses to undercooked meat from cull dairy cows who had been fed subtherapeutic antibiotics.[88] This case was a bit more shocking because the antibiotic in question was our old friend chloramphenicol. The researchers found the bacteria to be resistant also to penicillin, tetracycline, and ampicillin.

The California case was another "smoking gun" to show the dangers to human health caused by subtherapeutic antibiotics in animal feed. Still no action was taken to prohibit the practice. After years of scientific war over the issue, the authorities, it seems, are numbed and have lost interest in the subject. Meanwhile, antibiotics are more widely used than ever, despite the claims of the beef industry. Maybe feedlot steers don't get antibiotics because hormone implants are the drug of choice. But dairy cattle, calves, and other species are receiving them. Now that authorities are checking, they are finding residues of antibiotics in milk across the country.[89] If it is true, as opponents claim, that the constant use of drugs in animal feeds is breeding drug-immune diseases, we can look forward to more and more epidemics of food poisoning and fewer and fewer "wonder" drugs to treat them.

Old-Time Protection vs. Brave New Farm

At this point you are probably wondering a couple of things: Why, if things are so bad, aren't we seeing more death and disaster? Why, if things are so bad, isn't our government taking action to get animal drug abuse under control?

To the first question there are several responses. For one, there is some death and disaster, as we have just seen. Nevertheless, agribusiness, like any industry under fire, will vigorously fight those who point fingers. Agribusiness will use a simple, standard defense: "No proof." This leads us to the second response: Some kinds of death and disaster come gradually over a long period of time and hence are hard to link to a specific cause. Cancer and some of the degenerative diseases are good examples. One who suffers, say, stomach cancer from long exposure to residues of carbadox or SMZ in milk, hamburger, and pork will be unable to prove that causation in either a medical laboratory or a court of law. Such causation can be established probably only by years of epidemiological studies each of which requires hundreds of cases and additional dozens of years before results are accepted as conclusive. Thus agribusiness will have several decades of easy drug use before any are scientifically proven to cause human death and disaster.

And there is a third response to those who wonder why we aren't seeing more human health problems as a result of animal factory methods: No one is looking. The human health problems are out there, we suspect, but researchers are not accustomed, as yet, to seeing them linked to animal food production. People have colds, flu, nausea, diarrhea, and other illnesses all the time and no one thinks that they might be caused by animal drug residues or animal-food-borne bacteria. Thus the health problems—and very likely some deaths—occur, but there are no surveys, no studies, no data to show why. Salmonellosis is perhaps

From the crates to the conveyor line.

Into the killing room.

Bleeding.

Scalded and plucked.

the only exception. But it is the only food-borne disease that must by law be reported to CDC. Officials there say that while some forty thousand cases are reported to them each year, they believe that most cases are not reported and that as many as four million Americans may suffer salmonellosis annually.[90] Now that this one disease is proving to be strongly linked to drug-dependent factory methods, we suggest to health authorities that it may be just the tip of the iceberg.

Now the second question: Why isn't the government providing protection? Let's face it; government regulation has not been very popular in the last decade. The prevailing official mood seems to be that industry is most productive when it is free from bureaucratic meddling. And, historically, some industries have had relatively less regulation than others. Agriculture is foremost among these, as it involves food, farming, families, and other traditions that have been seen as "good things" for the government to coddle more than to control. For most of its existence, USDA has been more of a coddler than a controller, more of a booster than a regulator. Morevover, with assets at an estimated one trillion dollars, agriculture is agri-megabusiness. It is America's largest industry and probably its most politically powerful; USDA's efforts at regulation would be like the tail wagging the dog.

We should keep USDA's historical role and mindset in mind as we examine the federal meat and poultry inspection and grading sustem. Note that while these programs are designed ostensibly to protect consumers, they are administered by an agency with a record for passivity in that role. USDA is simply not a consumer protection agency. USDA policymakers have always seen themselves as more aligned with agriculture than with consumers, and they tend to see their programs more as a service for agriculture than as a service to the public. In conflicts between consumer interests and agricultural interests then, USDA will tend to lean more toward its client's side (although its officials will probably feel caught in the middle).

Within the vast realm of animal agriculture, USDA and the FDA hold up the two main safety nets between agribusiness and the consumer. The FDA's Center for Veterinary Medicine operates the first safety net. CVM is responsible for regulating drugs and medicines administered to food-producing animals. Thus CVM can be seen as an administrative filter designed to keep toxic substances from reaching food-producing animals. Its regulatory authority reaches those who violate federal food and drug laws and regulations. USDA's Food Safety and Inspection Service (FSIS) is the second safety net and is set up at slaughter-houses and egg- and poultry-processing plants. Where animals and commercial eggs are received from producers, USDA's inspectors stand ready to condemn or approve and grade animal products before they are sent into the stream of commerce.

CVM's ability effectively to screen out the flow of toxic substances that go to factory-farmed animals is not without flaws. As we noted in the previous section, factory farming now depends on ever more potent and broadly bioactive chemistry. We predict that, one way or another, factory farmers will find what they need to maintain profitable factory conditions. The "milk-fed" veal industry is the best case in point; it operates on a number of dangerous drugs—none of which is approved for nonruminating calves—obtained illegally and administered illegally. We suggest that there is a direct relationship between the extent of potent drug use and the degree of intensification in animal husbandry systems. In factory farming, we have created a monster, and a drug-hungry one at that.

Both CVM/FDA and FSIS/USDA have had plenty of criticism over the years for their inability to keep the supply of animal foods free from drugs, chemicals, and germs. CVM has had its share of criticism recently in the form of the Weiss committee's report discussed above. The report concluded with seven recommendations to the Secretary of Health and Human Services that could help clean up CVM's role in the animal drug mess. Essentially, these would require FDA to

- inventory all unapproved drugs, remove them from the market pending safety tests, and stop encouraging the use of unapproved drugs;
- withdraw unsafe drugs;
- review approved drugs periodically;
- set up an independent human food safety office solely responsible for consumer interests;
- crack down on illegal sales of drugs;
- in general, enforce the Food, Drug and Cosmetic Law and regulations to the letter in the interests of public safety.

FDA has responded to these recommendations by saying that it is compiling the drug inventory but that it will not remove unapproved drugs from the market for safety tests because "most of [these] have been available for many years prior to the animal drug amendments" of the food and drug laws.[91] FDA said it would continue its policy of dealing with products with safety concerns as the need arises. FDA noted that there are currently eight products of concern, but complained about the time and resources necessary to remove a product once it is out there on the market. FDA noted the example of DES, which took seven years to remove. It ruled out cyclic review of approved drugs, saying that its policy is to review them on a "for-cause basis."[92] The agency declined to establish an office for human food safety. FDA said it was trying to step up efforts to control illegal sales but that it has "insufficient resources to correct the problem" and is turning to the states for help.[93]

In the wake of the Weiss hearings and report, a telling drama unfolded. Dr. Joseph Settepani, a professional scientist at CVM, was transferred to, as they say, administrative Siberia. From a post at FDA headquarters in Rockville, Maryland, where he worked in his specialty, organic chemistry, Dr. Settepani was "detailed," or temporarily transferred, to another line of work in a trailer at the agency's research facility in Beltsville, Maryland.

Dr. Settepani was a key player in flushing out evidence of FDA/CVM's laxity—or servility—in enforcing animal drug laws and regulations. He was a "whistle-blower"—one who serves the public interest by speaking out when a government agency is not doing its job. The Weiss hearings might not have been held had it not been for Dr. Settepani. His many memoranda dissenting to FDA/CVM's open-door animal drug policy were found in agency files during a routine review by an investigator for the House Committee on Government Operations. Things looked amiss to the alert investigator, he reported back to the committee, and the hearings were scheduled. Dr. Settepani's memos helped Congressman Weiss and the other committee members understand the problems and focus discussion on these issues at the hearings. His memos and other written work were favorably cited in the Weiss report thirty-six times, and the committee noted that no other FDA official found any of Settepani's work to be unreasonable or ill-founded.

Dr. Settepani's "temporary" transfer to the Beltsville outback looked fishy to Congressman Weiss, so he wrote to FDA Commissioner Frank Young and asked him to look into the matter to see if Settepani had been transferred against his will, as a reprisal for expressing his scientific judgment. One administrative thing led to another and soon Dr. Settepani's personnel grievance, supporting affidavits, and the story of the animal drug mess at FDA/CVM lay before the secretary of the Department of Health and Human Services (DHHS). The secretary asked one of DHHS's divisions, the U.S. Public Health Service, to set up a special committee to conduct a "scientific review of concerns about the animal drug evaluation process [of the] Center for Veterinary Medicine."[94]

(Dr. Settepani's personnel grievance, like many such legal and administrative proceedings, remains unresolved. After about a year at his "temporary" job in the trailer at Beltsville, Maryland, the post was made permanent.)

In April 1987, however, the DHHS special committee reported its findings. Called the Lin Report after its author, Dr. Samuel Lin, the committee chairman and an assistant surgeon general and deputy assistant secretary for health, the report listed eleven recommendations to FDA. Briefly, FDA is supposed to study whether there is a need to set up a new division charged "with the specific responsibility for human food safety"; to take a hard, close look at its tacit encouragement of drug uses not in keeping with label restrictions; to "further study the indiscriminate [subtherapeutic] use of antimicrobials"; to tighten up traffic in OTC drugs, and to take other actions that, in general, would tighten up control over all animal drugs.[95] The Lin Report indicates an official lack of confidence in FDA's ability to review questionable drugs on a "for-cause" basis:

> The committee is not persuaded that a structured and accountable system of setting causal review priorities exists within CVM. This conclusion is based upon the nature of CVM's response to the Weiss Committee report, the review of presented documents, and on the testimony provided. Furthermore, the committee concludes that once a drug receives approval, the process for withdrawal is too long and the legal requirements imposed . . .

are too onerous to allow CVM to carry out its responsibilities to act expeditiously to protect human safety. While we recognize that the interests of drug manufacturers need to be protected adequately, such a scientifically and legally imposed process is torturous and, in the longer view, potentially detrimental to public health and safety.[96]

If political pressure from consumers is raised high enough to counter that exerted by agribusiness, FDA may be forced to make the changes necessary to patch the holes in its safety net. The essential change needed is one of philosophy and mission. Throughout its hearings, the Weiss committee noted FDA's tendency to see its role as one more in service to agriculture than to the consumer public:

> The record of FDA's regulation of these drugs reflects that FDA's primary legal responsibility for protecting human health and safety has now been superseded by the objective of assuring the availability of new animal drugs. This is a serious conflict that suggests FDA's misunderstanding of its legal function.[97]

In the best-case scenario, FDA will reorient itself to more of a consumer protection organization and it will tighten up the lax policies identified by both the Weiss and the Lin committees. As we have repeatedly pointed out, however, even the best regulation of animal drugs will not eliminate residues in animal products and risks to consumers. It bears repeating again that factory farming depends on broadly bioactive drugs that often carry risks to human health. We think it is reasonable to assume that such drugs will continue to be used even if FDA is radically reformed. Even approved drugs contribute risks to consumers of animal products. In fact, the studies show that most residues are caused by *normal use* of approved drugs, and we believe not even a perfect FDA can do much about it. One recent study of the causes of residues in cattle and pigs cautioned:

> Although major changes in attention to withdrawal times and medication records will likely eliminate much of the drug residue incidence, drug residues will still be a problem. Biologic variability associated with the whole population of food animals will almost ensure this. Further, certain diseases (e.g., inadequate renal function, simple dehydration) and drug administration practices (e.g., failure to rotate injection sites sufficiently, injection into fat rather than muscle) will contribute directly to the problem.[98]

We can depend, then, on factory-farming methods to continue to supply us with residue-laden animal products—even if FDA has its safety net in the best of order.

This leaves us at the mercy of the second safety net: the USDA's meat and poultry inspection program carried out by its FSIS division. As we said, USDA historically has shown more allegiance to agricultural producers than to consumers. This philosophy and perceived mission is unquestionably proper for most of USDA's programs, but it seems amiss at FSIS, the agency charged with the responsibility of keeping the supply of meat and poultry safe and wholesome. There are plenty of historical reasons to believe that FSIS will not easily transform itself into a consumer protection agency. A rather recent development makes it all the more likely that FSIS's mission will be more proindustry than proconsumer: Its new director is Dr. Lester Crawford, former head of CVM and the man most responsible for CVM's confusion of mission in regulating animal drugs. In its report, the Weiss committee was perplexed and frustrated with Crawford's sense of mission as expressed in his testimony. Crawford told the committee at one point, "We try to do our best to streamline the drug process so that we have drugs approved for every indication that there is out there."[99] To the Weiss committee, Crawford's priority list put factory farmings' drug needs well ahead of consumer safety. We are bound to wonder, then, what his priorities will be as America's chief meat inspector.

USDA/FSIS has been criticized by consumer groups for its meat and poultry inspection and drug residue testing programs. Essentially, the charges are that the FSIS system is behind the times, that the state of technology of flesh production is many laps ahead of that of flesh inspection. The image is one of high-tech factories mass-producing rivers of animal products inspected by hand, one at a time, by old guys wearing green eyeshades. That may be a bit overdrawn, but it does illustrate the situation.

The basic concept of individual carcass inspections was set down back in 1906 when drug residues were unheard of and the flow of flesh through slaughter-houses was a slow trickle compared to the torrent today. The carcasses of about 120 million cattle, calves, sheep, lambs, and pigs and over 5.5 billion chickens, turkeys, and ducks now go through the federal inspection lines each year. One departmental inspection service official admitted that "USDA has a huge prob-lem in trying to assure wholesomeness of product and still accommodate in-dustry's needs to automate processing of 10 billion pounds of production an-nually."[100] Since the rise of factory farming and mechanization of meat and poultry processing, the department has been struggling to maintain some sem-blance of adequate inspection under the old law's requirements; there have been revisions since, but the basic method of postmortem inspection has gone un-changed for thirty years.

An inspector in a typical broiler-processing plant has about one second to inspect each carcass for twenty-odd diseases transmissible to humans. Because the cost would be prohibitive, the USDA does not inspect each carcass for residues but takes random samples and turns them over to laboratories for analysis. Catching a residue-contaminated carcass by this means is a matter of chance. And by the time the laboratory test results are done, the meat is often out in the stores. The 1979 GAO study cited earlier in this chapter (see note 31) found that the actual incidence of illegal residues in meats and poultry was far greater than that reported by USDA. FSIS has since made some improvements, but there isn't an updated report to substantiate whether the chemical residue (and germ) control situation has really improved.

In a July 1985 report entitled *Meat and Poultry Inspection: The Scientific Basis of the Nation's Program,* NRC found that the situation had not improved that much:

- It is well established that species of Salmonella and Campylobacter are major causes of diseases transmissible to humans . . . [and] current postmortem inspection methods are not adequate to detect these organisms;
- The fundamental design of FSIS's residue monitoring program needs to be improved to ensure maximum protection. In particular, the committee questions the adequacy of sampling size and procedures, the basis for and the utility of tolerance levels for chemicals, and the basis for setting priorities for testing chemicals;
- The current residue testing strategy of FSIS to detect with 95 percent confidence whether or not a problem exists in 1 percent of the animal population is inadequate to eliminate consumer exposure to residues. Because millions of animals are slaughtered annually . . . , the chance of any animal being sampled in the United States is minuscule.[101]

Apparently FSIS was not able to make the necessary improvements in its safety net, because the meat and poultry inspection program was reviewed again by Congress's Office of Technology Assessment (OTA) in October 1988. In that report, OTA identified several problems with chemical monitoring and law enforcement:

- FSIS cannot test for most pesticides. Out of 227 pesticide ingredients FSIS considers of potential concern, FDA's four multiresidue tests together can detect only about forty (less than 18 percent). "FSIS has identified 10 highly ranked pesticides it would like to monitor routinely but cannot, using its multiresidue [testing] methods."[102]
- FSIS cannot stop contaminated food from reaching the market. "Existing analytical methods, when combined with sampling and reporting requirements, generally do not provide results fast enough to prevent commodities from reaching the market even after violations are found."[103]

One month later, November 1988, USDA's own Office of the Inspector General (OIG), an in-house watchdog agency, delivered an even more exhaustive review of FSIS's pesticide residue monitoring program. Among other faults, OIG found:

- FSIS was unable successfully to investigate pesticide violations in 79 percent of cases reviewed. "FSIS was unable to or did not take appropriate corrective action on 22 of 28 cases" where unacceptable levels of cancer-causing chlorinated hydrocarbons were detected. One contaminated sample is "indicative of potential widespread contamination."[104]

- FSIS allowed adulterated products to enter commerce.
- The sampling for the residue monitoring program was not random because some plant inspectors did not include all slaughtered animals in the sampling universe.
- FSIS is mismanaging a program under which industry members agree to develop their own quality and residue control measures. Of eleven agreements reviewed, eight producers had not fully complied, two had not implemented any of the required quality control procedures, and seven had not implemented any of the required production control procedures.
- "Nevertheless," USDA's inspector general continued, "FSIS reduced the amount of residue testing normally performed and had approved, without adequate verification, labels referencing the superior products produced under this program. Since periodic reviews were not being performed, FSIS had no independent means of assuring compliance by the participating companies and no assurance that the program effectively reduced the incidence of residue in meat and poultry products as it was intended to do."[105]
- FSIS has "completed initial ranking on only eighty-three (or 18.5 percent) of 448 compounds identified as either a pesticide, drug, or environmental contaminant which could be present in meat or poultry."[106]
- When FSIS found residues of chemicals other than those it was looking for, it did no follow-up in eleven of fifteen cases. In addition, "none of these [unidentified chemical residues] reported by field laboratories were properly investigated or documented."[107]

This is the pattern set by FSIS in carrying out the responsibility of ensuring the safety and wholesomeness of the nation's supply of meat and poultry products. To make matters worse, in the midst of all these critical studies and reports the Reagan administration instituted sweeping deregulation of the inspection system. That process was commenced by USDA Secretary Richard Lyng (1986–89), a Reagan appointee and the former president of the American Meat Institute, a meat industry lobby group. These moves troubled even the ordinarily probusiness *Wall Street Journal*: "[USDA] doesn't want to add inspectors. Instead, it wants to cut its force and to rely heavily on the industry to regulate itself with a kind of honor system."[108] The article noted that "critics wonder how effective plant employees will be as unofficial inspectors when federal officials often encounter hostility from plant owners and managers."[109]

Even the beef industry has taken a dim view of the "improvements" in the meat inspection system. A writer for *Beef Today* noted that in 1987 FSIS "sampled just 198 steers, 110 heifers, 272 cows and 37 bulls for antibiotic residues, and only 781 steers and 817 heifers for hormone residues. It sampled just 113 young chickens and 332 young turkeys for antibiotics."[110] This would lead a consumer advocate "to naively conclude that USDA tests fewer than 0.007 percent of the 28 million heifers and steers slaughtered annually, or only one head in every 14,000."[111]

Naive or not, many consumer advocates believe that FSIS/USDA does not rigorously sample and test the stream of animal products for residues of all of the dangerous chemicals now in use in agriculture. Officials say that more thorough sampling and testing would be prohibitively expensive. In the interests of economics, then, we are asked to take our chances when we consume meat, milk, or eggs.

Not the least of the problems with the inspection system is a history of corruption of inspectors by the packers and processors whose products they are supposed to inspect. The job of inspecting carcasses is grueling and the hours are long: twelve-hour workdays are common and they may be divided among several plants in an area. To keep the lines rolling, plant operators can influence inspectors to use their considerable discretion. For instance, under the law an inspector's overtime must be paid by the plant. Since plant operators decide how long their plants will operate, they can grant or deny overtime. It has been reported that "reasonable" inspectors are often allowed to take home free meat and are offered liquor and other gifts. Plant operators and inspectors have been prosecuted and convicted for this kind of low-level bribery, but critics say that it is so endemic to the inspection process that it is practically impossible to prevent.[112]

The net result is that corrupt plants turn out shoddy meat and poultry, much of which probably would have been condemned by uncorrupted inspectors. At such plants one or more conscientious meat inspectors may turn whistle-blower despite threats, harrassment, and assault by plant owners; some have been fired or given punitive job assignments by corrupted USDA higher-ups. This carrot-and-stick treatment of inspection officials sets up patterns that undermine the inspection system's effectiveness and dangerous products are permitted to enter stores and supermarkets. It discourages whistle-blowing and conscientious inspection and after a while it burns out the very people we want in the system. One California whistle-blower, a twenty-three-year veteran of USDA's inspection service who had seen corruption and suffered abuse from superiors and plant owners, finally lost his faith in the meat and poultry inspection program. During a special USDA review of shoddy inspection patterns in two hundred Los Angeles–area slaughtering and meat-processing plants, he swore in an affidavit: "Based on my experience in Los Angeles, my advice to the public is not to eat meat."[113]

Once in a while, an FSIS official comes along who departs from the norm of USDA officialdom and takes on more of a consumer activist role in carrying out his job. Robert Angelotti was such an official, and he was the head of FSIS until a "scandal" removed him in 1978. Angelotti was forced to resign his post ostensibly because he was accused of claiming reimbursement for two meals that were paid for by others. The underlying reason for getting rid of him, however, appears to be that he went around to meat-packing plants with an expert without notifying plant personnel and inspectors.[114]

In response to critics of the FDA/CVM and FSIS/USDA safety nets, the agencies usually point to supposed low incidences of contamination, but these figures can be deceiving. It could just as easily mean that they are not detecting all of the incidents. It could also mean that they tend, like all professionals, to cook the books a bit to protect their client (agriculture), to defend themselves, and to prevent stirring up a hornet's nest of public reaction. We are not saying that the agencies are doing the *worst* possible job (although many consumer groups and critics would probably agree that they are not doing the best job either). Our point is that when one considers the chemical-dependent methods and needs of factory farming, the agencies will never be able to guarantee the safety of the animal-derived food supply no matter how well they run their programs.

Profits First, Caution Maybe

The new farming methods present greater risks than ever before and the controllers of these methods can exert more powerful financial and political influence. As we shall see in chapter 7, the ownership of animal products industries is becoming more highly centralized. You can't judge the quality of your eggs, milk, and meat by a visit to Farmer Jones's farm; you have to take the word (in the form of advertising) of an agribusiness corporation or a well-heeled national promotional outfit like the Beef Industry Council or the National Dairy Council. These industries already know that the less said about some of their methods, the better. A study paid for by the Animal Health Institute, a trade association of manufacturers of factory drugs, chemicals, and feed additives, disclosed that

> consumers are totally unfamiliar with the practices of meat production. Moreover, they tend to resist acquiring such knowledge, and consider meat favorable as a meal/diet essential, but are discouraged from buying and serving foods with which anything they consider unpleasant has been associated.[115]

Throughout factory farm publications, from magazines for farmers to the slick annual reports of Pfizer, Dow Chemical, and the Animal Health Institute, there is a continuous tirade against "consumerism" and government regulation. Farming magazines that depend heavily on advertising placed by drug and chemical manufacturers feverishly attack attempts to control agrochemistry. At least one such magazine, *National Hog Farmer,* acknowledged its self-interest on the question of drug and chemical regulations, admitting that "we obviously have a stake in this matter."[116] Other magazines are not quite so honest and run articles claiming that the loss of antibiotics and other drugs "would cost the swine industry alone over half a billion dollars" and would increase costs to consumers by "at least $1 billion a year according to the most conservative estimates."[117] Their editors attempt to persuade farmers to fight the drug companies' battles;

editorials urge readers to "sound off and sound off fast" to government representatives.[118]

Would farmers lose anything if drugs and chemistry went under tighter controls? A 1978 study requested by the U.S. Senate's Agriculture Committee showed that farmers would benefit from a ban on antibiotics, tetracyclines, and sulfa drugs. "Total net revenue to farmers would be initially enhanced," it states, encouraging farm expansion for a few years after which production and prices would level off.[119] The report revealed the real reason why agromanufacturers are hostile to a drug ban. "Increased risks associated with feeding livestock in confinement production systems without low-level use of drugs," states the report, "could make such confinement production less viable."[120]

The controversy over the use of DES as a growth promotant set the pattern for attempts to regulate drug abuse: rising public concern about risks of drug use, followed by government action to ban or regulate those uses, followed by industry battles to hold the line against regulation. In 1970, DES was linked to vaginal cancer in women, and uses of the drug in humans were restricted. Then, in 1973, after traces of DES were found in the organs of slaughtered animals, the FDA banned the use of the drug in food animals. This ban was reversed by the courts after several drug companies sued the government, saying that the FDA did not follow the proper procedures in imposing the ban. Slowly but surely, the FDA came back with another attempt to ban the drug. This time the agency successfully steered through the administrative thicket and its prohibition on oral and implant uses of DES in food animals became effective on November 1, 1979. But industry, of course, wouldn't take this lying down. Two manufacturers of DES brought suit in the federal courts that challenged FDA's conclusions about the dangers of the drug and asked that its ban be lifted. They lost their cases and the use of DES in food animals remained illegal. Then the whole controversy ended and DES disappeared from the news and the public mind.

But it had not, apparently, disappeared from the drug lockers of beef feedlot owners in Texas. In the summer of 1980, a tip from a feedlot cowboy made its way to an FDA field office, then on to higher offices. When FDA got on the case, they found that hundreds of cattlemen had ignored the ban on DES, acting on their fearlessness of drugs and chemicals as well as deep-seated rural contempt for federal regulators. FDA veterinarians found many instances of cattle with too many implants, cattle with implants of DES and other hormones, implants in both ears, as well as other misuses of an already illegal drug. After all the investigations, it turned out that some 430,000 animals had been treated with DES illegally and nearly 30,000 had reached meat markets. FDA officials estimated that as many as 10 percent of cattlemen had gone on using DES illegally.[121]

The lesson to be learned from the case is that agribusiness manufacturers and the agribusiness press used their dollars and their influence to squelch what should have been the broadest social discussion of the effects of an agrochemical product. Using lawyers, scientists, and public relations experts, the agribusiness press selected information and arguments and molded an ideological package for free home delivery to farmers and other people farther down the line of profitability in agriculture. After years of drug industry self-serving propaganda on DES, the farm community was whipped into a fervent belief that DES was harmless and very profitable. Against this well-crafted belief, the federal regulatory position and ban was bound to meet contempt. In the end, farmers looked bad and they took the heat *and* the rap for the drug/chemical industry, which started all the trouble to begin with.

Eventually, most cattlemen got the message, and DES is no longer the hormone of choice in feedlots. As we have seen, it was immediately replaced with zeranol, testosterone, progesterone, and estradiol or other types of growth accelerators. Every now and then, though, DES rears its carcinogenic head. In 1984, FDA caught four upstate New York factory ("milk-fed") veal producers using it. The treated calves had already gone through slaughterhouses to fancy restaurants (where customers paid high prices for it, thinking they were getting the highest-quality meat). USDA/FSIS's meat inspection system did not pick up the DES; FDA found out about the illegal use, in the words of an FDA official, through another "system of intelligence."[122] By all accounts, DES is still used illegally by some European farmers even though it has been banned there since the mid-1970s.

History repeats itself, over and over again, like a long-running Broadway play. With the same basic plot, a drama plays repeatedly in continuing conflicts over other animal drugs and husbandry shortcuts. As always, the role of industry is to introduce another magic bullet—a new product that is amazingly profitable and absolutely harmless. A chorus of agribusiness scientists attests to the wonders of the new product. If industry buys enough heavy advertising, the farm press joins in the chorus. A few independents step forward to challenge the product's profitability and harmlessness, and they are isolated, shunned as naysayers, and derided as antitechnologists. Regulatory personnel sit timidly in the wings, watching the drama unfold. Usually agribusiness has seen to it that their superiors are political appointees chosen from the ranks of magic-bulletist, antiregulationist agribusinessmen. Then the regulatory mission will be quite clear to agency insiders, quite obscure to others. Should the challengers persist with their case until mainstream science and media take interest, agribusiness sends forth its indentured scientists and editors to hold the line. If both sides persist, the drama turns into a battle royal that can go on for years.

The battle royal over subtherapeutic use of antibiotics, for example, has been going on for over a decade now and it will keep going on until the challengers are able to bring overwhelming proof that it is harmful to public health. Then, of course, we will already have substantial populations of drug-resistant disease bacteria. Perhaps the danger is not of the sort that can be proven easily; it may take a health disaster to do so.

Meanwhile, other struggles over other magic bullets go on, with the powerful and self-assured forces of agribusiness profitability pitted against the broad but disorganized concern for safety. Usually profitability enjoys a long run until concern for safety rallies and brings enough pressure to take away one of the magic bullets. Until the bitter end, however, those who profit most from dangerous drugs will dogmatically maintain their harmlessness. Where profits are considerable, safety is not.

Even hotter now than the struggle over antibiotics is the one over BGH (or BST), which promises that dairy cows will produce from 10 to 25 percent more milk. BGH's manufacturers, most agribusiness scientists, most of the farm press, FDA, and many factory dairy farmers are convinced the BGH is completely safe and that it will boost farmer profits. They say BGH milk is identical to natural milk, that BGH is a naturally occurring hormone, and that it does not appear in the milk. Even if it did, they say, you would digest it and it would not affect your health.

Some scientists, however, contest these claims and say that BGH may be harmful to human health. It is not a "natural" hormone, they say; even FDA admits that BGH molecules can be up to 3 percent different in structure from their natural counterparts. Researchers have found increased levels of BGH in blood and milk of treated cows. In humans, BGH and its digested products could be absorbed from milk and could, particularly in infants, cause hormonal and allergic effects. Researchers have reported finding increased levels of cell-stimulating growth factors, apparently identical to those in humans, in BGH milk. These factors could cause premature growth and breast stimulation in infants, and possibly promote breast cancer in adults. BGH-treated cows are more subject to stress and bacterial infections, which will lead to use of antibiotics that can leave residues in milk. Also, the stress effects of BGH in cows could suppress immunity and activate latent viruses, such as bovine leukemia (leukosis) and bovine immunodeficiency viruses, which are related to the AIDS complex and may be infectious to humans. It is possible, too, that steroids and adrenalinelike stressor chemicals induced in cows by BGH treatment may contaminate milk and be harmful, particularly to infants and young children. Finally, the challengers say, fat and milk of cows are already contaminated with a wide range of carcinogenic contaminants, including dioxins and pesticides. BGH reduces body fat in cows and may be likely to mobilize these fat-stored carcinogens into blood and eventually milk.[123]

Much of the data on these problems is the property of the five pharmaceutical companies that are in the race to get BGH on the market first. Other researchers who would like to do independent studies of BGH effects don't have much time. With five hundred million dollars in anticipated annual sales at stake, the race is a dead heat and already close to the finish line. With so much invested in research and development, BGH manufacturers are more likely to push for sales than for safety.

The push for profits is constant, and it keeps risky products and procedures in business. The Weiss committee found plenty of examples at its hearings. For one, FDA bowed to cattle and sheep industry pressure to keep albendazole, a suspected human carcinogen, available for treatment of liver flukes. FDA could not approve it as a new animal drug because of its suspected carcinogenicity, so it arranged an "emergency investigational new animal drug" program as a "concession to the cattle industry."[124] Albendazole was sold on an "emergency" basis for five years until the drug and livestock industries could come up with a replacement flukicide, clorsulon. And the Weiss committee found that CVM cut corners in rushing clorsulon into approval.

The power of industry over FDA was apparent to the Weiss committee in the agency's handling of other risky drugs as well: methylene blue, which causes mutations and is a highly suspect carcinogen, was permitted—indeed promoted—to cattlemen for treatment of nitrate poisoning in cattle even though it had never been approved for use in food animals.[125] And for over eleven years, FDA permitted some two hundred formulations of sulfa drugs to be marketed without the agency approval required by law. This was because FDA apparently lacked the clout to force the drugs' manufacturers to supply all information needed for the approval process. The drug and livestock industries were able to get what they wanted, over, under, or around FDA.

At the moment, a family of drugs known as nitrofurans is still available to industry, even though for nearly twenty years they have been known to cause cancer. The drugs are used by the poultry and pig industries to control diseases and dysentery. The Weiss hearings revealed that for thirteen years FDA delayed action to remove them.[126] Removal hearings have been held, an administrative law judge has decided against the nitrofurans, and it is up to the FDA commissioner to implement the removal. For two years now, FDA Commissioner Frank Young has been sitting on the administrative law decision to remove these cancer-causing drugs. Insiders suspect that FDA is sitting on the case because industry needs the nitrofurans to take the place of drugs (dimetridazole and ipronidazole) already removed. Another "concession to industry" involving known cancer-causing chemicals.

Finally, as FDA's Center for Veterinary Medicine drags its feet in regulating cancer-causing animal drugs, USDA's Food Safety and Inspection Service is apparently doing the same in dealing with its own tribe of meat industry violators. In an attempt to crack down on meat and poultry plants that have been chronic violators of health, safety, and product standards, FSIS instituted what it calls the Intensified Regulatory Enforcement (IRE) program. IRE is intended to put the plant under close scrutiny to identify the problems and help managers correct them. It works if FSIS stays vigilant and follows through, but a March 1989 study of the IRE program by GAO found FSIS foot dragging. GAO found that the program had been successful in short-term improvements at plants, but that "long-term improvements . . . are less likely to occur for two principal reasons."[127] GAO found that FSIS "does not have an adequate follow-up" system for keeping after problem plants. The review found that after FSIS uses IRE to clean up a plant, it "graduates" the plant out of the intensive enforcement program and does not keep after the plant to ensure that it sticks to the improvements. GAO found that seven of ten "graduated" plants had slipped backward and become problem plants again, and that "FSIS had generally not taken corrective action against them."[128] Further, GAO found that "FSIS cannot ensure that all problem plants are being identified and considered for IRE because it does not have an adequate method to identify the universe of potential IRE candidates."[129]

Evidently, USDA/FSIS's intensive regulatory enforcement program is not so intensive. If the worst meat and poultry plants in the country keep slipping backward, we have to wonder about the real purpose of IRE. Could it be nothing more than window dressing now that the consumer public is concerned about drugs, germs, and pesticides?

So the battles go on over DES, SMZ, subtherapeutic use of antibiotics, BGH and PGH, the nitrofurans, and the other suspect drugs and chemicals needed by factory farming. No doubt they will continue indefinitely. The eventual outcome with respect to any particular product is unpredictable; we can, however, predict that agribusiness will push relentlessly for greater availability of highly bioactive drugs and chemicals. Meanwhile, consumers worried about the quality and safety of factory-farming products have at least one way out: they can follow the advice of the veteran meat inspector and quit eating them.

We feed medicated feed all the way to market.
—"Stick with Hogs," *Farm Journal*, March 1976, p. Hog-17

---

5 THE FOOD

FACTORY IN REVERSE

Wastage in Factory Production

Expensive facilities and utilities require high animal throughput for solvency. High animal throughput requires high-energy rations that are more directly edible by humans. . . . With fossil energy no longer cheap or plentifully available, and no energy panacea to replace fossil energy, can we subsidize meat production by large energy infusions to keep grain-fed meat a part of our American Heritage?
—W. L. Roller, H. M. Keener, and R. D. Kline, *Energy Costs of Intensive Livestock Production* (St. Joseph, Mich.: American Society of Agricultural Engineers, June 1975), p. 8

The current issues surrounding the adequacy of the American diet no longer center primarily on nutrient deficiency. Overconsumption of calories, fat, saturated fatty acids, cholesterol and sodium has become a serious problem for many consumers, and animal products have been implicated as major sources of these food components.
—National Research Council, *Designing Foods: Animal Product Options in the Marketplace* (Washington, D.C.: National Academy Press, 1988) p. 298

There is presently no disincentive in the U.S. marketing system to prevent the feeding of grain—when it is cheap—to the point that it causes overfattening of red meat animals. Until such a disincentive is in place . . . the industry will continue to produce animals with too much fat.
—National Research Council, *Designing Foods: Animal Product Options in the Marketplace* (Washington, D.C.: National Academy Press, 1988) p. 298

THE LIFE OF OF ALL LIVING THINGS—plant or animal—depends on a basic chemical process called photosynthesis. This process occurs in the cells of plants where, with the aid of energy from the sun, complex organic molecules needed for growth and other plant processes are built from carbon dioxide, water, and other simple molecules. Each time molecules are bonded together by photosynthesis, the bond becomes stored energy. When an animal eats plant material, digestion and other bodily processes break down these large molecules into nutrients and energy for its growth, body heat, movement, and other animal functions. Both plants and animals are able to build up a surplus of large, energy-laden molecules. Animals store theirs in the form of fats; plants store theirs in the form of proteins, starches, and oils that are usually most concentrated in seeds, nuts, and grains.

Agriculture is essentially human effort aiding the conversion of solar energy into food. Grain is agriculture's standard form of energy. Industry has its barrels of oil, agriculture its bushels of corn. We should prefer a mode of agriculture that is neither wasteful of this energy nor destructive of the environment.

Energy-Rich Factory Feeds

At present, most plant materials produced on American farms are run through animals to produce meat, milk, and eggs. We feed about 70 percent of our corn, 94 percent of our oats, 52 percent of our barley, 74 percent of our sorghum, and over 90 percent of our unexported soybean crop to animals.[1] Steadily rising demand for animal products over the years has forced more and more land to be devoted to raising corn, soybeans, and other grains. Grain is easily stored, ground, mixed, and measured and is more easily processed than the rest of the plant. Whether in whole kernels or ground and mixed with additives, grain can be conveniently pumped through the factory's automated feeding machinery.

Factory poultry and pigs must be fed rich, easily digestible grain concentrates because they have digestive tracts that cannot break down rough grasses, hay, and silage. The broiler industry boasts of the efficiency with which its fast-growing strain of bird converts grain to meat; but this dubious efficiency is achieved by using the highest-calorie grains. As we shall see, it is not really an efficient use of these grains at all. Less efficient still is the use of grain to fatten cattle, who can digest grass and other foods not digestible by humans. Because beef-factory farmers are paid by the pound, their production goal is to produce the heaviest animal in the shortest possible time. Feedlots are, in that narrow sense, efficient factories. But because of the grain-rich diets and no exercise, they are more fat factories than protein factories. A "choice"-grade beef carcass from a "well-finished" feedlot steer has about 63 percent more fat (and more calories and cholesterol) but less protein than a "standard"-grade carcass from a grass-fed animal.[2] Then, at the packing plant, supermarket, and kitchen, grain and energy are wasted when this fat is trimmed away.

Factory Efficiency?

Animals have biological limits on their ability to convert plants into other material. A pound of grain cannot produce a pound of edible protein because not all of the grain is digested into nutrients. Not all of these nutrients are absorbed into the bloodstream, and not all of those absorbed into the bloodstream are

A Texas feedlot.

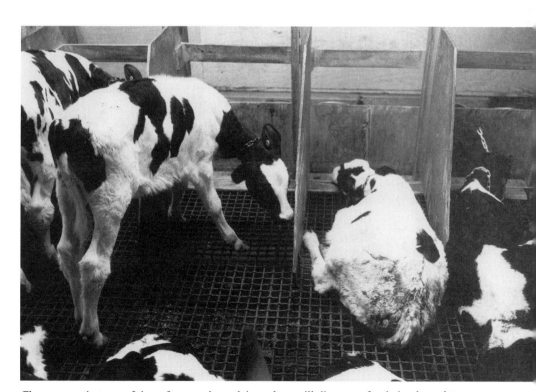

Chances are that one of these four newborn dairy calves will die soon after being brought to this confinement nursery.

converted into muscle. Some of the nutrients are burned up for movement, cell replacement, internal processes, and other nongrowth functions.

Not all of the animals that we feed end up on our tables. Unlike machines of metal or plastic, animals are perishable, and this perishability is a substantial factor in the cost of putting meat, eggs, and milk on American tables. After investments of time, energy, and resources, an animal—so industriously prepared into a walking food package—can be quite uncooperative: it can get sick and die. A study of Missouri pig farms revealed that over one-third of all pigs born on the farm die there as well.[3] Nearly two of every ten calves die in veal and dairy factories, and losses can run as high as half the calf "crop." Life is so hard in the cages of the automated layer house that about 25 percent of hens put in the cages die or are "culled" during an average eighteen-month laying cycle.[4]

Animal behavior, as factory farmers are only too aware, also adds to the unreliability of animals as protein machines. They don't always mate, breed, and turn out offspring in clockwork fashion. A missed heat period, a failure to conceive, or a miscarriage means that months of feed invested in the breeding animals brings no salable pig or calf, and no return. One pig expert estimates that each pig lost at birth represents a waste of about 130 pounds of feed used in feeding the breeding herd.[5]

If we are to analyze the real efficiency of animals as food machines, then, we must add in all grain and other food energy spent in rearing and maintaining breeding animals and all losses resulting from infertility and deaths. When these are figured in, only about 17 percent of the usable grain or food energy fed to a dairy herd is recovered in milk, and only about 6 percent of that fed to a beef herd is recovered in edible meat.[6]

But animals take in more than mere calories of energy from grain and feedstuffs. They also consume protein and other nutrients that could be used to nourish humans. Protein is poured through animals and lost at an astonishing rate. The accompanying table shows that animals are not very efficient at producing protein for us from the protein we feed to them. The figures are based on assumptions about fertility, mortality, reproductive rates, and production

Percent of Feed Protein Converted to Animal Protein

Animal	Percent
Dairy cow (milk)	22
Hen (eggs)	23
Broiler	17
Pig	12
Beef animal	4

Source: J. T. Reid, "Comparative Efficiency of Animals in the Conversion of Feedstuffs to Human Foods," in *New Protein Foods*, eds. Aaron M. Altschul and Harold L. Wilcke, vol. 3 (New York: Academic Press, 1978), pp. 116–43.

costs usual in farming systems. The figures for protein refer to the *whole* animal; the percentages for the edible portion would be even smaller.

The High Cost of Waste

The waste of grain and resources because of animals' inefficiency as converters is costly, but it becomes even more so in light of the unpredictable nature of animal production. Disruption of production schedules causes dollar losses to producers and consequently higher prices paid by consumers. Stress and disease, even when they do not cause death, make factory animals more expensive to prepare for market. In poultry, respiratory diseases cost producers $500 million and skeletal diseases another $300 million. In all, poultry diseases cost producers some $2 billion a year. Death losses from pig diseases cost producers over $1 billion a year, with respiratory diseases accounting for $400 million in losses. Dairy and beef producers lose the most of all. Cattle diseases cause over $4.6 billion in losses, with reproductive diseases making up $2.6 billion of that. Mastitis costs dairy producers $368 million and respiratory diseases cost all cattle producers $500 million.[7] In all, it is estimated that U.S. livestock and poultry producers lose some $8 billion each year because of diseases and parasites. This amounts to 11 percent of *gross* farm income from all U.S. animal and poultry production and adds substantially to the animal products food bill.[8]

Grain and other investments in animal production are wasted when animals are injured or killed in shipment from farm to farm and to the slaughterhouse. Increasing specialization in the cattle and pig industries has separated operations; there are breeders, producers of young calves and pigs, and producers who "finish" the animals to market weight. Cattle and pigs may be moved several times from farm to auction to farm and back again. Most animals are moved in crowded trucks and subjected to stresses from exposure in cold weather or overheating in warm weather. Crowding, jostling, and rough handling cause bruises and other injuries. These losses are enormous, according to a 1974 study on livestock transportation and handling practices. The authors estimated annual losses totaling one billion dollars from disease, injury, death, and weight loss in transit.[9] Factory animals are especially vulnerable to shipping losses; according to an expert, factory pigs are "more delicate than open-raised pigs. . . . They're not only tailless and cleaner, but much more nervous" and prone to stress-related deaths and injuries.[10]

Then there are the wastes at the slaughterhouse—losses from the human food chain because many animals and parts of animals are damaged or diseased. Under federal meat and poultry inspection (which accounts for over 90 percent of all animals inspected), animals are examined before slaughter for obvious signs of disease or abnormality. In 1987, nearly 20 million chickens and 808,000 turkeys were condemned at federally inspected slaughterhouse doors.[11] Another 474 million pounds of chicken, turkey, and duck meat were condemned after

Veal calves' carcasses.

slaughter.[12] In the same year, federal meat inspectors condemned 334,000 cattle, calves, sheep, lambs, and hogs.[13]

Factory methods add to this mountain of discarded flesh. The feedlot liver syndrome discussed in chapter 2 results in a great number of carcasses condemned at the slaughterhouse; liver condemnations alone amount to a ten-million-dollar annual loss to producers.[14] Nervous, "meat-type" factory pigs drop dead from stress either in transit or in meat packers' stockyards. The Livestock Conservation Institute, a meat industry service organization, estimates that upwards of eighty thousand pigs die each year on the way to the slaughter lines.[15] An estimated 8 to 10 percent of all hogs marketed have severe porcine stress syndrome (PSS), which produces what the pork industry calls PSE (for pale, soft, exudative) pork. In stressed pigs, high adrenaline levels and other chemical changes raise acidity in the animals' systems, which causes their meat to be pale and watery.[16] The PSE problem costs the pork industry an estimated thirty-eight million dollars a year.[17] Marek's disease—cancer—in chickens is the leading cause of condemned carcasses at processing plants; it is believed to be related to the stress of crowding and the supergrowth of birds in modern broiler factories.[18]

These tonnages of condemned flesh never become the food they were intended, nor does much of each animal that does pass inspection; heads, feet, and other inedibles amounting to about half the animals' live weights go with the condemned flesh into fertilizer, soap, and other by-products. Some of the flesh pile goes into protein supplements that go back to farms to "beef up" another round of animals. The animal factory as food factory is wasteful indeed. The meat industry tells us that nothing is wasted at the slaughterhouse, but all this really means is that they make extra money selling all of the nonedibles. It ignores the waste inherent in producing the whole animal in the first place.

Fuel for Factories

Agriculture, primitive or modern, has "ancillary" energy costs, that is, the energy or power used in manipulating the flow of solar energy through plants to the final food product. Energy must be spent in clearing, cultivating, sowing, weeding, harvesting, separating, and storing food—grain, let's say. Energy is spent in moving, grinding, and mixing this grain and in feeding it to, watering, and otherwise caring for the animals who eat it. Energy is spent in shipping, slaughtering, processing, packing, storing, and cooking the animal food products. We even spend energy in advertising these products.

Over the years, agriculture—American style—has moved away from human labor for these tasks and toward machine power. In the late nineteenth century, when resources for power and machines were cheap and wages were rising, agricultural planners began to choose machines for their convenience, control, and low expense relative to human labor. The history of the poultry industry sketched in chapter 1 illustrates this choice toward the capital side of the trade-off

Energy use: Continuous artificial lighting speeds growth and productivity in many poultry and egg factories.

between capital and labor in production. As a result of thousands of such choices over the years, we have evolved an agricultural technology that has increased overall productivity per farmer, but only by huge investments of energy from petroleum, coal, and hydroelectricity. American agriculture uses more energy in production than it puts out in the form of food. An American scientist, David Pimentel, has estimated that if the whole world were fed diets of food produced by U.S. agricultural technology, known petroleum reserves would be exhausted in thirteen years.[19]

Animal factories are especially gluttonous of energy. Energy is spent in manufacturing the buildings, hardware, and supplies for confinement systems; it is used to keep the machinery going and to maintain the "controlled environment."

In addition, the placement of animals in confinement creates problems that require energy for solutions. For example, pigs and poultry have more difficulty than some warm-blooded animals in maintaining body temperature. They easily get too hot or too cold. On a traditional farm, they could keep warm in cold weather by nestling in bedding placed in shelters. In hot weather, they could cool off in shady, damp soil. In the factory, however, when the environment becomes uncomfortable, the operator must use energy to adjust it, otherwise productivity falls. Large factory buildings packed with animals must have very powerful ventilators to keep foul air moving out and fresh air in. Sprayers, foggers, and, on some farms, air conditioners must be used in hot weather to keep crowded animals from overheating. Energy must be spent in moving feed in and wastes out. And waste must be treated if the farmer wants to avoid pollution problems and neighbors' complaints. Waste treatment requires additional capital expenditures for pumps, paddles, and other aerobic treatment equipment, and that brings higher monthly bills for the electricity to run it. *Farm Journal* wrote about

Energy use in a factory broiler house: The large disks are gas heaters. Automatic waterers hang from hoses, while the two pipes running the length of the building are automatic feeders.

a Kansas pig factory, for example, where 7,500 pigs excreted thirty tons of manure each week. With a king-size odor problem, the farmer had to install an aerobic waste treatment system that boosted his electric bills by ninety dollars a day.[20]

Heaters are necessary if young animals are to survive separated from the warmth of their mothers' bodies and dry bedding. Young animals are vulnerable to chills, especially on drafty, cold concrete or metal-slatted floors. To improve survival rates, farmers use electric heating pads and infrared lamps in pens and stalls. Even older, growing animals get chilly in factory buildings and when they do, they eat more and burn up more energy to maintain body heat. Farmers who want rapid weight gains on schedule have two choices, both costing energy: either turn up the heat or feed more grain.

More Waste

When the energy spent in running animal factories is compared with the protein and food energy they produce, the ratios show waste again. The food energy we get from pig factories is only about 34 percent and from broiler factories only about 14 percent of the fossil fuel energy used in production.[21] By way of contrast, the soybean and corn crops fed to these animals produce an energy dividend: corn produces nearly seven and soybeans nearly six units of food energy for each unit of fuel energy used in production.[22]

Now let's look at protein produced for each unit of fossil fuel used in production. If the corn and soybeans consumed in the pig and broiler factories were consumed instead by humans, for each unit of fossil fuel energy used in production we would get back nearly five times the protein produced by either the pigs or the broilers.[23] According to animal scientists at Ohio State University who have been studying energy costs in factory systems:

> [These data] forcefully bring to mind one obvious fact—man certainly doesn't grow animals to amplify our food energy availability! No knowledgeable person ever thought we did. Even the best of the animal enterprises examined returns only 34.5% of the investment of fossil energy to us in food energy whereas the poorest of the 5 crop enterprises examined returns 328%.[24]

Another measure of the energy costs of animal foods is the value of raw materials consumed in producing them. In the 1982 revised edition of her landmark book, *Diet for a Small Planet,* Frances Moore Lappé reported:

Energy use: Artificial daylight induces faster broiler production.

A detailed 1978 study sponsored by the Departments of Interior and Commerce produced startling figures showing that the value of raw materials consumed to produce food from livestock is greater than the value of all oil, gas and coal consumed in this country.[25]

According to the same study, the production of meat, dairy products, and eggs accounts for *one-third* of the total amount of raw materials used for all purposes in the United States.

We have accepted this enormous toll on energy and resources without question; indeed most of us never even knew of it. We have thought animal products a dietary necessity for so long that their environmental costs have not been considered. The time seems right now to reckon with those costs. And we know now that meat, milk, and eggs can do our health more harm than good, so the animal factory seems doubly unconscionable.

Agriculture is supposed to be the process whereby solar energy and resources are converted into food; animal factories, however, appear to be something else. They are, indeed, protein and energy factories in reverse and they are hungry, inefficient consumers of natural resources.

6   HIDDEN RUNNING

COSTS OF THE FACTORY

Who's Paying Them?

In recent times, the ill-defined "balance" of nature has dipped danger-ously and the environment has deteriorated alarmingly. One aspect of this deterioration is pollution from intensive animal production.
—H. A. Jasiorowski, "Intensive Systems of Animal Production," *Proceedings of the III World Conference on Animal Production,* ed. R. L. Reid (Sydney: Sydney University Press, 1975), pp. 369, 383

Runoff and percolation are not the only ways that feedlot contaminants can affect water quality. Beef cattle feedlots can contribute ammonia, amines, and odorous sulfur compounds to the atmosphere. Such com-pounds are potential pollutants to waters in the area and can have an effect on nearby plants and animals.
—Raymond C. Loehr, *Pollution Control for Agriculture,* 2d ed. (Orlando, Fl.: Harcourt Brace Jovanovich, Academic Press, 1984), p. 49

The wastes from the manufacture of certain animal drug products have created hazardous waste sites and contaminated drinking water supplies.
—John C. Matheson, "Environmental Studies and the Approval of New Animal Drugs," *FDA Veterinarian,* September/October 1988, p. 2

HUMAN ATTEMPTS TO MAKE animal agriculture efficient through factory farm-ing cause unexpected problems. Some of these problems are not easily over-come, and impose continuous risks and costs. We have already noted the increased risk of far-reaching accidents in the food chain like the PBB disaster in Michigan. And we have seen how blind, ruthless pursuit of productivity has created drug-dependent animal industries and contaminated meat, milk, and eggs. Thinking that we can protect ourselves from germs and drug residues, we pay for more and more patches on the government's safety nets. Alarmed, we pay for more and more research, both to "prove" the link between animal drugs and human disease and to cure the new food-borne diseases. The animal factory is productive, all right; it produces a lot of problems.

119

I've seen the U.S. situation, and would not swap our setup for yours. You use such massive amounts of antibiotics that if you dropped them, you would have a catastrophe.
—R. Wilmore, "Many Problems in British Antibiotic Policy," *National Hog Farmer*, October 1975, p. 28

A not so obvious problem caused by factory farm systems is the costly disruption of the complementary relationship between plant and animal agriculture. On traditional farms, most animals are unconfined and can disperse their wastes over the land with no detrimental effects. Odor problems are nonexistent because the wastes either dry or dissolve into the soil. Cycles for the exchange of energy and nutrients among soil, plant, and animal are continuous without risk of pollution and without additional inputs of labor and energy (see Fig. 6-1). On factory farms, animals and land are separated, these cycles are interrupted, and a complex of environmental problems occur. According to a leading authority on agricultural pollution:

> If the waste-land link is broken or is inadequate for all of the animal wastes at a feedlot, then environmental costs in the form of increased fertilizer use, waste treatment, resource loss, and alteration of other natural cycles occur [see Fig. 6-2]. If adequate land is not available to apply the wastes and grow feed for the animals, then feed must be imported. This in turn creates a further dislocation in the basic cycle since nutrients in the feed grown in one area are transported to another and result in waste management concerns in the second geographical area.

Factory Sewage

Animal agriculture is the greatest producer of sewage wastes in the United States. A sixty-thousand-bird caged-layer house produces about eighty-two tons of manure every week. In the same period, the two thousand sows, boars, and feeder pigs in a small factory produce nearly twenty-seven tons of manure and thirty-two tons of urine.[2] One of the new, very large superfactories—and they are becoming common all over the Cornbelt—with as many as fifty thousand pigs inside can produce over three thousand tons of manure and urine a week. In all, our farm animals produce about two billion tons of manure each year—about ten times that of the human population—and half of this comes from confinement operations.[4]

Not all animal wastes are the same. Animals fattening in factories are fed such liberal amounts of rich feed that they absorb only a fraction of the nutrients. Their wastes contain more protein, organic matter, nitrogen, phosphorous, and other material known to cause pollution problems than do the wastes of animals

FOOD, FIBER, SHELTER

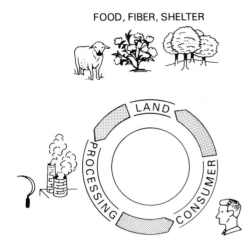

Fig. 6-1. The continuous cycle of resource use in nonintensive agriculture, where the land/animal/plant relationship is maintained and cautiously tended. Plants and animals are permitted to exchange energy, wastes, and residues according to natural cycles and rates, that is, without significant additional inputs of fertilizer, pesticides, drugs, fuel, etc. Productivity: moderate. Environmental damage: none.—After Raymond C. Loehr, *Pollution Control for Agriculture,* 2d ed. (Orlando, Fl.: Harcourt Brace Jovanovich, Academic Press, 1984).

Fig. 6-2. The broken cycle of resource use in intensive agriculture. The land/animal/plant interrelationship is severed and segmented. Each link is intensively manipulated by using heavy inputs of fertilizer, pesticides, drugs, fuel, etc. to boost selected growth rates and cycles and to override others. Productivity: high. Environmental damage: high.—After Raymond C. Loehr, *Pollution Control for Agriculture,* 2d ed. (Orlando, Fl.: Harcourt Brace Jovanovich, Academic Press, 1984).

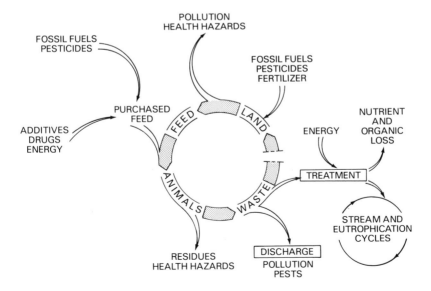

on normal diets.[5] Feed additives used in factories—antibiotics, copper, and arsenic, among others—make the manure a more potent pollutant. So the trend toward factories has brought us not only the new problem of dispersing waste, but a new kind of waste that is more polluting than ever.

Obviously this pollutant potency can create havoc in the local environment, with damage to air, water, and soil quality. Rich in organic matter, the waste uses up large amounts of oxygen in fresh water as it decays. Rich in nitrates, phosphorus, and other minerals, it encourages algae to grow, which takes up more oxygen. This causes streams to die, along with the fish and other life in them. In more and more areas, animal factories are being identified as major polluters. Runoff from storms has carried factory wastes to streams and groundwater, causing fish deaths and damage to recreational areas. In regions with high numbers of animal factories, constant smells and water problems are now common. These regions are straining to accommodate abnormal concentrations of animal numbers and animal wastes, and the land and waters simply cannot assimilate them.

If we want to see how bad the environmental damage can be, we can look to the Netherlands, where the industrious Dutch use factory farms to fuel their big export business in animal products. Environmental scientists there say that these farms produce ninety-four million tons of manure each year, yet the land can absorb only fifty million tons safely as fertilizer.[6] In the southern part of the country where most of the factory farms are located, air thick with ammonia is killing trees and natural vegetation. In a report on environmental damage in the area, *New Scientist* noted signs of stress in mighty oak trees and scraggly, bald pine trees.

> Tree tops droop as the walls of cells are weakened by excess nitrogen; and root systems are shallow because there is no need to search for nutrients deep in the soil. Fungi, such as *Diplodia pinea,* which healthy trees should shrug off with little damage, infect sickly trees from leaf tip to root. [The region] is a thick tangle of dead wood among the surviving greenery.
>
> All this is apparent to the untrained eye. Obvious only to the biologist is what has been destroyed forever of the original species of plants and insects that once flourished here. Gone are the heather *Erica detralix,* with its flower like a tiny pink bell, and the *Carex nigra* sedge.[7]

The name of this region is Rouwkuilen, which is Dutch for "place of mourning." In some areas the groundwater is polluted with nitrogen as far as thirty meters down, and people have been advised to quit using their wells. The green slime of algae fills streams, lakes, and canals. Poisoned by copper, cadmium, and zinc from animal wastes spread on fields, earthworms die and no longer aerate and enrich the soil; rainwater falls, but does not soak into the powdery ground. (Traces of these toxic metals must be put in feed additives to balance the diets of confined animals; free-roaming animals would pick up the necessary traces from soil and roughage.) The Dutch government's efforts to halt expan-

Droppings under egg cages.

sion of animal factories and put quotas on manure production backfired. Anticipating controls and quotas, Dutch factory farmers fudged records and inflated reports of animal numbers to establish plenty of leeway for expansion once the laws took effect. Now Dutch factory farmers are meeting their quotas by expanding facilities and adding animal numbers to pay for them, and the animal waste problem is growing worse than ever.[8]

The Factory as Neighbor

Factory farms stink. Up close, odors from wastes can be literally overwhelming. On first visiting factory farms—before our noses became "callused"—we felt fatigued and irritable for hours afterward.

Attempts to control odors with chemicals are being explored. There are chemicals to halt the biological breakdown process that releases odorous gases, chemicals to mask odors, chemicals to counteract one or more of the odorous components in waste, and just plain old deodorants. Chlorine, lime, potassium permanganate, and hydrogen peroxide have been used to hold down odor problems. In all, some twenty companies put out as many products supposedly helpful in controlling odor problems. In recent tests at the University of Illinois, none of these significantly reduced odors.[9]

Factory wastes attract sparrows, starlings, and insects, especially flies. In a letter to a farming magazine, one pig farmer complained: "I have a total confinement system that is eaten up with flies and I know it's a health hazard."[10] Complaints about excessive flies and rodents have been a major cause of litigation between factory farmers and their neighbors. These "pest" animals can transmit diseases to and from farms. But what problem can't be solved by one

A pig farm with waste-treatment ponds.

more feed additive? Sure enough, some commercial additives agribusiness companies sell contain hormones and toxins to hold down bird and insect populations around factory farms.

Because of factory farming's strong impact on the environment, there has been an increase in the number of lawsuits against factory farm owners. Neighbors of a Missouri cattle feedlot and pig factory claimed that runoff damaged ten acres of land, polluted two ponds, lowered milk production in their dairy herd, and caused the deaths of six cattle.[11] A Kansas pig factory was forced to shut down because of complaints from neighbors to state authorities.[12] In Minnesota, protesting neighbors and townspeople blocked construction of a large pig factory under local ordinances when the builder could not assure them that there would be no air or water pollution.[13] In Florida, runoff from the outdoor holding pens of huge factory dairies is contributing to the killing of Lake Okeechobee.[14] In Nebraska, a pig farmer was even overcome by the strong smells from a much bigger pig factory next door. National Farms, a leading contender in the agricorporate race to dominate pig production, put one of its three-hundred-thousand-pigs-per-year superfactories only a mile and a half from his house. He sued National Farms for damages. A jury deliberated just five minutes before awarding him $150,000 and ordering the company to relocate him. "They promised us it wouldn't stink," he said, "but it smells like rotten eggs. It's worse than living in a city sewer."[15] In Virginia, residents of a couple of counties petitioned their governments to block another agribusiness firm, Smithfield-Carrol Farms (of Smithfield ham fame), from building similar giant pig factories in their area. In one of the counties, citizens requested an environmental impact study to resolve questions about possible nitrate contamination of drinking water and pollution of rivers.[16] In Michigan, a community settled its lawsuit against Sand Livestock Systems, a major factory producer, after the company agreed to strict odor and waste disposal controls and to buy a nearby homeowner's property.[17]

Another leading superfactory corporation, Premium Standard Farms, which is based in Ames, Iowa, thought it would have no trouble in its own state—the country's biggest pork producer. Unfortunately, it chose a site uncomfortably close to a popular state park. Citizens and environmental groups kept up pressure on state officials until they denied the company permission to go ahead with construction of a waste-treatment facility, citing environmental concerns. Only temporarily frustrated, Premium Standard Farms went across the state line to Missouri, where it found an impoverished county eager to take it.[18] (Ironically, the Missouri county's poverty is part of the widespread economic blight that has crept across the heartlands as a result of agribusiness policies that choke family-sized farms with debt and costly inputs. It looks like the first order of agribuiness is to eliminate the competition. More on this in the next two chapters.) Premium Standard Farms' miffed president, Dennis Harms, told a reporter, "Iowa will suffer because of this."[19] Apparently Harms's only concern was for another kind of environment, for he explained the state's action by saying: "We perceive it as kind of an antibusiness environment in the state."[20]

As a result of the increase in pollution problems and the skirmishes between factory farmers and their neighbors, state and federal authorities have stepped in. The federal government's Environmental Protection Agency put forth a proposal in 1976 that would have regulated some 3,200 of the nation's 700,000 beef, dairy, and pig feedlots. A court decision later the same year expanded the scope of coverage to about ninety-five thousand operations. These rules, however, prevent only discharge of untreated wastes into navigable streams; they have not effectively ended the problems of odors and pests. Most states now have some kind of water and air pollution controls in place that can be applied to factory farms. Whether or not they will be in a given case often turns on how important the factory farms are to the area. Some states have specific laws and regulations that require producers to obtain waste permits, provide waste management facilities, and meet other standards. Other states have developed "codes of practice" or "good practice guidelines," which amount to official suggestions to factory producers. The only teeth in them is that an uncooperative producer may be more vulnerable to civil lawsuits for nuisance.

Solutions to waste problems lag behind the development of factory systems and add to the complications of farming. If farmers want the maximum fertilizer value from animal wastes, they must devote much time, labor, and energy to hauling and spreading the stuff on fields. But frequent field application is bound to cause odor problems and complaints from the neighbors. There are times, too, when field application is impossible, such as during the crop's growing season and when the ground is frozen or wet. Moreover, heavy tractors and equipment compact the soil, making it less able to absorb the manure and increasing the potential for pollution. An additional problem for some factory farmers is that they do not have enough land to assimilate safely all of the wastes their animals produce.

Farmers are in a bind. High land costs, lack of land availability, and other factors force them to concentrate animals in factories; but then they need additional facilities to get rid of the daily pileup without causing pollution problems. As one pig producer states the dilemma: "We've got two routes to go. Either disperse the livestock so we don't have to disperse the waste or concentrate the livestock and have problems dispersing the waste."[21]

Whether farmers decide to store, disperse, or degrade animal wastes, the facilities can be expensive and a chore to operate. Some factory storage facilities use forced air, augers, or pistons to push waste from factory buildings to tanks or holding ponds. Some farmers gouge out large, pondlike "lagoons" to hold wastes where bacteria digest everything into simple, nonpolluting elements. These anaerobic lagoons are the most labor free, but they can give off strong odors. If odors are a problem, farmers must pump in fresh water or use pumps and aerators to stir in oxygen.

The loss of nitrogen from animals' wastes is perhaps the most costly aspect of factory disposal systems. Field crops need nitrogen, and to provide it American farmers spread about ten million tons of commercial fertilizer each year at a cost of about $2.5 billion. Livestock and poultry produce enough waste each year to provide $1.5 billion worth of nitrogen fertilizer, but because factory farm

The concentration of animals, as in the case of these pregnant sows, takes much of the labor out of pig production, but the huge volume of waste produced creates serious pollution problems.

A waste-holding lagoon for a large hog factory.

methods of waste collection and disposal destroy nitrogen, only about half this amount is available for fertilizer. On the largest factory farms, intensive waste treatment methods cause even greater losses of nitrogen. In lagoons, for example, as much as 80 percent of nitrogen is destroyed by microbial and chemical action.

Most factory farmers aren't concerned about the efficiency and the greater ecological good of nutrient recycling. It is just too much trouble and too expensive to get nutrients back to the soil. One such farmer's comment is typical: "Until fertilizer gets more expensive than labor, the waste has very little value to me."[22] Such is the economic logic of capital-intensive American agriculture.

The Cost of Disease Control

Animal farming is more costly than growing plants because mammals and birds are susceptible to more diseases than plants are. And because they are closer to humans in evolution, these animals can harbor diseases transmissible to humans. Trichinosis, brucellosis, leptospirosis, and salmonellosis are just a few of the eighty-odd bacterial, viral, and parasitic diseases that we can catch from farm animals.[23]

Because of these threats to human health and the perceived "need" for animals in the human food chain, animal disease control programs at public expense began in the early 1800s. By about 1880, Congress established the Bureau of Animal Industry within the USDA "to provide means for the suppression and extirpation . . . of contagious diseases among domestic animals.[24] The bureau established a disease control scheme that used quarantine, killing, and burial or burning of entire herds and disinfection of premises in attempts to "eradicate" the diseases within the United States. "Eradicate," as disease control authorities use it, is a technical term and their definition of it does not mean that the disease-causing organism has been made extinct worldwide. It just means that its movement has been brought under control so that no new cases of the disease are reported in the United States.

Eradication campaigns are costly; they require veterinarians and other expert personnel and they provide the indemnity payments to farmers whose animals must be destroyed. Since 1934, when the campaign against brucellosis began, over $1 billion has been spent trying to wipe out this disease in U.S. cattle.[25] Efforts to halt just this one disease are costing the federal government about $33 million and the states another $25 million each year, and the end is not yet in sight. Occasionally, this eradication program bogs down and some experts believe that if eradication is possible at all, the cost may be prohibitive.[26] Hog cholera was believed to have been nearly eradicated until the spring of 1976 when an outbreak in eastern states sent government exterminators out with their emergency gear. They killed and buried twenty-four thousand hogs, and farmers were paid $3 million in indemnities. Then, in January 1978, the disease was pronounced eradicated by the Secretary of Agriculture. Total expenses to "eradicate" hog cholera came to over $140 million public funds.[27] Similarly, when exotic Newcastle disease struck poultry operations in southern California in the early 1970s, government disease control squads went to work. Twelve million destroyed birds, $56 million, and a year and a half later, the disease was adjudged "eradicated," although small outbreaks were reported in each of the next three years.[28]

As new animal diseases emerge, new eradication programs follow. Pseudorabies in pigs, for example, has been taking virtually entire herds on some farms in the Midwest since 1973. Representatives from USDA, the National Pork Producers' Council, and other groups have proposed a five-year eradication program that would cost $44 million.[29] Others have estimated that the program could cost state and federal governments as much as $90 million.[30] A new disease, African swine fever, has reached the Western Hemisphere and, because there is no vaccine and no treatment, government and industry are already discussing an eradication program. If the disease takes hold in the United States, experts estimate that the cost of a five-year program could reach $290 million.[31]

Of course, we aren't arguing that it would be better to let the animals die and save the money. We are simply trying to point out the irrationality in our practice of maintaining huge populations of food animals. These reservoirs for diseases will continue to generate higher food costs—whether from rising costs of control programs, veterinary services, and medical supplies or from wasted grain and other investments when the animals die. The choice is not between animal deaths or disease control; we could just as easily reduce our reliance on animal agriculture with its costly problems.

Although disease control programs were conceived of and have been justified on the grounds of public health, many of the diseases under control measures

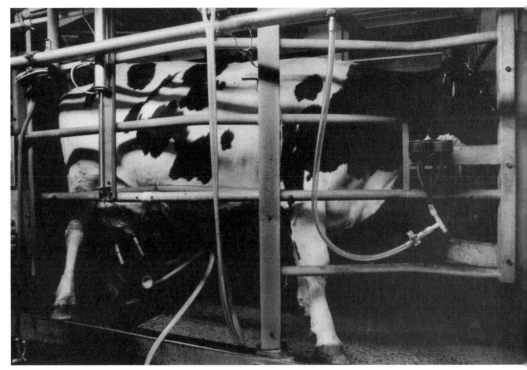

Milking.

have no effect on humans. Rather, the control programs pay out public funds to reduce the true cost of animal production. They constitute a public subsidy to farmers and the meat industry.

The Cost of Too Much Milk

Like the meat and poultry inspection program, the milk price support system is another publicly funded prop for the animal industry. While the inspection program keeps meat prices artificially low by covering the cost of inspection out of taxes, the milk price support system keeps consumer milk prices artificially high. Under this program, the federal government sets minimum prices that must be paid by processors to milk producers. To guarantee that all milk sells at these prices, the USDA buys all unsold (surplus) milk at announced prices; this system keeps farmers in the dairy business when they would otherwise be producing other crops. The "benefit" to consumers is that they have more than enough milk to go around. So much, in fact, that 135 million pounds of butter, 257 million pounds of cheese, and 547 million pounds of nonfat dry milk had to be removed from the market by the government during the 1986–87 marketing year and added to inventories from the previous year.[32] After donations to foreign and domestic food aid programs, sales to the army, and sales of nonfat dry milk for use as a protein supplement in animal feeds, the government had a total of 1.2

billion pounds of butter, cheese, and nonfat dry milk in storage at the end of the 1986–87 marketing year.[33]

The program persists because of the raw political power that dairy industry money can buy. Of all the special-interest groups, the dairy lobby has historically been among the biggest contributors to the campaigns of those running for federal government offices, and officeholders have returned the favor.[34] According to government records, taxpayers shelled out almost $1 billion in the 1986–87 fiscal year to buy surplus butter, cheese, and dried milk.[35]

The Cost of Factory Tax Breaks

For years, government tax policy has subsidized the factory approach to animal farming and promoted specialization at the expense of diversity and versatility in farm systems. It promoted hardware rather than human inputs to production. In many states, for example, [portable confinement units are not considered buildings or real estate and are not subject to real property taxes.] Until 1986, highly specialized pig and poultry factories and hardware qualified for the "investment credit" deduction from income taxes. All-purpose, conventional farm buildings did not qualify. [Farmers who maintained their old-fashioned barns and animal shelters did so without the tax advantages their factory-building neighbors had.]

Federally guaranteed loan programs have been misused by officials to fund large cattle and pig factories. Testimony at hearings before Senate committees revealed that the financing practices of the Small Business Administration (SBA) and USDA's Farmers Home Administration favored factory systems to the economic disadvantage of family farms in violation of the Food and Agriculture Act of 1977. SBA had set its own size standards that permitted funding of operations with up to one million dollars a year in gross sales, and was routinely financing pig factories in the top 1 percent of sales volume.[36]

Nebraska's Center for Rural Affairs has identified five basic features of the tax laws that have fostered the rise of factory farming and other kinds of industrialization in agriculture: [corporate tax rates, cash accounting, capital gains rules, investment tax credit and accelerated depreciation (when applied to taxpayers with farm income—not all of whom are farmers living on farms—these provide incentives for constant expansion), and farming practices that use capital more than labor.] In his revealing book, *Family Farming: A New Economic Vision,* the center's cofounder and codirector, Marty Strange, explains how these tax features have changed dairying:

> Used to their fullest advantage, these combined tax subsidies go a long way toward explaining why there has been so much expansion in the dairy industry, and especially why there have been so many new, large-scale facilities built in the southeastern and southwestern regions of the country, areas not traditionally known as dairy country. Before 1986, a corporate

dairy farm in the 46 percent tax bracket could use the tax rules to garner $170,000 in tax subsidies on a $1.05 million investment in a five-hundred-cow dairy. That's a subsidy of *$340 per cow in the herd* [italics in original].

In pork production, the same rules have applied in the same way, leading to a revolution in the way pork is produced.[37]

Thus, the more the money invested in specialized confinement buildings, the more generous the tax favors. We taxpayers have had to make up for the taxes reduced by those favors; in effect, we have been paying for some of the forces that have brought on the capital-intensification of animal production. The Tax Reform Act of 1986 eliminated the investment tax credit, tightened up cash accounting of farm income, and cracked down on abuses by those who used farm losses as tax shelters. It barely touched accelerated depreciation, however, which leaves a powerful financial incentive to choose capital- over labor-intensive farming methods. In any event, the 1986 tax reforms were too little, too late. The capital-intensive, or factory, revolution was by then a fait accompli.

From Public Interest to Private Gain

Who pays for the scientists and officials who are leading agricultural technology toward the use of more hardware and energy, employment of fewer and fewer people, greater specialization and vulnerability, and monopoly control of food production?

We do. The bulk of agricultural research in the United States is conducted by the tax-supported "land grant" college complex and the USDA. Composed of sixty-nine state universities, their colleges of agriculture, experiment stations, and extension services, this complex employs over thirty-five thousand people at an annual cost of nine hundred million dollars of public funds.

This system was set up to serve the needs of consumers, family farmers, and farm workers; but one of its main jobs now, it seems, is providing expertise to the largest agribusiness and food industry corporations. Public funds supported a Cornell University project to develop mechanically deboned poultry "meat"—pulverized bone, cartilage, and flesh—so that industry could put it in hot dogs and luncheon meats and fetch a better price for slaughterhouse leftovers. Scientists at the University of Georgia used public funds to perfect a mechanical broiler harvester that herds birds onto a conveyor belt and out to the trucks. At the request of a Georgia broiler company, the university's poultry science department started a program of offering workshops to a single company's management personnel who, in turn, "tailor the program to company grow-out programs."[38] In other words, the university provides a publicly supported consulting firm for Georgia's broiler companies.

In defense of such blatant service to agribusiness, university scientists usually claim that these projects are privately funded by agribusiness concerns, which

have a right to get what they have paid for, and that this helps each department's overall research activities. Yes, it does, but the arrangement also influences the nature of that department's overall research activities. The scientist or team of scientists who attracts fat grants from, say, the five companies who sell BGH will be smiled upon by higher-ups in the university and perhaps rewarded with a larger share of public funds for their other research. (It is safe to say that their work is not likely to be terribly critical of BGH.) Other scientists in the department will then want to "get in on" private research funds and will tend to plan projects that cater more to private than to public interests. Perhaps they will get too little private money for all of the work and the rest of it will be carried out with public money. In this way, in the words of a farm policy expert, private grant arrangements "give the scientist influence over the allocation of public funds. In short, the private grants leverage public funds."[39]

Many government and university scientists act as publicly supported inventors for industry. They develop a drug, machine, or system and then allow a company to turn it into a commercial product. Much of factory farming technology is developed in this way, and publicly supported scientists have no qualms about it. But they assure us that their tax-supported work to help agribusiness companies

A sheep-confinement system being developed at one of USDA's research facilities.

brings progress and improvement for everyone. Under such a system of technological development though, any benefit to farmers and consumers is coin-
cidental rather than intentional. Agribusiness, not farmers or consumers, makes
the vital decisions about what subjects should be investigated and what direction
technology should take. In the process, "scientific objectivity" has vanished and
the public has lost the benefit of expertise in finding the best technology for all
society.

The trend toward animal factories is highly touted for production efficiency
which, it is argued, keeps prices of animal products from skyrocketing. But there
are huge hidden costs behind this illusory efficiency. If the true costs of factory
farming were made visible, people would not be willing to pay them.

It may not be wise to fool mother nature, but it can be profitable.
—John Bailey, "This Device Can Boost Beef Output," *The Wichita Eagle and*
Beacon, November 14, 1976

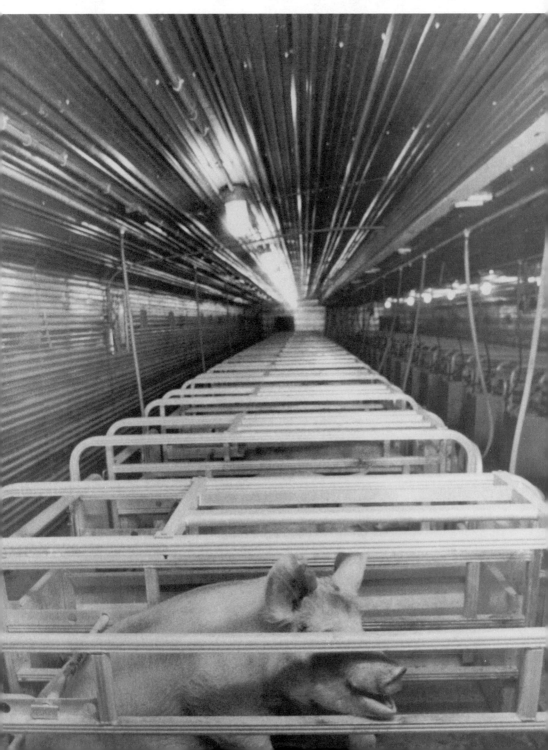

AGRIBUSINESS

The Farmer as Victim, or Who's Making the Real Money?

I think we need a systems-type research program in agribusiness . . . the kind that gave us the atomic bomb and put a man on the moon.
—Dr. John H. Davis, coiner of the term "agribusiness," quoted in "Agribusiness Needs of the Future," *Broiler Industry*, September 1976, p. 26

Meat, milk, dairy products, and eggs increasingly will be produced in confined large industrial-type facilities. The trend toward controlled and enclosed facilities, which is virtually complete for smaller animals such as hens and broilers, is increasing even for the larger animals such as beef and dairy cattle.
—Raymond C. Loehr, *Pollution Control for Agriculture*, 2d ed. (Orlando, Fl.: Harcourt Brace Jovanovich, Academic Press, 1984), p. 25

Big Boys Smell Profits in Pork: That's why giants like Tyson [Foods] are pushing to boost the number of poultry-style pork production outfits.
—Headline for a story by Ken Haggerty, in *Agweek*, September 4, 1989

THE HEART OF AGRICULTURE IS THE FARM, the place where plants and animals are grown. Like the heart, the farm sends out sustenance to the tissues of society—people and communities. The farm is deep in the heart, too, because its work is close to nature and is the basic life activity of producing food. And, compared to what most of us do for a living, farming is freedom—from bosses, time clocks, commuter traffic jams, and meaningless drudge work. On the farm, the family stays together and goes to work together. Farming is ideal—as work, a life-style, a place to live, and a place to raise a family. That is why many people want to farm and many others work so hard to keep on farming; they know a good life and good work when they see them.

This kind of farm, the small-to-moderate-sized farm operated by the labor of family members, is called the "backbone of American agriculture" because for

135

decades it has produced the great bulk of the nation's food. It is more than that, however. It is one of the wellsprings of American entrepreneurial, social, moral, spiritual, and practical values. Because it nourishes the rest of society in so many ways, the family-run farm is a valuable American institution and one that many people would like to keep viable.

It is also in serious trouble, as you probably know from newspapers, magazines, television, and movies. In the past decade, news of farm foreclosures, farmer suicides, and farm community poverty has made people aware that the backbone of American agriculture is nearly broken. Saving the family farm has become the newest cause célèbre—so much so that there is a danger now that sentimentalism and sensationalism will take the place of painful study of the causes of and patient search for solutions to the farm crisis.

Farm policy experts suggest a bewildering variety of explanations for the farm crisis, few of which can be understood by the average citizen—farmer or otherwise. When we try to follow the discussion we get hit with words like *commodities futures, parity, marketing orders, target levels, payments-in-kind,* and *vertical integration* and are soon lost. Then every expert has his or her favorite analysis, and each one contradicts another. As a result, the big picture is fuzzy, confusing, and apparently hopeless.

But it will not be hopeless if we can understand just a few of the *basic* forces moving against family-run farms. Members of Congress—virtually all nonfarmers—are trying to do just that in response to rising concern about the economic, social, and environmental problems associated with farming. A few years ago, they asked their Office of Technology Assessment (OTA) to study the situation and give them an overview of recent changes and current problem areas in agriculture. According to OTA, the period of change began around World War II, when tractors and other machines became available and began to replace draft animals and human labor:

> The increased mechanization of farming permitted the amount of land cultivated per farm worker to increase fivefold from 1930 to 1980. The amount of capital used per worker increased more than 15 times in this period. Total productivity (production per unit of total inputs) more than doubled because of the adoption of new technologies such as hybrid seeds and improved livestock feeding and disease prevention. The use of both agricultural chemicals and fuel also grew very rapidly in the postwar period. Agricultural production began to *rely heavily on the nonfarm sector* [emphasis added] for machinery, fuel, fertilizer and other chemicals. These, not more land or labor, produced the growth in farm production. The resultant changes have greatly increased the capital investment necessary to enter farming and have generated new requirements for operating credit during the growing cycle.

We add the emphasis above because most nonfarm people do not realize the power and significance of this sector, which we call *agribusiness.* This sector does not necessarily have to be the villain, though it surely has been a villain at times. It has surely been the prime mover behind the trend toward greater use of chemicals in farming. We have already seen how it influences animal drug policy and agricultural research agendas. There are plenty of similar examples to show that what is good for agribusiness is not necessarily good for farmers, consumers, and the environment. So in understanding some of the basic forces against the family-run farm, we must keep that in mind. Agribusiness, although it likes to wrap itself in the flag of family farming, has interests of its own, which are often in conflict with family farming (not to mention consumers, environment, et cetera).

A number of recent books, particularly Marty Strange's *Family Farming,* offer full discussions in easy language of all of the basic forces behind the unfortunate changes in agriculture. We urge anyone interested in food, farming, and the environment to read these and begin to understand the farm crisis and how it affects us all. A review of all of these basic forces would expand the scope of this book unbearably, so we must focus on animal production and how it figures in the problems down on the family farm.

Unfortunately, most farm policy experts miss the fact that the animal factory revolution has, in many ways, destroyed family farming. Some don't mention it at all; others mention it in passing, such as when they say that chickens are just another of the "crops" family farmers have lost to agribusiness. Because so few experts truly understand the vital role animal production plays in family-type farm economics, the significance of the animal factory revolution completely escapes them. To digress and speculate for a moment, we believe this blind spot is part of the larger blind spot people have when it comes to looking closely at how animals are exploited for food. It keeps them a good, safe distance away from the nuts and bolts of the unpleasant details concerning animal food production. This distancing defense mechanism makes it difficult for those people to understand what is happening to farm animals, to the animal farmer, and to animal production methods. Nobody wants to know. As a result, the animal factory revolution races ahead. It seems inevitable; it seems like progress.

In response to concern about the plight of family farming and their role in it, agribusiness leaders try to confuse us with semantics and reassure us with figures. The term "family farm" is made suspect. It is meaningless, we are told, because many of the nation's largest industrial farms are family-owned. But then, so is Ford Motor Company. For agribusiness, Frank Perdue, Oscar Meyer, and Jimmy Dean are family farmers. Next, the corporate, industrial farm is defended on the grounds that many true family farms are also incorporated and use high-tech industrial systems. True, many have moved under pressure from the forces lined up against them and have bought into the agribusiness way of farming. The aim of these word games is to make us think twice about using the emotionally laden term "family farm," for if we do, our display of ignorance and naïveté will embarrass us.

After the semantics come the figures games. We are told that the great bulk—some 86 percent—of the nation's 2.2 million farms are small and family-operated.[2] The figures show also that the very largest farms—those that sell more than half a million dollars' worth of farm products a year—add up to only 1.2 percent of all American farms.[3] Next farm census figures may be cited showing that the number of small-to-middle-sized farms (as defined by annual gross sales) is actually increasing. Thus, all looks well with the family farm.

These simplistic statistics, however, ignore the deeper realities of the changes in American agriculture. In fact, the apparent increase in the number of farms with small-to-medium annual gross sales is due to more and more farms making less and less money. Between 1969 and 1982, the smallest (those with under twenty thousand dollars annual gross sales) farms' already-small slice of the agricultural sales pie got smaller by two-thirds: it dropped from 17.2 to 5.5 percent of all farm sales.[4] Meanwhile, the largest operators are taking an increasingly larger share of agricultural earnings. At the top end of the scale are the farms that gross over two hundred thousand dollars a year. These are only 5.4 percent of all farms, but they took almost 54 percent of all farm income in 1982.[5] Between 1969 and 1982, their share of the agricultural sales pie grew by 20 percent: it rose from 45 to 54 percent of farm sales.[6] We should note here that these figures have been adjusted for inflation.

Even more telling about the changes in farming is a look at *net* farm income. The same 5.4 percent of farms that gross over two hundred thousand dollars a year are taking an even greater share of net. In 1969, they took 51 percent of all net farm income; in 1982, they took 84 percent. Their share of the net income pie got bigger by two-thirds. The very largest farms—the 1.2 percent that sell over half a million dollars' worth of products a year—made an even bigger leap toward dominating the market. Their share of net farm income in 1969 was 36 percent; in 1982 it had risen to 64 percent—a 77 percent increase.[7] Again, these figures have been adjusted for inflation.

If we look through these dry figures we can see that large-scale, industrial farming is taking over food production. This helps us understand why the smaller, family-operated farm is having such a hard time. There are many such farms, semantics and figures games aside. Maybe one cannot be defined to suit statisticians and tax lawyers but it can be identified by these characteristics: It produces a level of income close to the national average, the owners live there, their principal occupation is farming, and the owners provide virtually all of the labor themselves. It is a farm that can be managed by the average farm-skilled family and it can provide them with a standard of living and security enjoyed by the average American working family.

This is the farm that is going under in the current farm crisis. If we let it happen, we will have lost a lot more than jobs for rural people. The loss will extend into rural communities, to treatment of the land, animals, and environment, and inevitably to the food we eat. If we want to do something about this overall trend in farming—which includes the trend toward animal factories—we can start by trying to understand the forces propelling it.

Fig. 7-1.   In every type of animal production, the smaller farms have been losing their share of total production to the larger farms.—Office of Technology Assessment, "Dynamic Structure of Agriculture," *Technology, Public Policy, and the Changing Structure of American Agriculture* (Washington, D.C.: U.S. Government Printing Office, March 1986), pp. 91–106.

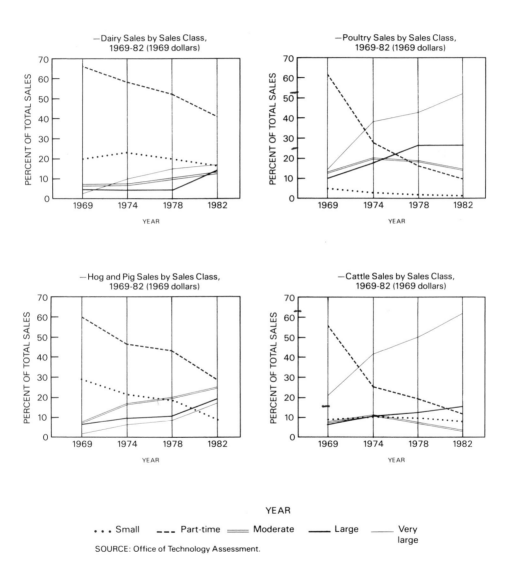

The broiler industry has kept chicken inexpensive by replacing farmers' labor with mass production in automated confinement buildings.

First we must see how farmers are caught in a current of economic developments that will either throw them off the farm or push them into bigness and specialization. A Kansas farmer who farmed land that had been in his family for a century explained how these developments force farmers into a dilemma.

> The returns to capital and labor invested in production agriculture are so low (and steadily growing smaller) that increased volume and specialization is the only alternative to a declining standard of living for farm people. The farmer who decides to stay small and keep farming has just initiated creeping bankruptcy.[8]

Bigger and Fewer

Prices of farmland rise because of demand for land from nonfarm interests and from established farmers with mortgageable land and equipment who want to expand. Big farms get bigger, the total number of farms declines, and all farmers must make an effort just to stay in farming. The big farmers increase farm productivity to cover the cost of added acreage; the small farmers, cut off from additional acreage that could improve their livelihood, must wrest even more from their land to make ends meet—if they want to remain farmers. At the same time, production goals get more elusive because the labor pool available to farmers is drying up; fewer and fewer people are skilled and reliable enough to do the increasingly complex kinds of work needed on modern farms—at wages farmers can afford.

[Changes in marketing of farm produce reinforce the trend to large-scale farming methods. Traditional local markets for farm products have been displaced by bigger, regional markets. In the interests of efficiency and, ostensibly, of health and sanitation, many states now require inspection of produce. Officialdom and agribusiness prefer to conduct inspections, standardized measurement procedures, and processing at a few large centers rather than at hundreds of small ones all over a state. In many states, health regulations and milk-processing companies require farmers to have special barns, equipment, tanks, and coolers that small farmers cannot afford.]

In dozens of subtle ways, blind belief in the myth that bigger is better has influenced farm policy decisions and forced changes in the way food is produced. With its twin brother, the God of Growth, Bigger is Better has long been the principal ideology of American industry, but particularly of American agribusiness. It has been most powerful because it is subtle, invisible, and not a "thing" that can be isolated and criticized. It has become a mind-set, a way of thinking, as a leading farm policy expert explains:

> Usually, the bigger-is-better influence in public policy is subtle. Explicit favoritism toward industrial agribusiness is rare. Instead, farm programs, tax rules, credit services and other instruments of public policy are weighted to seduce individual farmers to expand. Such policies are consistently designed to nourish the ambitions of the growth-minded farmer, to chide the reluctant, and to disdain those who are satisfied with enough. All farmers, no matter the current size of their farm, are encouraged to expand, to become "more efficient" for their own good as well as that of the public. And the policies offer no limits on how much expansion is good. There are no policies of restraint. No farm is big enough; every farm is too small. Growth, not simply bigness per se, is the policy objective of American agribusiness.[9]

The Bias Toward Agribusiness

When he was secretary of agriculture under Presidents Nixon and Ford, Earl Butz created the slogan for bigger-is-better agribusiness: "Get big or get out." The implication was that to be a good farmer you should constantly expand and increase productivity, yields, efficiency, et cetera. Actually, it was a very successful form of thought control, in that agribusiness forced its industrialist, expansionist mind-set onto yeomen—hands-on working people who had no real need for it. Agribusiness industries had a lot to gain from infecting farmers with the "new-think": greater sales of machinery, confinement buildings, chemicals, drugs, and other costly capital inputs; greater surpluses of cheap grain and commodities for export, for animal feeds, for processed food, and other agribusiness products. The greatest thing gained, however, was the massive political power to influence legislation and government policy. That power came in part from burgeoning agribusiness corporate wealth and in part from farmers themselves, who, imbued with new-think, used their credibility and favorable image with the public to preach the agribusiness growth gospel.

Many farmers did not fall for it; they stuck to their proven ways and still farm successfully today. But many others could not resist the promises of new-think and got caught up in the perpetual motion of borrow, buy, and build.

Agribusiness greased their way all along with plenty of incentives. They saw to it that government farm programs and policies favored size. For years, the bulk of tax-supported assistance to farmers has gone to the very largest operations. Throughout the 1960s, the top 20 percent of farms were getting over half the subsidies to corn, cotton, and other crops.[10] In 1975, only 16 percent of farms—the very largest—received almost half of the $530 million in payments to farmers; in 1987, the largest 4.5 percent of farms got 27 percent of farm payments.[11] The reason for the top-loading of payments is obvious: they are based on farm production, so the biggest producers get the biggest payments. To avoid the embarrassment of stories about big checks to wealthy landowners, government has placed limitations on payments from time to time. But, because it does not change the basis (production) for subsidies, top-loading keeps creeping back. As Nebraska farm policy expert Marty Strange explains it:

> The history of the payment limitation can thus be succinctly stated: The limitation is usually set so high that it affects almost no one, and if it threatens to discourage participation in acreage-reduction programs by driving larger farms out of the programs, it is raised or suspended. In short, Congress doesn't really mean to target the benefits of commodity programs to family-sized farms. It only wants to leave the impression that it does. Payment limitations are now a political ritual in every farm bill— obligatory and meaningless. Living the myth that bigger is better sometimes requires living a lie.[12]

In chapter 6, we saw how tax policies as applied to people with farm income have been a force for expansion and specialization. We should note one last force, one that is unknown to virtually all of the nonfarming public—over 97 percent of the population. Government farm-credit programs, originally installed to aid small farmers and to help people enter farming, have been subverted by agribusiness ideology to the point where they too serve primarily the largest operators who need them the least. Their purpose was to make credit cheap and available to struggling farmers who would not appear to be good credit risks and could not afford the interest rates of private banks and lenders. Over time, agribusiness used its political clout to fix things so that large operations could get the same credit deals. Now the situation has been made worse by the government policy decision to turn the lending over to private banks, with the government guaranteeing the loan. This makes banks, not farm policy administrators, the decision-makers in credit applications, and banks have been showing a tendency—as we should expect—to favor the large, specialized, productive, expansionist operations. Sooner or later, the agribusiness bias toward endless growth and large size creeps into everything.

In no way is the bias toward agribusiness subtle in farming magazines, agricultural college extension agents, and salespeople from the companies that supply products to agriculture. Together, these elements put forth an ideal of farming that represents their view of profitable or successful farming. The progressive farmer, the "pork all-American" or milk production champion, is the *publicity* one who goes all out for production and uses anything and everything to get it. Implicit in this ideal is the notion that the farmer should go into debt to acquire the latest in factory buildings, or equipment, chemicals, drugs, and services. To help farmers make expensive land pay, one farm magazine advises: "Consider intensification. . . . At the present time, you can put in improvements and expand livestock cheaper than you can buy more land."[13] The farm magazines, of course, are loaded with advertisements from manufacturers of buildings, equipment, drugs, and supplies used in factory systems. This advertising sets up powerful magnetic fields in the offices of the farm press and no doubt affects the movements of reporters' and editors' pens. This is not to say that agricultural journalists are personally corrupt, that is, that they are neutral on the issues but have "sold out" to agribusiness. No, we are afraid that most are "conscientious" about their views, having been infected with agribusiness ideologies somewhere along the way to their desk jobs. In much the same way, that infection enters veterinarians, animal scientists, agricultural engineers, and other professionals who spend their careers in public and private agricultural organizations. The mind-set—an unshakable faith in expansion, efficiency, specialization, and "agri-power"—is an unspoken job requirement. One needs it because people move from sector to sector within the agroindustries; today a lowly staff writer for *Successful Farming,* tomorrow a highly paid public relations coordinator for one of the giant grain companies or meat packers.

The agribusiness bias of the farm press has become so blatant that it is the butt of many jokes lately. Even farmers are sounding off about it and some of their letters to farm publications are printed. One told *Iowa Farmer Today:*

> Most ag journalists are not noted for investigative reporting. They have a tendency to treat big corporations, big commodity groups and large-scale farmers with unmerited deference. Partly because some day they may seek upward mobility, career-wise and financially, through previous contacts.[14]

Farmers' new insights into the agribusiness bias in the farm press is a bit too little, too late, however. That bias has been working invisibly, insidiously for over forty years and the damage is already done.

Most of the magazines have been hostile to alternatives to the agribusiness

Confinement technology in hog production is following the path of the poultry industry. As a result, independent hog farmers are being squeezed out by vertically integrated agribusiness corporations.

way of food production. When USDA proposed a total of three million dollars (only about 0.02 percent of its budget) for two projects to help stimulate local production (one would have helped promote roadside markets, the other would have encouraged community gardens in urban areas), both programs were blasted in *National Hog Farmer*. The editor wrote: "Why don't we just turn the Department of Agriculture over to the do-gooders?"[15] When a Washington, D.C.-based group, the Exploratory Project for Economic Alternatives, set forth a plan that would aid small farmers with subsidies and other incentives, *Beef* magazine said that "the best thing that can happen to this report is that it be consigned to molder away in some file cabinet and forever be forgotten."[16]

Animals: The Perfect Cash Crop

As we noted early in this chapter, animal production has always been the key enterprise for small farmers and beginning farmers. And after they are established, animal production continues to make the most important contribution to their farms' stability and success: steady cash flow. This is especially so if the farm is a narrowly diversified one with few dependable plant crops. We regret the need to emphasize this again: animal production is *key* to farming of the kind now being destroyed, and at the same time—ironically—being promoted by those seeking more natural, low-input, sustainable agricultural systems. One needs to understand this in order to appreciate how the trend toward animal factories is a destroyer of that kind of farming.

Farmers now have a steady flow of expenses; they have payments for land, buildings, machinery, fuel, and, of course, living expenses. They must produce some crops that generate a steady flow of cash. Field crops can make money, but they are dependent on market and weather uncertainties and are slow and seasonal in coming. Animal production has always been the main source of cash flow on many farms because it provides a *steady* flow of salable commodities.

Today's day-to-day cash requirements, however, can hardly be met by traditional methods of animal farming. Thus begins the capital-expansion spiral into factory systems and methods. First, flock or herd size must be increased substantially if more money is to be made. But then labor requirements impose limitations unless the farmer can afford to invest in factory buildings and equipment. The expense will be prohibitive unless the farmer is willing to maintain a very large number of animals and push them through with factorylike speed and efficiency. During the pig factory building boom of the 1970s one hog expert explained the pressure to produce: "With a $1,000 investment per sow you want to get as many pigs out of the buildings as possible. It's a far cry from a $50 individual house and some fencing used in the past."[17] The whopping costs of capital intensification of animal production, then, are spread over the herd or flock. To ensure profitability, the farmer must employ a full arsenal of factory methods, including crowding, speeding cycles, use of drugs and growth promotants, and the other factory management tools.

These forces, combined with the agribusiness ideology, have produced the specialized factory farms of today. The operation represents a huge capital investment and it requires intensive management, both of which take up all of the farmer's time and resources so that he or she cannot run a genuinely diversified, resource-balanced, ecologically integrated farming operation. Worse still, these specialized, capital-intensive operations tend to become chronic overproducers of broilers, eggs, pork, milk, and other animal products. These products glut markets and hold down prices to all producers. Then those with small numbers of animals in labor-intensive systems find that they are making too little money for the effort and they sell off their animals. Thus the specialized operations proliferate and take over markets from small, diversified producers. Soon agribusiness companies either buy up the specialized operations—or contract with them to raise company animals to company specifications—and become "farmers" themselves, as Cargill, the grain company, ConAgra, the feed company, and many other seed, feed, and chemical companies have been doing since the 1960s.

Factory Farm: Labor Efficient?

Still, many family dairy, hog, and beef farmers buy into factory expansion to try to stay in farming. They find that factory systems are not at all cheap.

Estimates for setting up pig-confinement facilities range from fifteen hundred to two thousand dollars per breeding sow. The cost of setting up a family-size dairy farm can easily run over three hundred thousand dollars. These estimates are for the cost of confinement buildings and equipment—none includes the cost of farmland or animals.

To keep their heads above water, then, farmers must devote more time and energy to farming than ever before. This is the irony of "labor-efficient" factory farms: the financial burdens are so great that farmers must work harder than ever to meet payments. Farmers now go to night school to learn stockbroker tactics like "hedging" and to understand futures trading and other market intricacies. Their headaches are worse than ever and many farmers know it. A Kansas farmer told a magazine writer:

> I just wish you could tell us how to get smaller. I'm from the generation that took to farming because of the life-style, and if we made a living that was okay. The best time I ever had farming was when I used horses and came home every evening at five to help Eileen in the vegetable garden. But there's no time anymore.[18]

"Small" farmers have to hustle like the business executives in cities whom they have so often ridiculed. But unlike executives and stockbrokers, farmers don't get such a large return on their investment and they must put in long hours of hard work to get it. For all of their six-figure balance sheets, farmers still do the hard, dirty work of agriculture while the rest of agribusiness makes the easy money supplying them, lending to them, and reselling their products. No wonder so many farmers get disgusted and quit farming for other work.

We've got a huge investment; we can't afford to let it sit idle. The building has to be working for us all the time. That means keeping it at capacity all the time.

—Neil Beck, Iowa pig farm manager quoted in Warren Clark, "Have We Broken the Hog Cycle?" *Farm Journal*, October 1976, p. Hog-34

What's Wrong with Bigness and Mechanization?

The history of the poultry industry provides the best illustration of what happens as animal production systems increase productivity through capital intensification. Because of the demands of expensive equipment, only large companies can afford to enter the business and to expand production; when they do, smaller operators are gradually squeezed out. A poultry industry magazine reported in 1975 that expansion in the egg business "is being done mainly by the large complex-type operations or corporations made up of producers, hatcheries or processors."[19] The magazine reported "very little, if any expansion" of small (thirty-thousand-bird), individually owned egg farms.[20] In the ten years since this book first appeared, the biggest egg producers have gotten bigger and the smaller ones have all but disappeared. In 1979, there were 6,106 egg producers; by the end of 1988, 1,668 were left. Nearly *three-fourths* of America's egg farmers quit—or were squeezed out—over the past decade! That is over 4,400 egg farmers—all of them at the smaller end of the farm-size spectrum. Over 2,000 of these farms kept under 3,000 hens; 1,300 of them kept under 10,000 hens, and 640 of them kept under 20,000 hens. Most of these smaller egg farms were independent farmers—the last of the "mom and pop" egg farms that used to supply the nation's eggs. Over this ten-year period, every category of egg operation lost producers except the two largest, those with half a million to one million hens and those with over one million hens. The number of the very largest operators doubled, from eighteen "farmers" to thirty-seven.[21] The predictions of ten years ago have become reality: some thirty agribusiness corporations now produce the bulk of the country's eggs.

The broiler industry started the revolution in factory animal production and it has led the way ever since. What has happened there is a harbinger of things to come in the other animal industries. What did the agribusiness takeover of broiler production bring us?

Cheap Chicken Flesh. In constant dollars, adjusted for inflation, the retail price of chicken dropped from sixty cents a pound in 1956 to twenty-seven cents in 1981.[22] As a result people are now eating more chicken than any other meat. In 1946, the typical American ate four pounds of chicken a year; in 1987, sixty-three pounds a year.[23] There is no question that chicken meat is cheaper than ever. But have we considered all of the costs involved in keeping that retail price low? The rest of this list reflects some of these.

Frankenstein Chickens. The God of Growth was called upon to do something about the chicken so that agribusiness could make more flesh from less feed. A "genetic marvel," the agribusiness chicken now swells up to market weight on half the feed, in half the time it did fifty years ago. It is also a metabolic basket case. Some birds suddenly squawk and die from "flip-over syndrome," a sort of heart failure experts attribute to the abnormal growth rate. Bred for chunky bodies, many birds can barely walk on their flimsy, underdeveloped feet and legs. In the broiler sheds, they squat most of the time or breaststroke their way, lizardlike, across the litter floor.

Germy Chicken Flesh. The price of chicken has been kept down largely by sophisticated, labor-saving machinery in the processing plant. The chicken conveyor line circles through the plant at speeds of up to ninety birds a minute. It stuns, kills, scalds, defeathers, decapitates, bleeds, eviscerates, dismembers, and packages chickens with the help of poorly paid workers along the disassembly line. Relentless line speeds ensure token inspections and shortcuts in sanitation; birds are "rinsed" in what has been described by CBS television's "60 Minutes" as "fecal soup." USDA studies say four of ten chickens reach stores contaminated with Salmonella bacteria. Studies by "60 Minutes" and Canada's ministry of health say that 58 to 66 percent are contaminated.[24]

Disabled Workers. A comprehensive study of the broiler business by the Institute of Southern Studies found that reckless line speeds and repetitive work operations made poultry processing one of the most dangerous occupations in the country. The injury rate for poultry plant workers is higher than that for either construction or mine workers. In 1986, it was one of the five most dangerous jobs in the country. Workers suffer skin diseases, tendonitis, carpal tunnel syndrome, white finger, ammonia exposure, infections, stress, and back injuries. Work on the chicken disassembly line is dangerous, boring, and brutal, yet the wages are among the lowest in the food industry. You can't complain about poultry plant workers driving up the cost of chicken, though: wage costs contributed only 3.3 cents toward the 1980 retail price of 72 cents a pound.[25]

Farmer Peonage. Until about the early 1960s, most chickens were grown by independent farmers who sold to independent processors. Then the feed, grain, and agribusiness corporations began buying up feedmills and processing plants and luring farmers to raise chickens on contract. The farmer owns his/her land and buildings, but the broiler "integrators" own the birds and feed. The houses must be built and maintained according to company specifications, which keeps most farmers perpetually in debt. They have to please company inspectors if they want to keep the flocks coming in order to meet mortgage and maintenance costs. The average grower makes about two thousand dollars per broiler house per year, before taxes. For a grower tending the usual three houses, that provides an average wage of $2.88 per hour.[26] According to a North Carolina grower, "You are a serf on your own land."[27]

A Chicken Cartel. Virtually all broilers are grown by farmers dependent on contracts with the powerful broiler integrators. Cutthroat competition among them also helps keep chicken cheap. A generation ago, there were hundreds of integrators. A decade ago, some fifty companies did 90 percent of the business; today forty-eight companies do virtually all the business. The top three—Tyson Foods, ConAgra, and Perdue Farms—produce 38 percent of all broilers sold in the United States. In 1989, Tyson Foods became the country's largest broiler company when it won a takeover struggle against #2, ConAgra, to buy out then #3, Holly Farms. Tyson, like Perdue, uses a family-owned farm image to dominate markets. It built its two-billion-dollar-a-year market processing McNuggets for the McDonald's fast-food hamburger chain. Corporate head Don Tyson is said by *Forbes* magazine to be worth $330 million. Frank Perdue, whose company dominates eastern markets, is estimated by *Forbes* and *Fortune* to be worth between $200 million and $500 million. The two lobbied the House Ways and Means Committee during tax reform debates in 1987 to approve an amendment they had requested. The measure was to allow them to use accounting procedures to keep three years of unpaid taxes because their huge businesses qualified as family farms. The two "family farmers" got to keep $500 million between them, according to the Institute for Southern Studies.[28]

The trend to more costly production facilities, whether they be animal factories or field equipment, dictates that only the biggest, wealthiest operators with the most expansionist philosophies will control food production. Everyone else, presumably, will end up working for them if and when jobs are available. As poultry industry history indicates, there will be fewer and fewer jobs available as the trend advances because these interests prefer to eliminate labor wherever possible. In the twenty-five years before 1975 for example, broiler production increased fourfold while labor requirements were reduced by 65 percent.[29] Poultry industry experts dote on elimination of labor; in 1977, *Broiler Industry* boasted that "automation can halve plant labor in three years."[30]

The price of chicken, then, is artificially low, for it does not reflect the true costs of production. If we include costs that can be measured in dollars (for example, fair wages for growers and the medical expenses of injured workers and consumers who come down with salmonellosis) chicken would not be so cheap. Other costs—especially those to the chicken itself—are not easily measured in money. Thus, it looks like the agribusiness takeover of the chicken industry boils down to one rather large social and financial transaction: it destroyed the livelihoods of thousands of families, it made chicken flesh cheap, and it made a handful of families megamillionaires.

Pigs and Cows Are Next

Pigs have been called "mortgage lifters" by farmers since the nineteenth century for their reliability in bringing in cash for the farm household. Now independent farmers' last sources of cash flow from animal production are going the same way as the poultry industry. They already see the handwriting on the wall. As one Missouri pig farmer put it:

> We've lost the chickens, we've lost the turkeys and we've lost cattle feeding as far as the individual farmer is concerned. The only thing that is left is hogs. It's just a matter of time.[31]

Specialization has spread throughout the pig industry. As in the poultry industry, pig raising is being divided up as companies take over the various stages of production. "Farrowing corporations," like poultry hatcheries, supply young animals to growers, who feed them to market weight. Some line up client farmers, require them to build finishing facilities to their specifications, help them arrange financing, and provide weekly management advice. Land grant schools are doing their bit to pave the way for specialization and corporate intrusion into pig farming. They have already made pig farming complicated; now they offer courses and degrees in factory management to add to the supply of trained help needed by the largest factory pig operations.

Large agribusiness companies, especially the broiler corporations, are getting into the factory pig business. A Pennsylvania company, Pennfield, began back in 1971 as a feed company. It expanded rapidly into factory production of broilers and eggs and has since built a pig factory "as a test program to demonstrate that we can get the performance we need to move into hogs."[32] Tyson Foods, not content with its leveraged buyout of independent poultry farmers, is aggressively going after pig farmers. A story about it in *Agweek* says it all in the headline: "Big Boys Smell Profits in Pork; that's why giants like Tyson are pushing to boost the number of poultry-styled pork production outfits."[33] According to the report, Tyson has already contracted with the farmers of seventy thousand breeding sows to produce pigs for slaughter at its plants. Grain giant Cargill, also the nation's largest egg producer, is making the same moves. Evidently the corporate race to take over factory pork production is on. British Petroleum's newly acquired feed company, Purina Mills, is lining up farmers to raise hogs by contract. The author predicts that if the trend continues, "the role of the traditional family hog farmer may be greatly diminished—if not eliminated—by the year 2000."[34]

Farmers and hog experts fear that it may be too late to reverse the trend. The large integrators already have too much muscle in the marketplace, and they get financial advantages that smaller, independent producers cannot get. Among the strongest advantages are the cost-cutting deals they can make with feed companies and meat packers. For some time now, the big-volume animal factories have

"The high capital investment it takes to raise pigs today may force the producers out who aren't ready and able to take on the debt load required to raise hogs in confinement units."—Jerry Peckum, loan officer, Iowa Production Credit Association, quoted in "Have We Broken the Hog Cycle?" *Farm Journal*, October 1978, p. Hog-34.

been getting discounts on bulk feed purchases and receiving premium prices from packers for delivering large loads to slaughterhouses every week. And as one worried independent pig farmer points out, "The feed companies don't really have to make a profit on the hogs they feed. They are happy if they can sell their feed and break even on hogs."[35] These are among the ways the biggest corporate pig "farmers" make money coming and going. They draw bigger profits, reduce the overall price of pigs, and make pig raising unprofitable for independent farmers.[36]

It is this kind of size-based muscle that gives corporate hog operations their edge, not the "efficiency" they boast of in the media. Bill Haw, president and chief executive of National Farms, Inc., is typical of corporate factory producers' chauvinism about the "efficiency" of large-scale animal production. Haw sees parallels between the chicken industry and his firm's operations, which took in one hundred million dollars in 1987 from its super-hog factories and -cattle feedlots. "Efficient production almost always passes to the marketplace," he says.[37] The son of a doctor, Haw left banking to run National Farms. If a profile of him in *Missouri Alumnus* is accurate, he carries what may be charitably described as a low level of sympathy for ordinary farmers ruined by the mid-1980s farm crisis. Of their financial troubles, says Bill Haw, "Farming should be based on economics instead of emotions. . . . Most farmers do the same thing year after year, then cry to the government when they need help."[38]

Like many agribusinessmen, Haw is unable to see his own government benefits and top-loaded financial advantages because they are invisible—embedded in the thick fabric of agricultural policy through years of agribusiness domination. Crying to the government for help is not necessary when you ride high on the waves of less-obvious advantages and benefits.

Meanwhile, the trend to factories is making it hard on ordinary producers. A study of Missouri farmers revealed that while some producers were increasing production by building new factory facilities, almost half were cutting back or quitting, and many had no plans to expand. When asked about their reasons, they cited problems associated with the trend toward factory production; these included "diseases, breeding difficulties," and "high capital investments."[39] According to *Successful Farming*, "Basically the study emphasized a national trend: more hogs and fewer hog producers."[40]

Can agribusiness corporations take over pig production as they have poultry? It's been thought that these animals need too much care and attention to be trusted to hired help, but corporations, with university help, are trying to change that thinking. The factory systems are nearly perfected and the skilled help to run them is in training. Two agricultural experts have been following the trend toward factory specialization and expansion for the past several years. One of their studies concluded:

> We have the feeling that the technology, organization and managerial capacity is now available and in place to slowly but surely change drasti-

cally the structure of the hog business. It may well be true that someone can be found "to sit up with the corporate sow."[41]

America's remaining pig farmers are running scared. Farming magazines contain letters from farmers and various articles that reveal the panic about what corporate integration of pig production will do to the future of their farms. Pig farmers at a recent farm conference heard a speaker tell them: "If you're average, you're going to be out of business."[42] One farmer wrote to the editor of a farm magazine: "We are destined to be like the poultry industry, with no independent producers. . . ."[43] Another wrote: "Each corporation that produces 300,000 hogs a year puts 300 guys like me out of business."[44]

The fears are real. According to the National Pork Producers Council, the industry has lost 40 percent of its farmers in the last five years.[45]

The same fears are spreading to dairy and beef producers. Beef packers are buying up feedlots and contracting with feedlot operators to raise cattle for them. This trend is all the more scary because both the packing and the feedlot industries are getting more and more concentrated. Of over forty-two thousand feedlots in thirteen major cattle feeding states, the two hundred largest produce about half of all fed cattle.[46] Only three major packing companies, ConAgra, Excel, and IBP, now slaughter and sell 70 percent of all feedlot cattle.[47]

They seem to be following in the poultry industry's footsteps already. A couple of years ago there were four big packing companies. ConAgra bought controlling interest in one of the four, Swift, and then there were three. In short order, ConAgra bought up two of the biggest feedlot operators, Montfort of Colorado and E.A. Miller, Inc. One of the other Big Three is Excel, which is owned by Cargill, Inc. Cargill is one of the world's five largest grain companies and an agribusiness firm that we keep running into at every turn. Only a few years ago, the U.S. Supreme Court allowed Cargill to take over Spencer Beef, a large meat packer, against the complaints of Montfort of Colorado and other feedlot operators.[48]

These trends, and fears that BGH will accelerate them, have independent dairy farmers worried. In the past decade they have seen the megadairies crop up in Florida, California, and the Southwest. Traditional, independent farmers are aware that the big milk factories can more easily adopt expensive new technologies than they can. They fear that BGH will give the megadairies one more big edge. BGH has been the major theme in farm state newspapers and magazines over the past four years. Most of the articles and letters center around what is likely to happen to dairy farmers once the drug hits the market. Most analysts predict that the market will be flooded with even more surplus milk for several years, which will make small operations too unprofitable to maintain. The entire industry seems to be afraid that the idea of hormone-made milk will turn off consumers and ruin the market for milk and dairy products. In Vermont, Wisconsin, and Minnesota, dairy farmers have introduced legislation that would ban the use of BGH.

Under the layer cages.

BGH bans notwithstanding, the big factory dairies alone are an ominous sign that the independent dairy farm is going the way of egg, broiler, turkey, and pig farms. Farmers now are aware of the tax breaks, feed price breaks, premium prices for volume production, and other advantages of the megafactories. They know what they are up against, and what they will have to do to stay in farming. A young dairy farmer in Georgia told *Dairy Today,* "If we want to stay and survive here, we'll have to add cows and then probably work people in shifts like factories. It looks to me like that's the answer to surviving in dairying without diversifying."[49]

Like the now-extinct small egg and broiler farmers before them who relied on small-scale animal production for cash income, many of these small beef, dairy, and pig farmers will be lost to agriculture. As we keep emphasizing, when small, diversified farmers lose their cash flow from animal production, they lose their farms as well.

"Farmers" vs. Consumers and Farmers

The broiler, egg, dairy, and meat packing industries have all reached the level of capital concentration and monopolism that gives them the market muscle to influence prices through restraints on competition. Forty-two of the broiler industry's largest firms, under the canopy of their National Broiler Marketing Association, were accused of restraining competition in the 1970s in a suit brought by various supermarkets, distributors, wholesalers, hotels, fast-food outlets, and states that bought their chickens. All but three of the firms agreed to a settlement under which they paid out at least thirty-two million dollars in damages to the plaintiffs, but they admitted no guilt to charges that they conspired to fix, maintain, and stabilize broiler prices.[50] Scarcely a year after the settlement was reached, the NBMA members voted to dissolve the organization.

The largest egg-producing firms formed an organization a decade ago called EGGMAR to help centralize marketing, to "prevent price erosion," and to bring "more price stability" to egg marketing; as a producer "cooperative," it is legally exempt from the antitrust laws.[51]

But monopolism is legal if it's done right. Like the egg industry, the milk industry takes advantage of loopholes in the antitrust laws designed to protect "farmer" cooperatives. Associated Milk Producers, Inc. (AMPI), and Land O'Lakes, for example, are high on the Fortune 500 list of the nation's wealthiest corporations, but they are "farmer cooperatives." The giant cooperatives form even bigger federations that monopolize market areas. In 1971, AMPI controlled more than 70 percent of the market in fourteen midwestern market areas designated by the USDA.[52] In the 1970s three federations controlled 80 percent of the New England milk supply, and one federation controlled 70 percent of New York–New Jersey milk.[53] This situation inhibited competitive milk pricing and kept milk prices to consumers at about 20 cents a gallon higher than the competitive price would have been otherwise.

Laws favoring cooperatives are supposed to give farmers a voice and some muscle in dealing with distributors, but these laws are exploited to the hilt by agribusiness for profit at the public's expense. Co-ops are not so good to farmers, either. Their big-business tactics of merger, expansion, and vertical integration have created costly, centralized bureaucracies that reduce farmer control as well as farmers' net share of co-op income. Agricultural economist Truman Graff of the University of Wisconsin estimated that only about 51 cents out of every dollar spent on milk ends up in the pockets of co-op member dairy farmers; the rest goes to advertising, lobbying, salaries of executives and staff, and other operating expenses.[54] The big co-ops deny membership and marketing benefits to small, independent dairy farmers because they don't turn out a large enough volume of milk. Thus the big factory dairies have an enormous competitive edge over small producers—so much so that the latter are now nearly extinct.

The term "farmer cooperative" has a nice, democratic, American ring to it and the concept could be good both for working farmers and consumers. But, as with so many other labels, the reality behind it is somewhat different. In trying to compete with market-dominating corporate distributors and wholesalers, cooperatives have turned to professional management for expertise, and corporatism has rubbed off. Management interests now overshadow farmer interests. A strict

At last the special day has come.
She is so very proud
As she looks down at her very
    first egg
She clucks and clucks so loud.

It is usually only a few days after she is in the laying house that she lays her first egg. Chickens do actually 'cluck' or 'sing' after laying an egg . . . it really seems to make them happy. Incidently, there are no roosters (male birds) in these laying houses. The hen just lays eggs naturally. The rooster is required for a fertile or hatching egg.

The cow now goes with many others
To the pasture to drink water and eat grass.
Some may stop at the salt box
To take a lick of salt as they pass.

In the summer the cows are turned out to pasture to eat grass. The dairy farmer keeps a salt box in the pasture because cows need salt. Cows also need a lot of water. It is important in helping them to digest food and to make milk. Water also helps to keep the cow cool in the summer. She may drink as much as twenty gallons of water a day.

profit orientation prevails. Farmer-members, like stockholders in a corporation, play only a small role in cooperative decision making. Often the co-op management asks corporate executives to sit on the board, invites food firms and conglomerates into partnerships, and even solicits agribusiness corporation membership. Farmer-members have let co-ops slip from their control.[55]

The Hard Sell: Moving Factory Products

An array of animal industry organizations now tries to push up demand for animal products with slick magazine and television advertising and other promotional techniques. You may remember the beef industry's "Real Food for Real People" and the American Dairy Association's "Milk Is a Natural" television spots. These groups are funded by farmers from a cut of their checks when they sell eggs, milk, or animals. They are supposed to be producers' organizations, but, like farmers' cooperatives, they benefit and are led primarily by the largest operators. In 1976, for example, when beef industry leaders pushed for a "checkoff" scheme (percentage contributions taken from farmers' sales to provide promotional funds), they failed to get the necessary two-thirds vote because of opposition from small- and medium-sized cattle farmers. On the heels of that attempt, a new "Beeferendum" was drawn up and the vote required for approval was reduced to a simple majority.[56]

The beef industry's checkoff brings in seventy-three million dollars each year.[57] The money is spent according to the wishes of a "Beef Research and Information Board" made up from the ranks of key cattle producers. The whole scheme was set up by an act of Congress; the USDA appoints the board members and supervises the vote. USDA administers the program and our U.S. District Courts enforce the laws establishing it. This looks, sounds, and smells like something official and in the public interest. But it isn't. The lion's share of the money raised goes for "consumer education" (advertising of beef), the "information" component of the program.

The other animal products industries also use checkoffs to raise money for "research" and "information." With names like National Egg Board, National Council on Egg Nutrition, and National Dairy Council, these organizations bolster the persuasiveness of their campaigns by conveying to the public an image of an entity that is official, authoritative, and a servant of the public interest. The National Egg Board, with the American Egg Board, estimated it would take in $6.3 million in 1979 and over half of it would go for radio and television commercials and other advertising.[58] The dairy industry's United Dairy Industry Association, which includes co-ops and dairy promotional organizations, has some $28 million a year to spend on "research" and other promotion.[59]

The biggest agribusiness corporations, of course, spend additional millions advertising their own brands of beef, chicken, milk, and the other animal products. Here again, the consumer pays a premium for the heavily advertised brands, getting little more than a vague psychological satisfaction in being a consumer of the "best." For all of Frank Perdue's boasts in advertisements about his chickens, it appears from the Consumers Union survey mentioned in chapter 4 that his chickens are, after all, no different from any others. But advertisements for branded and trademarked animal products bring profitable results, according to the president of a large meat-packing firm:

> The evidence leads to the consumer message. That's the future . . . the obvious direction. Add value to the products, give them a trademark. . . . Oscar Mayer has led the way. . . . They get 20¢ more for bacon than anyone else.[60]

Animal industries are adopting other kinds of information control in a reaction to attacks against animal agriculture for its wastefulness and for the health risks associated with its products. *Confinement* magazine showed this defensiveness, claiming that "foods of animal origin are under continuing attack in this country by a broad army of uninformed physicians, misinformed media people and various health-food nuts."[61]

Animal industries appear to be worried that younger children may not have sufficiently robust appetites for meat, milk, and eggs should they wonder, as they are prone to, about where these products come from. To head off such anxieties, they are sending pleasing messages to children about animal production methods. The dairy, egg, and pork industries sponsor coloring books and other materials for children that show farm animals in anthropomorphic, comic book fantasies. There is no hint, of course, of feed additives, stress, crowding, or debeaking.

The Care and Feeding of Experts

Animal agribusiness controls not only demand and markets, but the course of agricultural technology as well. Here its job is not so difficult; all it must do is provide money for the right research. Research on capital-intensive factory methods and systems is naturally high on its list of proper research subjects, as we have seen.

Sometimes agribusiness doesn't have to donate money; its products do just as well. At the University of Illinois, for example, where scientists tried to perfect sheep factories:

> The high-profile aluminum floors were furnished by the Aluminum Company of America. The ¾-inch #9 Saf-T-Mesh was furnished by Wheeling Corrugating Company. The stainless steel plank was furnished by Behlen Manufacturing Company. The low-profile aluminum floor was furnished by Danforth Agri-Resources, Inc.[62]

Once the design is perfected, the firms can realistically expect that their products will go into the manufacture of these factory systems.

Agribusiness firms also use the personal approach to mark the proper subjects for research. Many scientists, like all professionals whose careers thrive on reputation and ego gratification, respond well to recognition and back-patting. Knowing this, agribusiness interests dole out scrolls, plaques, titles, and cash awards to scientists for their work. By watching who gets the awards, we can tell which lines of research are deemed worthy. For instance, the scientist who developed DES for use as a growth promotant in feed has won a string of awards, distinguished professorships, and honorary fellowships; he is credited with having "brought science to what had been an 'art'—feeding cattle."[63] Agricultural manufacturers and suppliers like Ralston-Purina, Merck, Pfizer, Shell Oil, and Upjohn, trade associations like the American Feed Industry Association, farm magazines, and industry promotional groups are among the award givers.

Agricultural support industries can rely on a few scientists and quasi-professional organizations to provide expert advocacy when the dangers from pesticides, antibiotics, and other products are exposed. Foremost among these is the infamous Council for Agricultural Science and Technology (CAST). CAST is, indeed, agroindustry's "truth squad"; according to a member scientist:

> The attacks on use of food additives and pesticides have been occurring for years. To counter the emotionalism toward agriculture and to be a spokesman for scientific truth . . . [CAST] was formed in 1973.
> It consists of 22 scientific societies, composed of 60,000 agriculturally oriented scientists, making it possible to amass scientific truth quickly and getting it to the right place to dispel developing problems.[64]

CAST's funds come not only from its member societies but also from agricultural trade associations and manufacturers of fertilizer, drugs, and pesticides—including American Cyanamid, CIBA–GEIGY, Dow Chemical, Eli Lilly, Mobil Chemical, Monsanto, Shell Chemical, and Stauffer Chemical. In its first seven years, CAST published more than seventy reports on agricultural matters; the majority downplayed the possible dangers involved in modern agricultural practices. CAST's proindustry bias was demonstrated in a dispute with six scientists it hired to study and report on the use of antibiotics in animal feeds. The scientists' report stated that the practice increased bacterial resistance to antibiotics. CAST reworded their statement in its summary to indicate that the use of antibiotics "might" have that effect. The six scientists quit the study panel in protest. One reportedly believed that the whole purpose of CAST's study project was to produce a document that would be used to counter the FDA's case for a ban on the use of antibiotics in animal feed.[65]

The real parties-in-interest, then, behind present capital-intensive factory farming are the companies that do business in all of the systems, supplies, and products it requires. For decades now, these special interests have influenced research, technology, and opinion—both public and expert—in their own interests rather than in the interests of all farmers or of the public as a whole.

Experimental sheep-confinement unit, Ohio State University, Wooster, Ohio.

Metabolism study at USDA's Meat Animal Research Center, Clay Center, Nebr. "There's no question that drugs and growth promotants are 'where the action is' so far as current research is concerned."—Carey Quarles, Colorado University animal scientist, quoted in "A Look at New Drugs and Future Trends," *Broiler Industry,* January 1977, p. 24.

8 FACTORY

ETHICS

The Moral Cost
of
Animal Factories

In 1968 the amount of humanly edible protein fed to American livestock and not returned for human consumption approached the whole world's protein deficit!
—Frances Moore Lappé, *Diet for a Small Planet*, rev. ed. (New York: Ballantine Books, 1975), p. 3

At higher egg prices, crowding always resulted in greater profits.
—Robert H. Brown, "Toe-Clipping May Help Hens, Improve Returns in Crowded Cages," *Feedstuffs*, May 27, 1985

I think there's tremendous potential to engineer bacteria that could be introduced into sheep so they could digest all sorts of things—sawdust, industrial byproducts, etc.
—Hudson Glimp, U.S. Department of Agriculture animal scientist, in "Farm Animals of the Future," *Agricultural Research*, May 1989, p. 10

Risks are connected with the increasing intensivation [sic] of our animal husbandry. Already years ago Riemann and Peters (1974) mentioned: "Continuously the animal is made more and more subordinate to technical development. It becomes a product that passes through certain phases of production. Enormous technical possibilities are thus created, but at the same time great danger for the animal arises."
This intensivation [sic] implies that the animals live in housing systems with a small area per animal and without any litter. In the present intensive animal husbandry it can be seen that the animals have problems in adapting. The appearance of apathy and abnormal behavioral patterns point at a disturbance of animal well-being. A quick treatment can be enough for the somatic part of health, but is no efficacious measure for problems concerning physical and social health. Behavioral studies make it possible to register the physical and social problems of the animals.
—R. G. Bure, "Measuring the Well-Being of Pigs in Different Housing Systems," *Livestock Environment II: Proceedings of the Second International Livestock Environment Symposium* (St. Joseph, MI: American Society of Agricultural Engineers, 1982), p. 428.

THANKS TO WESTERN DIETARY HABITS, decades of nutritional misinformation, and—more recently—aggressive advertising campaigns, the average American consumes over 840 pounds of animal products each year (see Fig. 8-1).[1] About three-fourths of this weight is comprised of egg and dairy products, so in this area there is little waste and little difference between retail weight and weight of the edible portion. By our calculations, this provides the average person with about 70 grams of protein each day.[2] Under the conservative guidelines set down by the World Health Organization (WHO), the average adult needs about 33 grams of protein each day. Thus, those who consume animal products are consuming over twice the protein needed for adequate nutrition. This from animal products alone—on top of the protein one gets in cereals, legumes, nuts, vegetables, and the other nonanimal foods consumed daily. In fact, most of us get all the protein we need each day from these nonanimal foods, so the protein from animal foods is really superfluous.

Because of the addiction to animal products, then, our average American adult runs two (actually three, if you count the nonanimal protein) times as much protein as needed through his or her body each day.

This overindulgence in animal products is wasteful in many ways, and it is now well-known to be harmful to human and ecological health, too. Of course, the animal industries' primary interest is ever-growing sales and profits, so they can hardly accept this rapidly building knowledge. Their only response is to push us doggedly to consume even more. They—the animal protein pushers—are the original Diet Dictators, and they have, at times, been rather more militant than their contemporary critics.

Why Are Americans Addicted to Animal Products?

In the nineteenth century, the westward expansion of the United States opened up vast new lands that attracted millions of people from hungry, land-scarce Europe. Huge herds of cattle grew fat cheaply, grazing on grassy plains. Cowboys and cattle drives brought meat-on-the-hoof to railheads in Kansas, Missouri, and Nebraska to feed the demand for meat in America's growing cities. At the same time, American society was still largely rural. Land and forage were cheap and a few farm animals provided a reliable and plentiful source of food and some cash income for the farm household; it was not difficult to develop and satisfy an appetite for meat. Waves of immigrants took readily to the new country's meat-based diet, a diet that had been beyond their means in the Old Country. By the turn of the century, Americans were eating about sixty-five pounds of beef, sixty-five pounds of pork, and sixteen pounds of poultry per person each year.[3]

Soon thereafter, grasslands, woodlands, and pastures fell victim to the need to turn out the numbers of cattle, hogs, and poultry required to feed the growing American population. Prairies were plowed under and forests cleared to grow grain and fodder to feed expanding populations of these animals. As more and more land was converted to raising animals, environmental conflicts arose. The diverse biocommunities of prairies and woodlands lost their habitats to monocultures of corn, wheat, alfalfa, soybeans, or other crops; some species became extinct, others intruded into new areas where they caused dislocations, and still others remained to plague farmers with predations on their crops and livestock. The last would face diminishing chances of success against state and local forces that rallied against them. States established bounties on predatory animals and local communities organized hunts and trapping campaigns to clear the land of crows, rabbits, groundhogs, hawks, and other "varmints."

Science + Business = The American Way

Early in the twentieth century, the science of nutrition began when vitamins and other nutritional elements were identified and their role in health discovered. In the 1920s, the meat-packing industry, with USDA cooperation, began its meat promotional campaign in the public schools, touting their product as practically synonymous with protein, sound nutrition, and good health. The government's involvement in pushing animal products stemmed from an agricultural policy that promoted animal production as a means of increasing farm cash income.[4]

Then, in the 1930s, a tragic form of malnutrition was observed in African children. It was called by its African name, kwashiorkor, and it was discovered that protein deficiency was a major cause. Soon, wherever malnutrition was spotted, nutritionists painted it with the brush of protein deficiency. Actually, much of the malnutrition was simply marasmus, or a plain lack of food and calories. USDA put out charts and other materials that advised consumers to choose from among twelve food groups. Three of these were animal products: dairy products, eggs, and "meat, poultry, and fish." Under intense pressure from livestock interests, these became the "Basic Seven" food groups during World War II. Under continuing pressure from meat and dairy interests, the seven food groups were reduced to the "Four Food Groups" in 1956. Meat and dairy products constitute two of the four, with the implication that these foods should make up half of our diets.[5]

I believe it's completely feasible to specifically design an animal for hamburger.
—Bob Rust, Iowa State University meat specialist quoted in Gary Vincent, "Hamburger Cattle," *Successful Farming,* October 1977, p. B-15

The emphasis on animal protein in diet should have been a passing fad once nutritionists learned better, but the industrial interests concerned saw to it that it stuck. Until very recently, most nutritionists would not stray from dogma on the necessity of animal protein. Their doctrinaire approach, fanned by industry promotional propaganda, led to a steady rise in consumption of animal products as people became more affluent after World War II. Not to eat meat began to appear downright un-American. In 1946, a book entitled *Meat Three Times a Day* proclaimed:

> To argue [that people should substitute grains for animal protein] is to misunderstand the spirit of Americans and what lies back of our country's greatness and productivity. Instead of talking about how low our meat consumption can be cut . . . we should be working at increasing it to a pound a day or even more.[6]

This exaggerated role of animal protein in diet has had tragic consequences. Many poor people have inadequate diets because they are led to spend a disproportionate amount on expensive animal protein. It is estimated that about a million Americans rely on pet food for a significant part of their diet, instead of buying cheaper, more wholesome beans, grains, nuts, and other foods.[7] For their part, the more affluent have had their lives shortened by a diet too high in protein and animal fats and too low in roughage.

Heresy and Subversion

The assault on the meat-equals-health citadel began in about 1970 with the publication of Frances Moore Lappé's brilliant book *Diet for a Small Planet*. Her book exposed "the incredible level of protein waste built into the American meat-centered diet."[8] She raised the ethical issue posed by one country's addiction to the luxury of animal protein while much of the rest of the world starves. Lappé explained how American demand for meat causes half our cropland and upward of 90 percent of our corn, oats, barley, sorghum, and soybeans to go to the fattening of our meat animals and how those animals return only one seventh of these grains back to us in edible meat, thus wasting the other six-sevenths of this grain (118 million tons back in 1971).[9] In addition, the rich Western countries' demand for meat results in plant proteins becoming too dear for people in the poorest, hungriest countries. Lappé urged those concerned to change to meatless diets, to eat lower on the food chain, and to take other steps in the direction of a rational use of our world's agricultural resources.

Lappé's book and subsequent revisions have sold over a million copies and have raised a controversy that still lives. Just as Rachel Carson's *Silent Spring* lifted awareness of environmental pollution, *Diet for a Small Planet* opened eyes to the relationships among Western diets, world hunger, and environmental despoliation. In the wake of the book, newspapers and magazines ran features about the controversy and the new dietary awareness. The meat industry got into a dither over all of this "antimeat propaganda" as many people moved toward vegetarian diets and eating less meat. In this changing climate of dietary consciousness, a jump in meat prices in 1973 led to consumer boycotts, and per capita meat consumption fell back to 1967 levels.

DAILY FOOD GUIDE
some choices for thrifty families

MILK GROUP
some for everyone

MEAT GROUP   2 or more servings

VEGETABLE - FRUIT GROUP
4 or more servings

Dark
Green

Deep
Yellow

Citrus
and Tomatoes

others

BREAD - CEREAL GROUP
4 or more servings

everyday eat foods from each group
EAT OTHER FOODS AS NEEDED TO ROUND OUT MEALS

The four basic food groups according to USDA. The chart implies that meat, milk, and eggs should make up half our diet.

Meat industry leaders may have considered Lappé's book harmless heresy, but the drop in consumption was not good for business. They saw to it that the downturn in meat consumption did not last long. The propaganda organs began rolling to nip America's sudden new guilt over meat eating in the bud. If we cut back on meat eating, they argued, farmers would cut back on grain production and there would be less food for everybody. This was more threat than reasoning; it assumes that cropland and grain freed by reducing animal consumption would never be diverted into human food production. Meat advocates claimed that animals produce food for humans from forage inedible by humans, so that land too poor to support human food crops can produce food in the form of meat. Regardless of that fact, however, about 70 percent of all beef cattle are fed humanly edible grain and other concentrates in the finishing stage. Moreover, this argument ignores the wasteful practice to grain-feeding poultry and pigs. Because these animals are unable to digest forage, roughage, or plants from poor cropland, they compete directly with humans for food. Counterattack propaganda to the contrary, livestock still consume about three-quarters of our grain crop and take up cropland that could either support other plant and animal life or provide people with a sensible, healthy, and more varied diet.

Meat Revival Evangelism

In 1975, a record corn crop lowered grain prices and cattle started going back into the feedlots. Meat eaters, tired of the affronts to their moral integrity, began to fight back and to call for a return to the old-time steak religion. The politics of protein took a sharp swing to the right and the meatless diet came to be considered a subversive activity. Soon, meat consumption per capita and meat industry gross profits climbed to all-time highs.

Then, the meat barons suffered another round of assaults on their citadel, this time by health experts. The 1970s brought forth mounting evidence that linked excessive consumption of animal products with heart disease, stroke, cancer, diabetes, gout, osteoporosis, and a host of infectious diseases. Much of this evidence was presented before the Senate Select Committee on Nutrition and Human Needs in hearings during 1976. In January 1977, the committee announced its "Dietary Goals for the United States," containing recommendations that Americans decrease consumption of meat, heavy fats, whole milk, butterfat, and eggs. Before the ink dried, the Meat Board and the National Cattlemen's Association were stirring up pressure to have the report withdrawn on the grounds that there was "insufficient scientific evidence" to support the recommendations. They managed to force the committee back to the hearing rooms in March 1977 to take down "supplemental evidence" on the dietary question. Later that year, the second edition of "Dietary Goals" appeared—minus the "eat less meat" language but otherwise substantially the same report as before. Then, in September 1979, the surgeon general of the United States issued a report entitled *Healthy People,* which recommended that people eat less meat and make other dietary changes along the lines of the original "Dietary Goals." On its heels came another report, from the American Society for Clinical Nutrition, echoing the conclusions of both of these reports (one of the panelists recommended that meat be used only as a condiment).

The 37 million elementary and 15 million high school students in the United States constitute a special [National Livestock and] Meat Board audience.
—*Meat Board Report, 1974–1975* (Chicago: National Livestock and Meat Board, 1975), p. 23

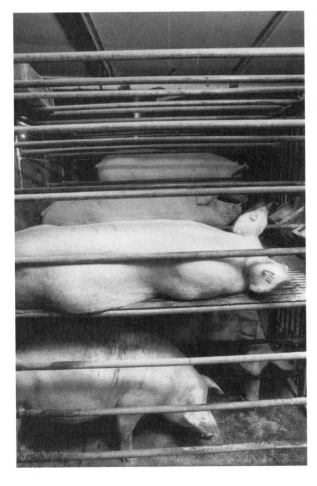

"They can still eat—total darkness has no effect on their appetites."—Harry Sterkel, Jr., "Cut Light and Clamp Down on Tail Biting," *Farm Journal,* March 1976, p. Hog-6.

The flood of published dietary studies and reports continued right into the 1980s, and the scientific consensus built that saturated fat, cholesterol, and too much protein are significant contributors to cardiovascular disease, cancer, and the other major killer diseases in the Unites States. Of course, these dietary recommendations were carefully worded: No one at that time could say that meat, milk, and eggs were the major sources of saturated fat, cholesterol, and excess protein in our diets. Anyone who directly blamed animal products became a target for the wrath of the animal industries and their scientific truth squads.

Fortunately for the American diet, however, a few well-qualified experts on human health wrote popular books in the 1980s incorporating the information from previously published scientific reports and studies. They were able to cut through all the scientific and political bureaucratese to state that there is no real need for animal products in the human diet and the less of them you eat, the better your health is likely to be. Nathan Pritikin's popular books helped get the point across, as did Harvey and Marilyn Diamond's best-selling book, *Fit for Life*. In 1983, *The McDougall Plan,* by John A. McDougall, M.D., and Mary A. McDougall, L.P.N., reviewed the mountain of scientific evidence and explained how the most health-supporting diet is one without animal products. In 1987, John Robbins—scion of the Baskin-Robbins ice cream empire who declined the offer to carry on the family business—published his visionary book, *Diet for a New America*. In a single volume, Robbins explained how a diet rid of animal products helps heal the human body and soul as well as our seriously wounded planet.

For those who may question the validity and objectivity of these popular books, we suggest that they peruse the National Research Council's latest opus, *Diet and Health: Implications for Reducing Chronic Disease Risk,* published by the National Academy of Sciences. This institution is known for its cautious and conservative investigative reporting. Although the language is guarded to avoid attacks by the animal products, sugar, alcohol, and tobacco industries, the 1989 report only bolsters the validity and credibility of Pritikin, the Diamonds, the McDougalls, and Robbins. Here is a summary of *Diet and Health's* conclusions:

- A high-fat intake is associated with increased risk of certain cancers, especially cancers of the colon, prostate, and breast.
- Saturated fatty acid intake is the major dietary determinant of the serum total cholesterol and low-density lipoprotein (LDL) cholesterol levels and thereby creates risk of coronary heart disease.
- Dietary cholesterol raises serum total cholesterol and LDL cholesterol levels and increases the risk of atherosclerosis and coronary heart disease.
- In intercountry correlation studies, diets high in meat have a strong positive association with increased atherosclerotic coronary artery disease and certain cancers, notably breast and colon cancer. Such diets are often characterized by a high content of saturated fatty acids and cholesterol.[10]

Through the careful language and cautious conclusions we understand at once that meat, milk, and eggs are some of the main contributors to the two diseases that kill more people each year than any others coronary heart disease and cancer. By way of contrast, let's see what *Diet and Health* concluded about the role of nonanimal foods in diet:

- Diets high in plant foods—fruits, vegetables, legumes, and whole-grain cereals—are associated with a lower occurrence of coronary heart disease and cancers of the lung, colon, esophagus, and stomach.
- Such diets are low in saturated fatty acids, cholesterol, and total fat, but are rich in complex carbohydrates (starches and fiber) and certain vitamins, minerals, trace elements, and nonnutritive constitutents, and these factors probably also confer protection against certain cancers and coronary heart disease.
- Compared to nonvegetarians, complete vegetarians and lacto-ovovegetarians (those who eat milk and eggs) have lower serum levels of total and LDL cholesterol and triglycerides.
- High-carbohydrate diets, which are high in plant foods, have a comparatively lower prevalence of non-insulin-dependent diabetes mellitus.
- Epidemiologic and clinical studies indicate that a diet characterized by high-fiber foods may be associated with a lower risk of coronary heart disease, colon cancer, diabetes mellitus, diverticulosis, hypertension, and gallstone formation.[11] [Authors' note: Animal products contain no fiber.]

Thanks to the National Research Council and the hundreds of studies that have come out over the past couple of decades, we can say rather confidently that, contrary to popular beliefs fostered by the animal industries, animal products do more harm than good in the human diet.

The animal industries may hope the worst is over, but they are not taking any chances. The great war over a sensible diet is on. As part of their strategy, animal industries generate myths about protein and stimulate appetites for more and more meat; at the same time, they gesture to "rising expectations" and the "need to supply superior animal protein" to the rest of the world.

It would be naive to expect long-range objectivity about diet, nutrition, and world resources where short-run profits are so easily made. The truth is that the carefully fostered American meat addiction creates market conditions that ensure the wasting of grain on livestock. Farmers often simply make more money on corn in the form of flesh. According to *Beef* magazine:

> The corn you feed your hogs during January, February and March will be bringing you about $3.90 a bushel! That's almost double what you'd get for it if you were to sell it as cash corn rather than as pork.[12]

Meanwhile, the misapplication of technology and the misappropriation of resources go on. Because of exorbitant animal production, each Westerner uses up to six times more grain per day than a citizen of the hungry world. While an estimated one billion people are chronically hungry, American animal agribusiness squanders energy and cropland and pours whey, dry milk, fish meal, oil seeds, and other materials potentially nutritious to humans into livestock feeds to produce hefty animals quickly.

It is true, as the livestock industries are quick to point out, that under present economic conditions there is no guarantee that if grain and resources were diverted from our livestock, they would be distributed to the world's hungry. Changes more far-reaching than personal dietary preferences in affluent countries must be effected if world food supplies are to be shared more fairly. Still there is a danger that our wasteful habits will spread to other countries.

American animal agribusiness is working feverishly to spread them. Industry promotional organizations are working with the USDA to expand exports of meat and animal products. Farming magazines like *Farm Journal* praise the efforts of developing countries in "climbing the protein ladder":

> In fact, enlarging and diversifying their meat supply appears to be a first step for *every* developing country. They all start by putting in modern broiler and egg production facilities—the fastest and cheapest way to produce nonplant protein. Then, as rapidly as their economics permit, they climb "the protein ladder" to pork, to milk and dairy products, to grass-fed beef, and finally, if they can, to grain-finished beef.[13]

The Soviet Union, Egypt, China, and many other countries are expanding their animal populations, increasing the grain drain, and placing an even greater burden on the environment. American agribusiness support companies are only too happy to send their consultants and salespeople to these countries to help them set up American-style animal factories. One has to wonder, and worry about, where all of the grain and resources to keep these factories running will come from. American agribusiness knows. It's all part of the plan to build markets for the grain, drugs, hardware, and animal "seedstock" provided by the same companies and folks who brought *us* factory farming.[14]

Can we afford to let them get away with it? With the world population now at five billion and expected to double early in the next century, can we afford to waste cropland and destroy food by running it through animal factories, whether here or elsewhere? Will we realize too late that the entire world cannot "climb the protein ladder" to America's wasteful dietary standards? Why should we pass on to the rest of the world a diet that is known to produce obesity, coronary heart disease, atherosclerosis, cancer, and other deadly and costly diseases? Japan provides the best example of what happens to the health of a country when it turns from its traditional diet to the American diet rich in meat and animal products. Meat industry dollars and taxpayers' dollars are paying for programs to encourage the Japanese to buy more U.S. meat, milk, and eggs. Japan is already buying half of our meat exports each year. Two years ago the British medical journal *Lancet* reported that Japanese deaths from heart disease, diabetes, and other American diet-related maladies have risen dramatically in the past twenty-five years.[15] The tragic myths of the "superiority" of animal protein and the "efficiency" of its production in animal factories must be destroyed before it is too late.

Down (and Out) on the Farm

Among the less visible, less tangible costs to society from overreliance on factory farm technology is the disruptive impact this mode of farming has on rural communities. As we saw in chapter 7, the poultry industry's "progress" shows how the animal factory revolution destroyed independent family farmers. As late as 1959, nearly 60 percent of all broilers were grown by independent farmers and sold to processors on the open market.[16] Now virtually all broilers are produced by "contract growers," most of them former independent farmers who agree to provide space and labor to grow company birds on company feed, following company specifications. Farmers who can get the loans to put in the required buildings and equipment find that they don't make much money for the huge debt load and long hours of labor that are the consequences of their new company affiliation. And many independent farmers are squeezed out of business by their inability to get the necessary capital. Once farmers become "poultry peons" tied to big companies, they must keep the chickens flowing—even when losing money—just to meet payments on their mortgaged farms and homes.[17]

Now we know that pig farmers and the communities they live in are headed for the same fate. One study of the pig industry concluded that if big companies gained control of the whole business, from selling feeds to marketing the meat, "producers would lose 5 to 10% in net incomes, rural communities up 12% in level of economic activity. And consumers would pay up to 12% more for pork."[18]

The decline of small farms has caused drastic dislocations of society, from the rural areas directly affected all the way to the urban core. Rural communities lose people and vitality, while urban areas see increased crowding, welfare burdens, and unemployment as the expropriated farmers seek new livelihoods. At the beginning of World War II, there were 6 million farms and an independent farm labor force of nearly 11 million in the United States; today, there are 2.2 million farms and an increasing force of hired farm workers.[19] Much of this shift in population was caused by political and economic policies that made life difficult for small, family-run farms, particularly the policy of mechanization in agricultural production. In what has been commonly described as "economic cannibalism from within agriculture," family farms were replaced by corporate farms that could afford the machines and new production methods. Small, labor-intensive farms, with the families who lived on them and the diverse crops and animals they raised, were phased out. "Their practices and levels of production did not satisfy the policymakers' plans so they had to be replaced by agribusiness.

The land and animals could be forced to produce much more, and human labor could be more productive in the service of a corporation's goals. Family farms were seen as a drain on the economy and their occupants were pushed out to bloat the cheap labor pools around the urban areas of the industrial North.

Despite all the pressures toward size and specialization, a few people still realize the value of their small-scale, family-run, diversified farms, and keep them productive and profitable without the massive inputs of capital and energy used on agribusiness farms. But agriculture experts perceive these farms as aberrations from the norm. When an article appeared in *Farm Journal* extolling the virtues of the "natural tide of history" (the trend toward large, energy-intensive farms), several readers protested.[20] The big farms, they complained, are able to get the good land that could make the difference between success and failure for smaller farmers. One reader wrote: "I hope that sometime, such leaders of agriculture as *Farm Journal* will wake up to a consideration of the social and ethical factors involved."[21]

Although the factory revolution may have kept meat, milk, and egg prices down (as we shall see in the next chapter, they are not substantially cheaper than animal foods produced in safer, more humane systems), these relatively lower retail prices do not reflect the entire cost of factory production. What if animal agribusiness were required to compensate the farm families ruined financially by the factory revolution? What if it had to pay for the suicides and stress-related illnesses now epidemic among farmers who are trying to keep their farms? What if agribusiness had to foot the bill for the economic blight and social dislocation its revolution has brought to America's rural communities?

Animals Are Not Machines

There is a final ethical cost to the animal factories. We assume that animals were put here for us to use as we please. But no good reason can be given for regarding animals as things. They are not things. They can feel pain. They can suffer frustration and boredom. They have lives of their own to lead. Much of the "progress" in factory farming methods raises an unsettling ethical question: Do we have the right to make animals live miserable lives just to satisfy our taste for a diet so rich in animal products that it is bad for our own health? In a very literal sense, we are killing ourselves through the consumption of animals raised factory-style.

Think for a moment about the whole picture surrounding our dependence on foods from drug-dependent factory animals: At the center of the picture, of course, is the damage to our own health, including the potential for coronary heart disease, cancer, atherosclerosis, diabetes, and the other diseases discussed above. Then, as we saw chapter 4, there are the additional dangers to our health caused by some of the drugs, hormones, and other chemicals that make up the animal factory's medicine chest.

An issue not as readily addressed, however, is the enormous toll in lives of animals. Consider first the 5.5 billion slaughtered each year—every death demonstrably unnecessary, virtually every death met in terror and pain.

"We consider that calves should have sufficient room to be able at all ages to turn around, to groom themselves, and to move without discomfort."—*Report of the Technical Committee to Enquire into the Welfare of Animals Kept Under Intensive Livestock-Husbandry Systems,* Command Paper 2836 (London: Her Majesty's Stationery Office, 1965), paras. 147–9.

But the animals slaughtered are not the only victims. Consider the experimental animals used by agricultural scientists in their efforts to build an efficient animal food machine. Consider the experimental animals used in laboratories where pharmaceutical scientists try to develop new drugs to control factory animal diseases. Or consider the experimental animals used in the laboratories of agribusiness companies and government agencies where drugs, pesticides, and other agricultural chemicals are "tested," tests through which we are assured potentially lethal products are safe for use in the food supply. Then consider the other millions of laboratory animals used by biomedical researchers each year to try to find cures for the chronic killer diseases caused in part by our animal-based diets.

Although it can be mistaken for a play on words, it is accurate to say that we are killing masses of animals to in turn kill ourselves. Yet every round of killing, at the slaughterhouses and in the laboratories, is said to be necessary—necessary for human health and betterment. One winces at the use of the word "necessary" and strains uncomfortably in search of its meaning.

In view of all this killing and its cumulative effect on human health, can we say that our civilization is humane? Can we say that we care for the earth, for its cycles and processes, and for all of the beings who keep it a living planet?

More than a few farmers, veterinarians, and others close to what is happening

"Ten years of confinement raises more questions than answers."—Dale McKee, Rio, Ill., pig farmer, quoted in *Hog Farm Management,* March 1979, p. 124.

in animal agriculture have a dim view of the factory revolution. In a letter to *Farmer and Stockbreeder,* an English farm magazine, a Coventry veterinarian wrote this response to a report on then-new cage systems for pigs:

> May I dissociate myself completely from any implication that this is a tolerable form of husbandry? I hope many of my colleagues will join me in saying that we are already tolerating systems of husbandry which, to say the least of it, are downright cruel. . . . Cost effectiveness and conversion ratios are all very well in a robot state; but if this is the future, then the sooner I give up both farming and farm veterinary work the better.[22]

Fortunately, these views are shared by some professionals in the United States. Shortly after the first issue of *Confinement*—the now-defunct omnibus factory farming magazine—came out, a retired farm veterinarian sent in a thoughtful letter. In part it read:

More and more, I find myself developing an aversion to the snowballing trend toward total confinement of livestock. . . . If we regard this unnatural environment as acceptable, what does it portend for mankind itself? . . . How can a truly human being impose conditions on lower animals that he would not be willing to impose on himself? . . . Freedom of movement and expression should not be the exclusive domain of man. . . .

What [then] of human behavior in [the future]? Will it sink to the nadir of contempt for all that is naturally bright and beautiful? Will all of us become tailbiters without recognizing what we have become?[23]

A greater wave of objection to animal factories began in the 1980s when the animal rights movement exploded. All of a sudden, animal agribusiness had a noisy new critic with a disturbing message for the public. The major media ran stories about how veal calves were made sickly and anemic to produce fancy "milk-fed" veal. The egg industry, already nearly floored by the cumulative scientific evidence about cholesterol's role in coronary heart disease, now took some punching about caged, debeaked layer hens. Animal agribusiness had enjoyed decades of public ignorance of its factory methods, but animal rights advocates diligently brought out all of the unpleasant details. The public's interest in factory husbandry methods was sparked by two things: shocking living conditions for animals and the factory animal's extensive dependence on drugs and chemicals. Worse yet for agribusiness, the media understood that the two were inextricably linked.

Animal agribusiness went through all of the classic defense mechanisms in an effort to deal with the animal rights onslaught, from avoidance, to denial, to rebuttal, to propaganda. Aware of the sweeping legislative reforms of animal husbandry systems in Europe (where the uprising against animal factories arose ten to fifteen years earlier than in the United States), American agribusinessmen are busy "educating" the consumer public through propaganda about the facts of life on the modern farm and preparing themselves for the legislative struggles to come. The first sector of agribusiness industry to prepare for the fight was the one with the most to lose: the feed industry. The American Feed Industry Association (AFIA), which, as the name implies, is a trade organization of feed and additive manufacturers, sent one of its officers out on the circuit to stir up alarm in producer organizations, veterinarians, ag schools, and others involved in animal production. He warned of "a growing insurgency" and that the animal rights movement is "not out to change what you do but to stop what you do."[24]

In addition to sending out its circuit-riding Paul Revere, AFIA worked with the American Farm Bureau (which is actually a farm insurance company) and other agribusiness concerns to create and coordinate a couple of organizations whose purpose is to hammer out the agribusiness and factory farm position whenever animal welfare, rights, animal drugs, or related issues are raised. One is called the Animal Industry Foundation (AIF), which is headquartered in AFIA's Arlington, Virginia, offices. AIF puts out a booklet entitled *Animal*

Agriculture: Myths and Facts. All of the booklet is in very large type, of the sort used in books for young children. In very, very fine print at the bottom of the last page, the booklet concludes:

> This book is published by the Animal Industry Foundation. The Foundation is a non-profit educational association dedicated to educating the American public on current agricultural practices. The Foundation intends that this book be used for educational purposes only.[25]

Inside, the booklet tells us that factory stalls and crates "are designed for the welfare of the animal" and refers to the restriction as "protective restraint."[26] And, oddly, we find agribusiness using the words "natural" and "unnatural"— terms that it denounces in other discourse: The AIF booklet tells us that "castration may be necessary to avoid fighting and unnatural behaviors in young animals" and that pigs' tails are cut off "to end a natural tendency toward tail biting."[27]

The other animal industry propaganda organization is called the Farm Animal Welfare Council (FAWC), a cleverly chosen name that dishonestly implies an official, perhaps governmental, concern with the welfare of farm animals. FAWC also operates out of AFIA's offices in Arlington, Virginia, and those of the American Farm Bureau Federation in Park Ridge, Illinois.

Recognition of the importance of propaganda and doublespeak has spread throughout animal agribusiness. The United Egg Producers (UEP) has developed bird welfare guidelines "for dealing with animal welfare advocates and environmentalists."[28] According to UEP, most factory egg farms can be called "family farms"—a description that inspires guilt in, and thus helps to deflect criticism from, urban-dwelling activists. The guidelines amount to no more than a summary of current egg factory systems and management practices. Most manipulative is the guidelines' discussion of what the egg industry called "forced molting" before animal rights came along. Now it is called an "induced molt" and although, as we saw in chapter 3, it can shock, stress, and kill hens by depriving them of food and water, it is made to sound peaceful and relaxing for the birds:

> Since laying hens will enter into a natural molt period after 8–10 months of producing eggs, it is considered sound management to induce this molt so that all the birds are molting at the same time. To accomplish this molt, it may be necessary to put the birds on a diet program in which feed consumption may be regulated for a period of time, allowing the birds a period of rest.[29]

Under the UEP guidelines, debeaking is now called "beak trimming," and it is said to be done to remove the "sharp tips" of birds' beaks to prevent them from hurting each other.

Lessons in doublespeak and euphemisms are being packaged and sent around now that factory practices are visible. Producers are told to avoid words like "crate" or "cage" when talking to the public. Factory farmer advocates write to farm magazines to spread the word about the latest euphemism, like "maternity bed" or "nest." One magazine columnist advised that "we must try to avoid hostile, emotive words and phrases like crate, teeth-clipping, tail docking, slatted floors, cages, etc., because the public, our customer, is put off by them."[30]

The hysteria about animal rights/welfare is not suffered by all in the animal industries, however. A *Farm Journal* survey showed that pig farmers' biggest fears are of competition from big corporate pig factories. Some 37 percent feared that they would be put out of business by big factories and poultry-type integrated operations; only 2 percent felt threatened by either animal rightists or consumer trends.[31] Other surveys and coverage of the animal rights controversy indicate that the greatest paranoia about "welfarists" occurs in animal scientists, drug and feed manufacturers, and others at the highest echelons of agribusiness. Farmers themselves appear to be more worried about the real threats, especially the creeping displacement of independent farming by a handful of vertically integrated agribusiness firms. In another article on the trend, *Farm Journal*'s *Hogs Today* talked to a Kentucky pig farmer who was pushed out of poultry farming in the 1960s and now feels that his days are numbered as a pig farmer. We thought his strategy for survival was interesting; he told the magazine:

> If I were a small hog producer I'd join every animal rights group I could find, and support them with my money. I'd help outlaw crates and slotted-floor confinement buildings, forcing hog production back outdoors or onto straw.[32]

His views are shared by a longtime agricultural journalist and former editor of *Farm Journal,* Gene Logsden. In a guest editorial for the magazine, Logsden argued that the animal rights movement is good for animal farming and that all the arm waving and paranoia are misplaced. Wrote Logsden: "Which is more a threat to your independent business as a family livestock farmer: animal rights or animal megafactories? Think about it."[33] Logsden understands that "if the animal rightists have their way, the livestock industry will return to the smaller, family-sized farms." He concludes:

> Obviously, at some point the grave problems of overconcentration in the form of disease, pollution, transportation and loss of independent farmers turns animal mega-manufacturing into animal maniac-manufacturing. Far from harming animal husbandry, the animal rightists might prevent it from committing suicide.[34]

Even some agribusinessmen are beginning to get the animal rights message. Early in 1989, one of the editors of *Meat Processing* urged the industry to cut its losses and dump the crating of calves: "Instead of fighting over whether it's bad, or how bad it really is, the entire industry—from grower to end user—should unite in a public repudiation of the entire concept of confinement."[35] His editorial called the present veal confinement system "unnecessary and out-moded."

No less emotional and controversial are the battles over the use of BGH and the patenting of animals "invented" by the new biotechnologies. In both cases, many farm advocates believe the developments will only speed the trend toward the takeover of animal farming by agribusiness and pharmaceutical companies. They will also speed the trend toward reducing animals to food machines, and inefficient ones at that. The argument will be that they can make animals more efficient, but as we saw in previous chapters—especially chapter 5—animals are inherently inefficent converters of plant protein and energy. So why try to push them so? When these biological limitations are well-known, it seems to us unethical to devote research and technology toward a goal of unlimited animal productivity. It also seems rather ridiculous when we consider the impacts of animal production on the environment and human health.

Not the least of ethical considerations are the impacts of productivity-obsessive research and technological development on farm animals. Our agribusiness broiler chickens and turkeys are crippled, blow-up flesh bubbles. Our modern factory dairy cow is a walking metabolic disorder, a giant milk organ on four legs, with all of the physical diseases and discomforts that go with disorder. BGH, patenting, biotechnology, and other new high-tech devices now promise to push these animals and others up another notch or two, for even more efficiency and productivity. Even if the same technologies succeed in eliminating animal stress and actual suffering—and we very much doubt that they will—the efforts are deeply misguided. If what is wanted is safe, healthy, efficiently produced food, it is neither necessary nor sensible to manipulate animals to reach that end.

The animal factory revolution began because animal production was becoming more and more expensive; it was a last-gasp effort to hold onto our increasingly costly addiction to animal protein. It was a blind struggle against biological and economic realities, and it has run its course. Naturally we want efficiency and productivity in agriculture and in our food delivery system. But when sows are routinely dosed with hormones and surgically scraped to extract greater productivity and efficiency in protein production, doesn't one wonder whether this end might not better be achieved in another way? When calves are forced into an anemic, neurotic condition just to satisfy the gourmet's desire for pale flesh, increased productivity is not even the goal. Productivity for, and catering to, the whims of the market may be all right in the plastics or automobile industries, but it can be cruel and abusive when the factory model is applied to animals.

Moreover, one must challenge any claims of productivity and efficiency in a mode of agriculture that has inherent in it so great a waste of land and resources. As we have seen, there is no real human need being satisfied by these methods, just old habits and unhealthy appetites for rich food. The evidence requires us to examine closely our notions of human need and necessity. The claim of necessity is frequently invoked where our use of other animals is concerned. The "necessity" so often turns out to be entirely unnecessary, and is, in fact, merely an easy way for us to salve our guilt. A belief in the "necessity" of it all makes any bloody business easier to carry out. Guilt-balming is tricky, self-defeating, and often backfires in unexpected ways. It would be much healthier to recognize which of our dealings with other animals are morally indefensible and to make our way without them.

Animal factories are one more sign of the extent to which our technological capacities have advanced faster than our ethics. We plow under habitats of other animals to grow hybrid corn that fattens patented, genetically engineered animals for slaughter. We make free species extinct and domestic species into biomachines. We build cruelty and disease into our diet.

Our failure to accept animals as beings entitled to ethical consideration in their own right is a barrier to any genuine sensibility in our relations with nature. We lose much that is dear in the process. As two writers who took a look at poultry factories concluded:

> We would insist that economics aside, the story [of the industrialization of chickens] has a much deeper moral: Unrestrained technology, fueled by the desire for larger and larger profits, exacts a price in terms of human values that we can no longer afford to pay. There are invisible costs as well as visible ones in the destruction of chickens.[36]

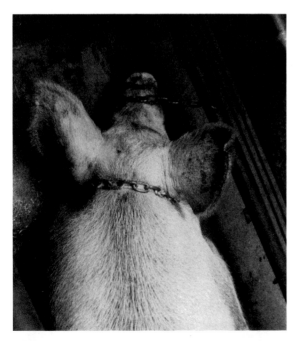

"In principle we disapprove of a degree of confinement of an animal which necessarily frustrates most of the major activities which make up its natural behavior. . . . An animal should at least have sufficient freedom of movement to be able, without difficulty, to turn around, groom itself, get up, lie down, and stretch its limbs."—*Report of the Technical Committee to Enquire into the Welfare of Animals,* para. 37.

There are many, many costs in our present methods and systems of food production. Agribusiness experts would have us know only the benefits. They use "cost–benefit" analyses to justify the use of antibiotics in feed or chemical growth promotants, or nitrites to cure meats. They assert that the benefits to consumers from these uses outweigh the risks involved. But if this sort of test is to have any validity in agricultural affairs, it must take *all* the costs of factory methods into account: costs to the health of consumers who dine on fatty, chemically dosed, antibiotic-fed animals that never exercise or see sunlight; costs to the environment from the pollutant effects of animal wastes; costs to our limited stores of fossil fuels; costs to the starving people whose lives might be saved by the food and resources we are wasting; costs to the land, which is forced to produce more and more crops to be turned into meat; costs to wildlife, whose habitat is destroyed to grow feedstuffs; costs to the quality of life for farm families who, getting no support from the USDA or the agricultural research establishment, can no longer compete with big business and must leave the land; costs to the animals themselves, confined, crowded, bored, frustrated, manipulated, and deprived of their natural lives; and finally, costs to our own self-respect.

We do not pretend to be able to quantify these costs. That problem we leave to the agricultural experts who are so fond of cost–benefit analyses. But we are confident that if adequate account is taken of the costs of the ruthless application of technology to animal rearing, they will decisively outweigh any benefits we obtain from animal factories.

"Good veal has always been difficult to find. But recently a Dutch process has come to our shores and is giving us a limited quantity of much finer veal than was generally available before. . . . The process consists simply of taking calves from their mothers' milk to small stalls, where they are fed with vitamins and powdered milk that contains no iron to darken the flesh. Also, the calves are kept comparatively quiet during their milk regime. Thus, they have delicate whitish-pink flesh and clear fat and are deliciously tender."— James Beard, *American Cookery* (Boston: Little, Brown & Co., 1972), pp. 331–2.

Figure 8.1. Per Capita Consumption (Pounds) of Animal Products, United States, 1979–87 (Retail Weight)

Item	1979	1980	1981	1982	1983	1984	1985	1986	1987
Beef	78.0	76.4	77.1	76.8	78.2	78.1	78.8	78.4	73.4
Veal	1.7	1.5	1.6	1.7	1.6	1.8	1.8	1.9	1.5
Lamb/mutton	1.3	1.4	1.4	1.5	1.5	1.5	1.4	1.4	1.3
Pork	63.7	68.1	64.9	58.5	61.9	61.5	62.0	58.6	59.2
Total meat	144.7	147.4	145.0	138.5	143.2	142.9	144.0	140.3	135.4
Eggs	35.1	34.4	33.5	33.5	33.0	32.9	32.2	31.7	31.6
Chicken	50.3	49.8	51.3	52.7	53.4	55.2	57.6	58.7	62.7
Turkey	9.9	10.5	10.7	10.8	11.2	11.3	12.1	13.3	15.1
Total poultry products	95.3	94.7	95.5	97.0	97.6	99.4	101.9	103.7	109.4
Total dairy products (in milk equivalent)	548.0	543.4	540.9	555.5	572.4	581.2	592.7	590.6	598.2
Total animal products	788.0	785.5	781.4	791.0	813.2	823.5	838.6	834.6	843.0

From U.S. Department of Agriculture, *Agricultural Statistics 1988* (Washington, D.C.: U.S. Government Printing Office, 1988), Table 680, p. 494.

9 IN PLACE OF

ANIMAL FACTORIES

Toward a Better Way of Life for Consumers, Farmers, and Farm Animals

Food is a cultural, not a technological, product. A culture is not a collection of relics or ornaments, but a practical necessity, and its destruction invokes calamity. A healthy culture is a communal order of memory, insight, value, and aspiration. It would reveal the human necessities and the human limits. It would clarify our inescapable bonds to the earth and to each other.
—Wendell Berry, "Land Reform Starts on the Land and in the Heart," *Environment Action Bulletin*, October 19, 1974

It is time for the meat industry to stop nipping at the edges of [the drug] issue. It is time to stop "recommending" that livestock be weaned off drugs. It is time to give consumers the safety they demand—and have a right to—in their meat supply. It is time to halt subtherapeutic feeding. Completely.
—Steve Bjerklie, Editor, "Let's Get Meat Off Drugs, *Meat and Poultry*, April 1987, p. 6

Severson emphasized that producers have been long the guardians of their animals' welfare and long the protectors of the land and water and "are doing a great job." However, he said that the consumer's perception ultimately will decide the issues, and if the feed and feeding industries fail to get their message across to consumers and legislators, producers will have to respond with new environmental and husbandry practices.
Those responses will involve laws limiting or prohibiting large confinement operations and requiring certain environmental and husbandry practices that will make compliance less costly for diversified family farms and nearly prohibitively expensive for large confinement operations.
—Rod Smith, "Kent Feeds: Consolidation Is Evolution of Technology, Provides Time to Respond," *Feedstuffs*, October 30, 1989, pp. 22, 24

FACTORY METHODS OF ANIMAL PRODUCTION are not, as some agriculture experts claim, the inevitable result of a "natural tide of history." They are the product of decades of government policy and corporate profiteering. Although the trend is reversible, the forces behind it are well entrenched. Therefore, there can be no immediate end to factory methods; it will take patient struggle to bring sanity and humanity to farming. In the meantime, farmers and consumers can begin by stopping their own contributions to the progress of factory farming.

Both farmers and consumers must learn more about the vast no-man's-land between them: the systems of manufacturers, carriers, distributors, wholesalers, and others that supply farmers and deliver food to consumers. At present, each side tends to have a short-sighted view of agriculture. As buyers, consumers are concerned primarily with food appearance and pricing at the supermarket. For them, farmers and their problems seem far away; consumers deal with food only as it comes from the store. As sellers, farmers concern themselves with prices at the market for their crops. Too many, unfortunately, have been swayed by agribusiness companies into blaming their problems on "consumerism" and governmental regulation. Neither farmers nor consumers would grumble so much if they understood the more important problems that lie beyond their points of sale or purchase.

The very first obstacle to be eliminated, then, is the phony war between farmers and consumers. As in conflicts between the races or sexes, it is easier to blame or ignore the other side than it is to recognize the pervasive, hidden attitudes and economic forces that make life miserable for everyone. Geographic separation may make it impossible for farmers and consumers literally to join hands, but they can join minds and recognize that they are the most important parties in people's most fundamental social activity: the conversion of energy and resources into food.

Primarily, agriculture should provide people with a sensible, healthy diet. Our national agricultural policy should promote the kinds of farming that do so, and it should guarantee information, technology, and economic incentives to people who want to run these farms. There are many dedicated, progressive people in consumer, food, and farm organizations and in the USDA making efforts toward this sort of agricultural policy. But they are up against agribusiness interests that see agriculture primarily as a provider of profits and balancer of trade deficits. These interests control agricultural policy and technology, and they want to keep it that way. As the fray intensifies in the next few years, profood and farm people will need a lot of popular support. Consumers and farmers alike will be subjected to propaganda and threats of increased food prices from those who dominate farm and food policy. It will be necessary to go to some trouble to get information and analysis on the issues because newspapers and magazines, reliant as they are on food-establishment advertising, are not likely to be consistently objective.

A movement for these changes is already under way and it needs your support. In their book *Food First,* Frances Moore Lappé and Joseph Collins wrote:

On college campuses, in religious organizations, among certain state and national legislators, in co-op movements, and among ecology and natural food groups there is a feeling that food is the right place to start to focus attention and energy for change. . . . This is definitely not a movement only of young people. It includes farmers' groups that have been fighting many of the battles we have just discovered for decades. Now they have new allies.[1]

Let's look now at some specific steps that can be taken by consumers and farmers to reverse the present trend toward factory farming.

What Consumers Can Do

The first priority for the consumer is to question the alleged necessity of animal products in diet. Chances are you eat far more of these products than are recommended even by present meat-oriented standards, because (1) you have been hooked on the protein myth, and (2) you have acquired tastes for them that have made them your main foods. There is plenty of evidence that this over-consumption of animal products does more harm than good. Excess protein is not stored for a lean day as are fats and carbohydrates; it must be turned over, "metabolized," by the body and eliminated as waste. If you have too much protein in your body, your metabolic rate "idles" faster than normal, shortens the life span of some cells, and contributes to premature aging. Urea, a by-product of protein metabolism, builds up in the bloodstream, burdens the kidneys, and increases the body's demand for water to "flush" the system. High-protein diets have been linked to neurological problems in children because of related effects on body chemistry. They are also believed to upset the body's calcium balance and to contribute to osteoporosis, a bone-thinning disorder that affects millions of elderly persons—especially women. By now it is virtually common knowl-edge that diets heavy in meat and animal fats have been linked to a higher incidence of heart disease, colon cancer, stroke, and other degenerative diseases.

Because of this evidence and the growing body of opinion that protein needs have been exaggerated, protein is now one of the most controversial elements in our diet. Books listed in the **General References** at the end of this book offer a more complete discussion of protein nutrition and dietary change than can be provided here, but a few brief points should clear up most of the myths about nutrients:

1. American consumption of animal protein alone is several times the amount recommended by the National Academy of Science and the National Research Council. Most of us could simply eliminate meat, milk, and eggs from our diets and still get all the protein we need from the bread, nuts, peas, and beans that we normally eat.

2. The NAS-NRC recommended daily allowances (RDAs) are calculated with a 30 percent safety factor to allow for individual differences or extra needs because of injury or stress. Thus, most of us need about two-thirds of the amount of protein that the RDA says we need.

3. The biggest myth of all is that protein from meat is "superior quality"—a designation fostered by the meat industry. Actually, your body needs not protein but eight amino acids that it cannot synthesize. Animal products have been adjudged "superior" because they supply all of these. But so do grains, legumes, nuts, and other plant parts, although one or more may be "low" in this or that amino acid. Hence the notion that plant protein is "incomplete." This fact makes little difference because people usually eat foods in combinations that supply all the essential amino acids. It's as complicated as a peanut butter sandwich. According to some researchers, the lesser amounts of amino acids in some plant foods may be adequate. These nutritionists look at "nitrogen balance" to assess protein nutritional adequacy. When the balance is positive, protein nutrition is considered adequate. Potatoes, corn, rice, and wheat fed as the only protein source in the diet have kept humans in positive nitrogen balance. Of course, no one recommends such a monotonous diet; it just shows another flaw in the thinking that we *need* "superior" or "complete" animal protein.

In spite of overwhelming evidence about protein nutrition, most people are still afraid of what will happen to them if they cut out meat, milk, and eggs entirely. This fear is traceable to the days when animal protein was believed to be somehow unique and vital to human health. (This, of course made meat-eating—and animal slaughter—"necessary.") If you decide to quit eating some or all animal products, your family and friends are likely to fear for your life and to badger you with all kinds of horror stories about "not getting enough protein." *Remember that, for American-style diets, the worst horror stories are about getting too much protein.* Nothing sudden will happen, but your body will age and deteriorate faster because of it.

Keep in mind a fellow named Dave Scott, a California scholar-athlete who has been the world's most physically fit human being for years. Scott has won Hawaii's legendary "Ironman" triathlon a record four times. He won it three years in a row, each year breaking his own records in the world's most grueling athletic competition—a race that includes a 2.4-mile ocean swim, a 112-mile bicycle race, and a 26.2-mile marathon run. Scott won't eat animal products because he knows how complex fat and protein molecules clog up his system and reduce his stamina. He knows from his own athletic experience and from his academic field, exercise physiology.

You may not want to follow Dave Scott's example completely, but he is very living proof that you can be healthy on a diet void of all animal products. If you are not willing to go that far at first, you can at least take better care of yourself and at the same time protest the animal factory revolution by refusing to buy factory-made meat, milk, and eggs.

You can start by refusing to eat "milk-fed" veal offered in fancy restaurants, and grain-fed beef. Chances are the pork, poultry, eggs, and milk sold in your supermarket come from factory farms, so you should look for them elsewhere. If you feel that you must have these products, cut down on your intake and get them from an "organic," "health," or "natural" food store, or try one of the food co-ops in your area. You may pay somewhat higher prices at these places, but if you cut down your consumption of animal products you will spend no more overall.

As you become a regular shopper in these whole-foods stores, let the owner/ manager know your concerns about meat, milk, and eggs. Most of these stores have traditionally been concerned only with "chemicals" in food and with narrow human health concerns. They need to know that more and more consumers are concerned about treatment of animals on farms, because, after all, there is a high correlation between crowding, restriction, factory productivity, and animal drug abuse. Ask them, for example, if the organic eggs come from crowded or caged hens. Some do, because the only concern is that the hens' feed is from organically grown grains. Humane concerns have not been a consideration in the whole-foods trade, but they must be included if we are to be fully conscious of how our food is produced. Make sure the store owner/manager understands your other concerns about farming, i.e., if the supplier farms are diversified and family-run, and how they manage wastes and other environmental impacts.

And wherever you buy food, whether at a supermarket, restaurant, or elsewhere, let the owner/manager know how you feel about factory-farmed animal products. You probably think your words will have no effect, but you might be surprised. If a supermarket or restaurant manager hears the same thing from even two or three people a week, chances are it will affect his or her ordering and purchasing decisions in time. You may not succeed in getting them to remove all factory-farmed products, but they might offer some alternatives where they would not have before. Then, as these alternatives are made more accessible, more people will buy them instead of the factory-farmed animal products.

If you have read this book with an open mind and a caring heart you are probably outraged by animal agribusiness and the factory revolution. You may be highly motivated to make changes in your diet and shopping patterns; you may want to carry your protests to your state officials and representatives in Congress. If you are so motivated, do what you can to make the larger public as concerned as you are about the cruelties to animals and dangers to the environment and human health associated with animal factories. That concern is already building, and the first few steps toward legislation and regulation are being taken. The trouble is, agribusiness is so powerful and so well represented at the state level and in Washington that these efforts generally fail to make a dent in factory farming. At present, these political efforts are rather frustrating.

This is where you—the consumer—come in. Agribusiness has you overpowered and outspent at any government level you choose. For business reasons, it will not allow any "animal welfarist" or natural-foods concerns to be institutionalized in law. Agribusiness is refusing to budge, even in the face of widespread consumer concern. Right now, for example, there is growing public demand to require the food industries to label foods so that consumers can more easily tell where the food came from and how it was produced. This concern arose when news about pesticide-ridden apples and other contaminated foods got wide exposure. The Alar/apple scare made people wonder so much about food safety that they began to demand accountability and began to shop where they could find it—at organic and whole-foods stores.

Agribusiness's response, for the most part, is to ridicule these concerns, to bombard food editors with disclaimers and assurances, and to beat down any efforts that would separate and label foods according to production methods and inputs. Some produce, for example, might be separated and labeled *natural, organic,* or *chemical-free.* Agribusiness argues that these changes are impossible because of the workings of the marketplace. Privately, it fears that separation and labeling will lead consumers to question—and avoid—the unlabeled foods produced by agribusiness methods.

So we will have to go over and around agribusiness. It may block us at the government level and it may saturate the media with self-serving lies about its practices, but we can simply boycott its products—especially its animal products. In time, some sectors of farming less tied to agribusiness may be weaned away from its awesome influence and get in sync with consumer opinion on animal production methods. In the meantime, if you are motivated by what you have learned in this book you can, at the very least, simply *refuse to buy* factory-farmed animal products. Since agribusiness refuses to make it easy for you to identify these by separation and labeling, then you can easily buy animal products only at food stores that can assure you about the animal husbandry methods of their suppliers.

For a guiding thought, you might want to follow the advice John Robbins gives in the introduction to his book, *Diet for a New America*:

> You don't have to be a vegetarian to be concerned about your health, and to want your life to be a statement of compassion. *It's not the killing of the animals that is the chief issue here, but rather the unspeakable quality of the lives they are forced to live.*[2]

But then you would be best off to give up animal products altogether. If your concerns and motivation are strong, getting rid of the animal products in your diet is probably the strongest statement you can make and the most effective individual action you can take. The food you consume three times or more daily is your most constant and intimate connection with the environment and the living world around you. If you reflect your concern for them in your food habits, you will be healthier in every way.

In choosing this route, be thoughtful of what you are "giving up." You may think immediately of loss, of never again savoring a bacon and cheese hamburger or the like. But appetites change with newly formed habits and you will soon not miss the taste and texture. You will come to recognize what you have "lost": grease, blood, cholesterol, and perhaps a few residues of dangerous animal drugs. Before long, you will realize how easy it is to live without a steady diet of meat, eggs, and dairy products. In fact, you will find that a meatless diet offers much more variety than the restrictive rite of flesh eating. There are plenty of good books on vegetarianism that discuss the benefits better than we can here; we have listed a few of them at the end of this book. Try a few vegetarian meals each week for a while and see if you don't find yourself leaning more and more toward these foods and away from heavy, meat-based meals.

You won't be alone, for the vegetarian trend is on the rise all over the country. Even the National Livestock and Meat Board acknowledges that the "slow, steady growth of vegetarianism . . . is not a fad."[3] A 1978 Roper poll indicated that the United States has about 7 million vegetarians and another 37.5 million people who are careful about their meat consumption, while 78 percent of the population acknowledges the merits of health, economic, ethical, and other reasons for being a vegetarian.[4] Apparently, long overdue changes in our diets are well under way for many people. If only we could get agriculture, food companies, restaurants, and the rest of the food establishment to make it easier for us.

To aid in the transition to a meatless diet, you may want to try some of the meat substitutes until your new appetites and culinary skill are more developed. *Tofu* (soybean curd) and *miso* (a product of soy and rice fermentation)—dietary staples in the Orient for thousands of years—are now available in many food stores. Several varieties of meatlike "analogs" made from textured soy protein are already available and steadily encroaching on the animal products market. Any of these can be used in place of meat in soups, casseroles, spaghetti sauce, and many other familiar dishes. It is true that some brands are heavily processed with artificial coloring and flavoring, but then so are processed meats. Look around; don't let the few "bad apples" keep you from looking for brands composed of wholesome ingredients.

The processes for extracting protein from soybeans, wheat gluten, and leafy plants are new, but they can supply wholesome, nutritious foods in convenient form without the problems associated with meat production. These processes could eliminate not only the waste of soil and grain, but the contaminants and other undesirable substances found in animal products. And direct conversion from plant materials would eliminate most, if not all, of the expensive disease control programs, pollution problems, and carcass inspections that go along with animal agriculture.

Some people are averse to any form of "processed" food. But there are good processed foods—bread may be the oldest. With a little artistry and culinary inventiveness, plain old beans, seeds, nuts, leaves, and other plant proteins could be turned into convenient forms with taste appeal and nutritiousness that would please the most reactionary taste buds.

These changes in food preference should help independent farmers and farm animals as well. Demand for a wider variety of foods should offer farmers more choices in raising crops, less vulnerability to environmental and economic forces, and, perhaps, better financial security. Lower demand for factory-farmed animal products should lower prices, which would make high-overhead factory systems unprofitable. Studies at Iowa State University show that a farmer using a pasture system can market six hundred pigs per year with lower production costs and with less than a third of the capital investment involved in a total confinement system.[5] Even agribusiness-oriented farm magazines advise farmers to go back to pasture and quit using expensive drugs and feed additives when farm prices fall. Apparently, present demand for animal products is still so high that the market is "fat" enough to support expensive, capital-intensive production methods. In a tighter market situation, small, independent, labor-intensive animal farms should have a competitive edge over the large agribusiness factories.

At any rate, consumer demand can make a difference. In Europe, some farmers have gone back to traditional systems because of public awareness of factory-farming methods. In Europe, many farmers have switched to free-range systems for chickens because they have learned that consumers prefer their eggs to eggs from cage-reared birds.

Individual dietary changes will not be enough, however. While you get your food shopping, preparation, and eating habits under control, you should work actively toward broader changes in agriculture and food policy. Since consumer demand affects food supply, we should begin making the following demands:

1. Demand a prohibition on the use of antibiotics, growth promotants, and other feed additives in animal agriculture. The FDA's efforts to ban or regulate these drugs are still under way, but they are being stymied by drug and agribusiness corporations. Without these shortcuts to genuine animal care and health, animal losses in crowded factories would be so great that factory systems and methods would not be profitable.

2. Demand an end to the public subsidies that prop up factory farming. If society is to subsidize agriculture, it could make much better choices about the kinds of production to be supported and the kinds of food to be produced.

3. Demand an end to tax-supported research and technological development of factory systems. The present funding scheme is one big boondoggle for drug and equipment manufacturers. Demand that this money and expertise be directed instead to work on farming methods that farmers can afford and manage, and ones that give consumers safe, wholesome food.

4. Demand local markets and food cooperatives where farmers and consumers can trade directly. Every community has a square or park where space could be set aside for outdoor markets. Find the food cooperative in your community; if there is none, start one.

5. Demand meatless meals and nonfactory farm products from restaurants, hotels, airlines, caterers, school lunch programs, and all other public food outlets. Let them know that you are aware of where food comes from and that you are worried about food produced by factory methods.

6. Demand labeling laws that would mark all factory-produced animal products. (Don't settle for a statement to the effect that the farming systems have been approved by an animal welfare organization; there are some that will rubber-stamp anything just to get their name around.)

7. Demand that supermarkets and other food outlets separate factory and nonfactory foods. There is precedent for this in state laws regulating the labeling and display of kosher foods and, in some states, "organic" or chemical-free foods.

8. Demand a tax on meat and animal products that would provide funding to subsidize the production of other crops. This would be no more absurd than our present policy of subsidizing the production of what are essentially luxury foods. If people want to continue to prop up costly, risky animal production, they should have to pay a premium and the premiums could be channeled toward the support of better foods and production methods.

9. Demand an end to meat industry propaganda in local schools; demand to know how nutrition is being taught to your children.

10. Demand a turnaround in USDA policy so that it puts good food and farm livelihood first. The present prevailing proagribusiness bias is a national scandal that has driven millions of farmers from the land and saturated consumers with junk food.

11. Demand land reforms and zoning laws that would restore small, diversified farms closer to populated areas. Too much of the cost of food goes to transportation, handling, and profiteering as food moves from the farm to the consumer.

12. Demand that food products be labeled to carry the name of corporations owning the brand line. This would expose the monopolism behind the myth of a competitive food industry—and the lie that your ham, eggs, milk, et cetera, come from good old Farmer Jones down on the farm.

13. Demand an end to the animal products industries' "checkoffs," which gouge consumers and small farmers for advertising that props up our wasteful diet weighted toward animal products.

Changes in Farming and Food Delivery

Getting away from factory-farmed animal products is easy because there are so many alternatives—so many other kinds of food and so many other kinds of farming. Usually when society rises up against a troublesome technology—like the automobile or petroleum products, for example—change is slow and difficult because practical, economical alternatives are not readily available. With animal factories, however, the situation is reversed: the safest, healthiest, and least expensive foods are the nonanimal foods; the safest, most environmentally sound, and least expensive farming systems are the nonfactory ones.

In our attempts to eliminate factory farming, we have to be careful not to create new problems. Independent farmers are in a precarious economic position, and abrupt, forced changes could ruin many who have invested in factory systems (although, as we shall see, many could easily return to traditional methods and still farm profitably). But we should be wary of an across-the-board substitution of traditional methods for factory methods. Although traditional farms are, in general, more ecologically sound, efficient, and humane than factories, there are gross exceptions. For example, the return of feedlot cattle to pasture and range systems, as advocated by some reformers, would sharpy extend the deforestation, overgrazing, desertification, erosion, and other environmental damage now being caused by these livestock production methods. In addition, animals maintained in the open in severe climates often suffer in stormy winters and hot, dry summers.

We cannot, then, expect to solve all of the problems discussed in this book simply by going back to traditional animal production practices. If we are to improve diet, environment, and the survival chances of independent farmers, we must reduce our reliance on animal production while promoting diversification in agriculture.

In the meantime, however, most farmers can raise animals successfully without using factory methods. There is ample evidence that traditional husbandry methods are productive and profitable. In fact, many farmers who had set up specialized factory facilities have, for purely practical reasons, abandoned them and gone back to more traditional methods. Typical of these is an Illinois farmer who, having too many problems with pig health and equipment maintenance in his total-confinement buildings, went back to small shelters with outdoor pens and runs. There are no furnaces, fans, or antibiotics on his farm now; he believes his pigs do better on fresh air, sunshine, and room to move about.[6]

Despite their bias toward animal factories, farming magazines contain occasional reports of pig farmers who have abandoned or modified strict confinement systems in favor of open pens, shelters, and bedding. In most cases, these farmers gave up on factory facilities because of their greater disease losses, poorer breeding performance, smaller litters, and higher energy costs.[7] In reference to the recent history of factory methods, one Illinois farmer wrote to *Hog Farm Management* that "ten years of confinement raises more questions than it answers."[8] Although the number of factory pig farms in his state had grown substantially from 1963 to 1975, the number of pigs weaned per litter did not change and the amount of feed required to produce 100 pounds of weight gain rose from 409 to 428 pounds in the same period. Moreover, on the farms surveyed, the 1975 pigs required about a month longer to grow to market weight.[9] Some farmers question factories and blind expansion, because they are discovering that "if we overcrowd our facilities, we must pay the price of slower gains, higher death losses and poorer feed conversion."[10]

Even a few animal experts are catching on to the false claims about the wonders of factory systems. Researchers at South Dakota State University found that pigs reared in concrete-floored shelters open to outside pens gained weight faster and more efficiently than pigs in slatted-floored confinement buildings.

The reasons for the difference, one of the researchers believes, are that the confined pigs were more crowded than the other group and were annoyed by bad air, noise, and other confinement conditions.[11] Studies at North Carolina State University showed that chickens reared in "loose" housing had these advantages over those reared and housed in cages:

- twenty more eggs per bird per year
- 3.9 percent higher rate of egg production
- 5.5 percent less feed required per dozen eggs
- 0.3 percent fewer large blood spots
- 1.9 percent fewer cracked eggs
- 3.2 percent greater livability
- seventy cents more income over feed and chick cost per bird housed.[12]

Although USDA, farm program planners, and agricultural academia at land grant universities show little interest in alternative animal husbandry systems, a few innovative farmers are very interested. Their interest has been stimulated in part by the family farm crisis and in part by growing consumer concern about pesticide and drug residues in foods. Their best efforts so far are reviewed in a book entitled *Alternative Agriculture,* compiled by the National Research Council's Board on Agriculture. The authors confirm what we said ten years ago: factory systems exacerbate disease problems, lead to animal drug abuse, and encourage the development of "magic bullet" veterinary products:

> Disease prevention through management has become an increasingly important research objective throughout the last decade. Nonetheless, technologies for disease treatment rather than management systems for disease prevention dominate current animal health systems. The subtherapeutic feeding of antibiotics and antibiotic treatment of diseased animals remain the mainstays of current animal health practices. Many alternative systems exist, however, and are widely practiced today. . . . Some major commercial producers maintain animal health with reduced or no prophylactic feeding of antibiotics. They are able to achieve this by modified production systems, including reduced animal confinement, improved ventilation and waste management systems, and, in certain cases, the use of alternative technologies.[13]

The NRC report explains that changes away from confinement toward outdoor shelters and pastures substantially reduce drug costs and veterinary bills. In one study cited, these costs in typical confinement pig factories were at least double those in a comparably productive pasture and hutch system. In another example, it has been shown in a USDA-sponsored study that veal calves in crates need five times as much medication—mostly antibiotics—as calves in hutch and yard systems.[14]

The NRC found that nonfactory systems are economically viable, too. Several major analyses of strict confinement versus pasture and hutch systems for pigs have shown that both produce the same returns. Factory producers can turn out greater numbers of animals, but their capital and overhead costs are high and cut deeply into profit per animal sold. Nonfactory producers may not crank out as many litters per year or as many pounds of meat on the same amount of feed, but their low capital costs and low overhead consistently produce higher profits per animal sold. The report notes that although alternative systems for poultry are profitable, they barely exist because of the drive for carcass uniformity by vertically integrated companies with highly mechanized processing plants. According to the authors, "[A]nimal science research at land-grant institutions has reinforced this trend, with little funding directed toward the understanding of alternative production systems."[15]

Dozens of studies and farmers' experiences show that there is nothing inefficient or obsolete about farm systems that afford animals more space, exercise, and freedom to move about. They pay off in several ways. Farmers need not pay for costly "health programs," growth stimulants, antibiotics, and other artificial means of propping up productivity depressed by factory conditions. With a much lower capital investment, these farmers have fewer dollars going out to banks, equipment manufacturers, and utility companies. Moreover, the farmers are not locked into specialization, but have flexibility in deciding what to produce.

Instead of policies that promote factory animal production, we need policies that allow the production advantages of alternative methods to come to the fore and enable farmers to make a good living using them. Among such policies should be:

Regulations Governing Livestock Production Systems and Methods. These could benefit animals, farmers, and consumers by requiring that animals be reared with a genuine concern for their health and welfare. Regulatory emphasis on sound husbandry techniques would eliminate the need for drugs, complex management, and isolation in expensive, crowded buildings. The need for greater amounts of specialized labor and the increased space per animal required to conform to the regulations should give small, independent farmers a better position in their competition against large, investor-owned agribusiness factories. A growing number of farmers and farm experts appear to understand this. Recall the pig farmer quoted in chapter 8, the one whose family had been squeezed out of poultry farming by agribusiness, the one who would tell other farmers in so many words: join every animal rights organization you can, help outlaw sow crates and slotted-floor pig factories, force pig production outdoors and onto straw, and you can help the small, family-sized farms. Recall Gene Logsden, the longtime farm journalist and farm magazine editor who argued:

> If large-scale animal factories continue to have their way, you will be slowly pushed out of the hog and beef business just as has happened to 95 percent of the chicken farmers.

On the other hand, if the animal rightists have their way, the livestock industry will return to smaller, family-sized farms.[16]

Logsden said he would bet "ten steak dinners that a farmer can raise 2,000 free-range chickens cheaper per unit than Frank Perdue can raise 2 million in his megafactories."[17]

Unfortunately, most farmers have been too brainwashed by agribusiness on the subjects of animal rights and government regulation. Most would mechanically oppose regulations on animal husbandry systems, and of course agribusiness would lead them all the way. Ultimately it will be up to consumers to assert their political power if we are to establish laws that will protect farm animals, produce safe food, and restore animal production to the family farm.

In Europe, where consumer opposition to factory farms is older and stronger than in the United States, several countries have established laws and regulations against factory practices:

Sweden. The most sweeping reforms of animal husbandry systems and practices to date were enacted in 1988 by the Swedish parliament and will be implemented over the next ten years. The new animal protection law requires that animal facilities provide enough space to allow all animals to lie down and move freely and that they be designed to allow for animals' natural behavior. Layer hens may not be housed in cages; dairy cows and breeding pigs must be released to pastures in the summer; dairy cows and young pigs must be provided straw or other suitable bedding material; and no animal may be kept tied or held in a way that does not allow freedom of movement. To ensure regard for animal protection and health, construction of new animal facilities and significant modifications of existing buildings must first be approved and inspected by local agricultural boards. The new law empowers the national board of agriculture to issue regulations or prohibitions concerning genetic engineering of animals, use of hormones and other growth-altering drugs, and breeding for characteristics that may cause suffering or alter natural behaviors. The essence of Sweden's new animal protection law is to require that "technology must be adapted to the animals, not the reverse."[18]

Switzerland. This country was the first to pass legislation regulating factory farm practices. In 1981, the Swiss enacted a law to phase out cages for layer hens by 1991. The law also required that veal calves receive iron and roughage in their diets. Pigs must be provided bedding of straw or other material, and restricted sows must be allowed exercise time periodically. Additional provisions establish standards for lighting, flooring materials, space, and other elements of the animals' environment.

The Netherlands. Holland's minister of agriculture has issued an order prohibiting the solitary confinement of pregnant sows in gestation crates. Pending legislation would prohibit tying down animals by breastbands or neck shackles.

West Germany. A court in the state of Hesse ruled in 1979 that battery cages for layer hens violated the country's law against cruelty to animals. A higher court later set aside the ruling pending the outcome of regulations proposed by the European Economic Community.

United Kingdom. Public outrage against factory farming first broke out in Great Britain. It forced Parliament to appoint a committee to investigate factory systems and practices. The Brambell Committee—nine scientists, agricultural experts, and others—reported back to the government in 1965. Among other things, it recommended the passage of a new law to safeguard animals with the following provisions: Set maximum stocking densities for the various species; prohibit debeaking of poultry; prohibit tail-docking of pigs; prohibit tethering and close restriction of veal calves and gestating sows; and require that veal calves be provided iron and roughage in their diets.

No such law was ever passed. Then, in 1981, the House of Commons Agriculture Committee published a similar report containing essentially the same recommendations. In addition, this report called for research into animal behavior under intensive conditions, an early end to veal crates, and changes in tax policy that would discourage factory systems and encourage alternatives. In 1987, Parliament passed a law banning the veal crate system effective January 1990. In 1988, the agriculture department announced regulations that require bedding for cattle and pigs and alarms on automatic ventilation equipment. The regulations did not touch battery cages and sow crates.

Europe in general appears to be close to some international agreement to phase out some of the worst factory systems and methods. In 1987, the European Parliament by an overwhelming vote passed recommendations that, if enacted by the European Economic Commission, would effectively eliminate factory farming. These include prohibitions on solitary confinement of veal calves and gestating sows; a phaseout of battery cages over a ten-year period; prohibition of routine castration, tail-docking, and other mutilations; and tighter regulations on handling of animals in transport.

For the United States we would urge similar regulations to protect animals immediately from the worst abuses while factory technology persists, but we think basic changes in agricultural direction and diet offer the only lasting, effective solutions.

Establish New Priorities in Agricultural Research and Technological Development. We should aim in the long run to phase out factory animal production altogether and replace it with more efficient, civilized food production and delivery systems that ensure a healthier, more varied diet. We will go into some of these more fully in the next sections, but we wish to stress here that new priorities should be established at once. We should no longer waste tax money and expertise on developing "super" cows and inflatable chickens for agribusiness. USDA and the land grant college complex should be put back on the job of developing systems and methods that are best for consumers, farmers, and the environment.

At the same time, agricultural experts should pay much more attention to farmers' innovations in livestock systems. It is a disgrace that the new alternative, *sustainable* agricultural methods, had to be, as *The New York Times* put it, "invented and developed by farmers over the last two decades almost entirely outside of the Department of Agriculture, agricultural universities and other institutions in American farming."[19] While a few university experts are interested in farmer-designed systems and help in improving them, the prevailing view has been to discount them as crude and unsophisticated. They are not, after all, ordinarily made of expanded metal, extruded aluminum, pumps, motors, switches, and other components put out by experts' favorite agribusiness grant-giving companies. They are not, in other words, properly "engineered" for mass production by an agribusiness manufacturer.

Some farmer-built systems use the simplest of materials, require the least labor and energy, and offer a high degree of animal comfort and freedom. Several examples stand out from our survey of farms and magazines, but one of the best was developed by an Illinois farmer who "thinks pigs come first in hog facilities."[20] Instead of restrictive farrowing crates, concrete slabs, and slatted floors, each of his sows and her litter has a "suite" that allows a varied environment and freedom of movement to find comfort. The young pigs can crawl into a wooden "hover" where bedding keeps them dry and, in cold weather, a light bulb provides extra warmth. At nursing time, the pigs join the sow on straw bedding in a dirt-floored farrowing stall. Unlike ordinary stalls, these have only one guard rail eight inches from the floor so the sow can step in and out of the nursing area. "It's not hard to see the first rail on the crate does the work for the sow, the rest just regiments her," says the designer/farmer.[21] After nursing, the sow can take a short walk outside to an outdoor "sun porch" where she has a dunging area. His building has no furnaces or fans, only small gas heaters over each sow that go on in very cold weather. Because his sows dung over outside pits, air in the building is fresh and the labor required to clean twenty-one stalls amounts to about half an hour—done once every other farrowing![22] So much for the "superior efficiency" of high-tech, controlled-environment, total-confinement pig factories.

Encourage Farming Closer to Consumers. With food prices rising, quality dropping, and residue fears growing, people are beginning to look elsewhere for food. And much to the chagrin of agribusiness, they are beginning to find it. Roadside and farmers' markets are reviving in and near cities around the country. Charleston, Savannah, New York City, Boston, Seattle, Washington, D.C., Hartford, Chicago, and other cities have successfully restored farmers' markets that enable local farmers to earn more for their labors without raising prices to consumers. Although these markets benefit all economic classes, they are of particular value to the inner-city poor, whose neighborhoods often contain few grocery stores and fresh-produce stands. Congress made a token effort to aid this renaissance when it passed the Direct Marketing Act of 1976, but the $1.5 million appropriated was a drop in the bucket compared to the millions in subsidies that go out to agribusiness methods of food production and delivery.

To supply these markets, much more could be done to encourage farming near cities. According to USDA's Economic Research Service, there are still large acreages of cropland reasonably close to most central cities.[23] Near many metropolitan areas, significant agricultural production goes on now, especially vegetable and fruit production. But there is a tendency for commercial development and municipal taxing policies to drive local farmers farther and farther away from markets and consumers. Hawaii, Vermont, Oregon, California, and the Canadian western provinces have established land-use plans designed to protect agricultural land from these forces. Maryland, Massachusetts, New Jersey, and other states have programs that preserve farmland by buying out the "development rights" to the land. Under these plans, the farmer can get money for the development value (the very temptation that forces many to sell out) of their land, yet still stay on it and produce food.

The protection of farmland near cities and the provision of direct markets should enable farmers to make a living producing a broader variety of cash crops instead of being stuck with animal production. But there will still be some demand for animal products while diets and appetites are shifting, and local, independent farmers could supply it without using factory methods. Small-scale poultry and dairy production using nonfactory methods could make a comeback with the growth of urban-fringe farming and direct marketing.

Revival of food production near population centers could have other benefits as well. Less energy would be spent on shipping, storing, and processing food; less energy would be spent as we shift to less capital-intensive methods. Farmers using more labor-intensive methods would have a large labor pool nearby to draw from; many of our unemployed concentrated in cities could have some relief from poverty, isolation, and boredom by doing farm work—especially at planting and harvesting time.

Encourage Low-Input Sustainable Agriculture. Prevailing agricultural systems and practices are destroying farm families and diversified farming methods; they are polluting the land and waters as well as our food supply. They depend on abuses of animals and nature to play the elusive game of maximizing efficiency and production. There has to be a better way.

There is, and it is the best news in years. LISA is entering the American agricultural scene. LISA, the acronym for low-input sustainable agriculture, is variously defined, but it is generally agreed to mean a kind of agriculture that tries to produce within the laws of nature without heavy doses of chemicals and expensive high technologies. In simplest terms, it is farming in accordance with ecological principles. For some, it means reducing the use of pesticides and chemical fertilizers. For others, LISA includes a broader view of "ecology" to include the people involved in farming, their communities, and the ultimate consumers of farm products. Under this broader view, "sustainable" would have to consider the impacts on these sectors as well.

Although most LISA advocates have not specifically addressed animal welfare concerns, animals would fare much better in a husbandry system based on LISA principles. For one thing, expensive solitary-confinement calf and sow crates with all their waste disposal and disease problems would not fit LISA standards. Animal health would have to be maintained by providing a wholesome environment, not by subtherapeutic antibiotics and routine injections of powerful animal drugs.

LISA is a hot topic these days, a buzzword in many circles. Just about everybody likes the concept except agribusinessmen, who fear the "low-input" part; for them this means reduced sales of gadgets, gimmicks, and magic bullets. Could it mean the end of the agribusiness era? LISA is also causing headaches in agricultural academia because ag scientists are smart enough to know how badly it is needed, but they have already sold their souls to agribusiness. In those circles, the strategy seems to be to support blandly LISA in principle, but work feverishly to narrow the concept and to fudge the definitions and goals to include as much of prevailing ways as possible. At a symposium on LISA at Iowa State University last year, animal scientists argued that a corporate-owned total confinement pig factory was "sustainable" because of its efficiency and productivity. Such thinking is quite prevalent, so LISA may well be co-opted while it is still on the drawing board.

You will probably be hearing a lot about LISA in years to come. Its definition, its direction, its very existence will be much wrestled over by all concerned with health, food, environment—in other words, just about all of us. You are as apt to be drawn into the wrestling as the next person, so you may as well come to terms with LISA, know what all the fuss is about, and be prepared to speak up about what concerns you. We urge agreement with those who define "sustainable" broadly to include concerns for people—farmers and consumers—and farm animals. We like the definition proposed by the Minnesota-based International Alliance for Sustainable Agriculture:

> A sustainable agriculture is ecologically sound, economically viable, socially just and humane.[24]

Under these standards, BGH-driven supercows that pump out more surplus milk for tax-supported government warehouses would not have been developed, and thousands of dairy farmers would still be on their farms. Most of the excesses of factory farm systems and practices would not exist, either, for none of them could be considered "low-input"—not to mention humane and socially just.

By various accounts, many farmers are already moving toward LISA-like agricultural methods, especially with respect to expensive chemicals and fertilizers. The USDA estimates that between twenty thousand and thirty thousand farmers have shifted away from conventional high-input methods. Other sources estimate that it is more like fifty thousand to one hundred thousand.[25] Many are motivated by concerns for their own safety as stories gather about farmers' health problems linked to years of handling dangerous pesticides. Many are concerned about the soil and the groundwater now that in some areas local officials caution them not to use the wells on their farms. Many are motivated by the higher prices they get when they sell a crop of organic oats or beans. Many are motivated by the disgust they feel toward ag school scientists, chemical companies, and county extension agents who they know have sold them an expensive bill of goods. Many, many farmers would like to move to LISA. Just about all environmentalists would like to help them do it. Just about all consumers would join in if they knew more about the issues.

How much does USDA and the current administration want LISA? Only about $4.5 million worth for 1990. This drop in the bucket amounts to only about one-half of one percent of a year's federal spending on agricultural research.

Create a New USDA Grading System. Most of the changes recommended above could be implemented with one simple, cheap device: a new, relevant USDA grading system for animal products. Just about everyone, from farmers to processors to consumers, realizes that the present grading system is a bad joke. It is outdated, incoherent, and makes everyone unhappy because it tells nothing important about the meat, milk, and eggs graded. From its beginnings in the 1920s, the USDA grading program has rated "quality" primarily on the basis of appearance and esthetics—something any shopper can do at least as well as the government. The grade rating tells the consumer nothing about where the food came from, how it was produced, its nutritional content, its purity regarding contaminants. In short, it tells us nothing about what concerns us most.

The National Research Council's report, *Designing Foods: Animal Products Options in the Marketplace,* criticizes the current USDA grading system as being out of tune with changing consumer attitudes. "In the animal products industry in general," the report states, "and in the meat industry in particular, 'high quality' has historically been associated with high fat content."[26] This is because the main determinant in the grading of red meat is the amount of intramuscular fat. The fattier the carcass, the higher the grade stamped on it by the USDA inspector. The NRC report confirms other indications that consumers are confused over food grading and know very little about the criteria used by USDA.

From what we know of consumer preferences, the best grading system would be one that informs us about fat content, nutritional content, drug residues, and, increasingly, animal welfare standards and environmental impacts. To be most effective, the system should feed information about consumer preferences back to farmers and food processors. Under such a system, consumer preferences, farm methods, and processing methods should gravitate toward the safest, soundest, healthiest, and most humane food and farming systems. Where animal products are concerned, the most telling information is how the animals were grown, fed, housed, and managed. The best grading system is one that gives us this information and lets us buy according to our concerns. Ideally, such a grading system would not rate hierarchically, i.e., "best" or "A," but it should simply tell us a few basic things about production systems and methods. We see four key concerns: farmer (who owns, where, size), environment, animal welfare, and human health and safety. If the grading system can tell us, for example, that the product came from a farm where drugs and antibiotics were not used to boost production, the last two concerns are addressed. If it can tell us that the farm was small, diversified, and practicing LISA, the first two concerns—possibly others—are addressed. If some of the more "pure" husbandry systems and farming practices incur higher costs and produce higher priced products, so much the better as that would give farmers an incentive to use them.

An immediate objection might be that such a grading system would be impossible to administer because of the difficulties in tracking food from farm to retail market. Another might be that it would require a prohibitively expensive staff of inspectors whose job it would be to monitor and evaluate farms. We can expect these objections from agribusiness, which has the greatest investment in the present system, which tells us nothing about what concerns us most. Agribusiness wants us to know nothing so it can tell us anything, as for example when it tells us that "milk is a natural." It is already pulling levers at USDA to nip in the bud the trend toward *natural* and *organic* labeling. It didn't mind as long as such foods were confined to organic and health food stores where all the "food nuts" shop, but now these foods are showing up in supermarkets and ordinary people are going to the organic and health food stores. So agribusiness is already fighting efforts to give consumers the information and choices they want.

It will be difficult to overcome the food establishment's political clout, but not its objections to a husbandry-based grading system for animal products. For one thing, USDA, state ag officials, farmers, and processors are already pushing for some of the same devices in an effort to control animal diseases and drug residues. They realize that if a Listeria outbreak or an illegal residue turns up at the consumer end, they have to be able to trace that product back to the farm. They know they must have this trace-back ability if they are to catch violators, correct problems, reduce incidence of contamination, and restore consumer confidence. So the government/industry/producer network is busily establishing producer codes, tattoo identification schemes, farm certification programs, and the other devices that make up a system for tracing animal products from the farmer up to the packager and back again. Since they are boasting so loudly about how effective these trace-back devices are in protecting consumers, they will be in an odd position to argue that they can't be done as part of a better grading system. But you can bet they will try, because their business is at stake.

An essentially husbandry-based system has been in place for the grading of milk since 1924. Administered by the Food and Drug Administration/Public Health Service, the Grade A pasteurized-milk program sets down detailed specifications for barn construction, equipment, cowyards, milking procedures, and other aspects of Grade A dairying. Farmers must follow these specifications if they want to be paid for Grade A milk. States are part of the scheme and their trained inspectors monitor farms to ensure that Grade A standards are maintained.

Thus we already have some of the elements of a husbandry-based grading system in place. It should be relatively easy to develop specifications similar to those of the Grade A milk system for other types of farms and animal products. If we stuck to the present hierarchical "A" rating scheme, a poultry farm, for example, would have to maintain facilities and methods geared toward maintaining animal health, growth, productivity, and profitability without the use of drugs, additives, antibiotics, or debeaking and other mutilations. Necessarily, this sort of farm would maintain smaller, less crowded flocks and there would be more labor involved in feeding, watering, providing bedding, and other animal care chores. These farms would probably be operated most successfully by families and individual owners who are willing to live on the premises and perform the labor. In the long run, small-scale, family, and LISA farming should be more financially successful and secure because it would be best positioned to produce the highest-priced grade of animal products.

Obviously many consumers are less finicky about fat content, nutrition, environmental impacts, et cetera, and more concerned with retail prices. They would probably choose the lower-priced grades of products from animals raised under less careful methods. Over time, the educational benefits of the grading system should influence them to buy the higher graded products, reduce intake, and still stay within their food budgets. Thus, a mere grading system could improve diets, reduce human health hazards caused by drugs and additives, and put some profitability back in small-scale and family farming.

For Farmers Only

Understandably, many farmers will look upon these proposals with fear and scorn. Many are intent on producing food exactly as they please and expect USDA and the food corporations to shove it down consumer throats. But consumers are getting more and more conscious of food, diet, and the environment and they are demanding changes. Farmers who really want to stay on their land and make a living raising food will have to become more attentive to these demands.

Farm people have become victims of their own isolation and independence. Many have contempt rather than regard for what goes on in cities where the consumers live, and many are loath to organize or join farmer associations. With these views, it's no wonder that the 2 percent of Americans who farm are an endangered species while agribusiness encroaches on their habitat. According to Chuck Frazier of the National Farmers Organization (NFO), "Farmers aren't sufficiently willing to cooperate by joining together and staying on a campaign long enough to get success in pricing their products. They have been burned too many times by organizers and individuals who sought power as self-appointed leaders." He also cites two general developments coming out of this broad discontent:

> They distrust government and many organizations, especially the leadership of government agencies and organizations. This attitude seems to be

growing. Secondly, when they do organize, farmers have recently tended to move into specialized commodity groups. As they do so, they dissipate their broad collective strength and stir up competition between different commodity producer groups.[27]

The natural forces of commodity marketing are the primary cause of this sectarianism and specialization in agriculture. With hard times nearly always in sight for independent farmers, they tend to turn to the one crop or type of livestock operation that provides the most security. Then they join with other producers of the same commodity to fight for subsidies, price supports, bans on imports, and other forms of Band-Aid protectionism that they hope will keep their commodity profitable for years to come. The "checkoffs" voted in by cattle, hog, and sheep producers are a good example of this kind of tunnel vision. Rice growers, potato producers, and cotton and wheat farmers all have similar commodity promotion campaigns, even though the demand for their products is relatively stable and constant. While farmers foot the bills for these campaigns, the advertising, media, and public relations firms that have the accounts are laughing all the way to the bank, where broad smiles greet them. In the final analysis, neither farmers nor consumers gain much benefit from the millions that change hands. It is ironic that farmers are among the loudest screamers against "government controls," yet they dare not whisper about the immense power that commodities traders and other agribusiness interests have over them.

Independent farmers who expect to stay in farming will have to snap out of their anarchism/individualism/isolationism and wake up to consumer, environmental, and other popular concerns. With a truly progressive attitude about food and environmental issues, farmers could gain a fair amount of muscle in coalition with groups working on these issues. Farmers who ignore these trends, or who fight for the narrow goal of making the agricultural status quo more profitable, can expect deepening powerlessness and an increasing trend toward expensive, complicated farming as agribusiness promotes its same old self-serving technology, and government slaps on controls in response to consumer concerns for the environment and food quality.

Toward a Healthier, Happier Future

Agriculture was a great advance for humans, but it spelled doom for much of the rest of the planet. Ten thousand years of human control over the soil has turned good land into deserts, monocultures, and weed patches. To feed ourselves—now over 5 billion strong and bound to double early in the twenty-first century—we destroy ecosystems with bulldozers, plows, and pesticides. Other beings, their habitats destroyed, have neither food nor shelter. Those that survive by adapting to our crops become pests and targets for our poisons, traps, and guns.

Progressive changes in our world view are necessary if we are to maintain a habitable planet. We should strive to limit the extent of our exploitation over animals and soil. While maintaining our hard-won level of civilization, we must extend the scope of moral consideration beyond our own species. We must limit the use of technologies that advance our own short-term success at too great a cost to other creatures and, in the long run, to ourselves.

If these proposals appear farfetched to some, that may be because the habit of maximizing short-term profit is hard to break. But we can halt the trends that point to ominous ends and start planning an improved quality of life. At the risk of seeming utopian, we propose the following:

1. We should stop expecting agricultural technology and food production to be the solutions to the world's ills. There are those who would intrude even deeper into seas, swamps, rain forests, mountains, and deserts to create more cropland to feed people. The problem is not that we don't have enough food to go around. We do. The world food problem exists because of inequities in distribution of food and resources that have grown out of unfair notions about people and property.[28] A few have too much while a great many have too little. Inevitably, those who have too little try to achieve the standard of those who have more than enough. As they do so, social strains occur, followed by increased demands on the environment as human levels of expectation and consumption rise. Instead of pushing for greater agricultural productivity, we should push for ethical, political, economic, and social progress that will equalize distribution of what we take from the earth.

2. Once we have done so, we could reduce human population humanely through family planning. High birthrates are directly related to poverty, malnutrition, and high infant mortality.[29] When a society begins to enjoy a better quality of life and sees its children live to maturity, people feel more secure and hopeful about life, and they desire fewer children as a result. Probably the surest way to head off predicted population increases and their toll on the environment is to divide more equally the world's food, health care, and beneficial technology within the next generation or two.

3. As equitable economic and social institutions are inaugurated and population growth reversed, we could undo much of what we have done over the ages. Many parts of the earth have been overpopulated for centuries. Many areas are so inhospitable to humans and agriculture that they should be off-limits rather than "conquered" and modified for permanent human habitation. An ethical land-use policy of "not for humans only" could end much of our competition with other species. Much of the earth's land now exploited for food and materials could be freed if humans abandoned animal agriculture. People now engaged in livestock production could be encouraged to turn to other means of livelihood. Over time, millions of acres of land could be returned to wilderness and natural diversity.

4. We should advance new ideologies and technologies of food production. Industrial technology in the hands of profiteers has allowed them to take over agriculture and give us corporate and factory farming. In response to these problems, many reformers favor a return to small, family farms. While self-sufficiency and small size may be beautiful compared to the corporate model,

this return to unyielding individualism and simple tools will not provide the answers. The technological solutions lie in employing the best that *each* scale of food production has to offer. Some people think that mechanization is the root of all evil and that it should be wholly replaced by small-scale, labor-intensive farming methods; others ignore what mechanization does to food quality and blindly advocate labor-eliminating machines as the ultimate liberators of all humankind. Sane food production will require both, in various combinations, depending on the crop and conditions. Factory farming shows that animals don't thrive on mechanical care. Juicy palatable fruits and vegetables don't survive agribusiness's mechanical pickers, so tough, bland ones are developed. But this doesn't mean that we must plant and harvest field crops by hand.

More people could be involved in food production in the future. While only 2 percent of the population farm for a living, polls indicate that over half of all Americans grow some of their food and millions of others would like to if they had access to land and assistance.[30] There may be more to this than a fight against rising food prices; there are emotional satisfactions from tilling the soil. People should not be separated from food production and alienated from the environment by either ideology or technology. Future systems of food production should allow people to participate according to their time and skills. Gardening, urban greenhouse farming, urban fringe farms, farmers' markets, and food cooperatives would provide opportunities if people had time, convenient transportation, and economic security to work in them more frequently. For large-scale production of fruits, vegetables, and staples such as cereals and legumes, we ought to consider cooperative farms. On these farms, a wide range of people could participate in the civic work of food production. Full-time farmer-residents could provide expertise and year-round supervision and could direct long-range planning and operations. Other specialists could be mobile, offering their skills on tours to many farms in different regions. Much of the low-skill work could be done by anyone who has the time and the desire to do outdoor work.

The popularity of urban gardening indicates that many city people enjoy such work as a diversion from office and factory drudgery. Arrangements with employers and other incentives could make it possible for those people to do similar work on the public's farms. These farms could distribute the responsibility and pleasure of food production more evenly throughout society. People could get to know other regions of the country, other kinds of work, and other kinds of people. In the process, urban-rural alienation could be reduced and the quality of rural life enriched by agricultural production that emphasizes sociality, public interest, and the sharing of skills, tools, and labor instead of feed conversion ratios and corporate profits.

Agriculture, our most vital activity, should also be a humane and rewarding occupation.

NOTES

Chapter 1

1. For poultry industry history, see generally Mack O. North, "Startling Changes Ahead in Production Practices"; Ray A. Goldberg, "Broiler Dynamics—Past and Future"; George E. Coleman, Jr., "One Man's Recollections over 50 Years"; R. Frank Frazer, "Strategy for the Future" and "Gordon Johnson Remembers"; all in *Broiler Industry*, July 1976.

2. "How Egg Industry Changed During the Last 20 Years," *Poultry Digest*, May 1978.

3. Ibid.; Mack O. North to J. B. Mason, September 18, 1976; and "90% of U.S. Layers Are Housed in Cages," *Poultry Digest*, July 1978.

4. Michael W. Fox, *Farm Animals: Husbandry, Behavior, and Veterinary Practice* (Baltimore: University Park Press, 1984).

5. Interview with a hatchery manager, Massachusetts, November 7, 1976.

6. American hatcheries produced 428 million egg-type chicks in 1987. United States Department of Agriculture, *Agricultural Statistics 1988* (Washington, D.C.: U.S. Government Printing Office, 1988), Table 512, p. 358.

7. Ibid., Table 501, p. 349.

8. North, "Startling Changes," p. 98.

9. *Agricultural Statistics 1988*, Table 509, p. 356. The table lists 5 billion 3 million broilers produced in 1987, but the total does not include the numbers from states that produced under 500,000 birds.

10. Assuming 240,000 miles to the moon and 2,800 miles from New York to Los Angeles and each bird to be exactly one foot long from beak to toes.

11. *Agricultural Statistics 1988*, Table 520, p. 362.

12. "Dynamic Structure of Agriculture," in United States Congress, Office of Technology Assessment, *Technology, Public Policy, and the Changing Structure of American Agriculture*, OTA-F-285 (Washington, D.C.: U.S. Government Printing Office, March 1986).

13. Jackie W. D. Robbins, *Environmental Impact Resulting from Unconfined Animal Production,* Environmental Protection Technology Series (Washington, D.C.: Office of Research and Development, U.S. Environmental Protection Agency, March 1978).

14. "Diseases Major Limiting Factor," *Hog Farm Management,* May 1976; V. Rhodes and G. Grimes, "A Study of Large Hog Farms," *Hog Farm Management, 1976 Pork Producers' Planner,* December 1975; and A. Jensen et al., *Management and Housing for Confinement Swine Production,* University of Illinois, College of Agriculture, Cooperative Extension Service Circular 1064 (Urbana-Champaign, Illinois: November 1972).

15. Tom Bodus, "Fewer Hands Control a Larger Share of the Nation's Hogs," *Pork '87,* October 1987.

16. Ibid.

17. V. J. Rhodes, C. Stemme, and G. Grimes, "Larger and Medium Volume Hog Producers: A National Survey," S.R. 223, University of Missouri Agricultural Experiment Station (Columbia, Missouri: University of Missouri, 1979).

18. Advertisement for Farmstead Industries, Waterloo, Iowa, in *Hog Farm Management,* April 1975, p. 1.

19. Ibid.

20. *Agricultural Statistics 1988,* Table 462, p. 313; Robbins, *Environmental Impact.*

21. Jess Gilbert and Raymond Akor, "Increasing Structural Divergence in U.S. Dairying: California and Wisconsin Since 1950," *Rural Sociology* 53, no. 1 (Spring 1988): 55–72; U.S. Congress, Office of Technology Assessment, "Emerging Technologies, Public Policy and Various Size Dairy Farms," in *Technology, Public Policy, and the Changing Structure of American Agriculture* (Washington, D.C.: U.S. Government Printing Office, 1986), pp. 189–202.

22. The figure is according to Food Animal Concerns Trust, P.O. Box 14599, Chicago, IL 60614, an organization that markets veal and eggs from farmers who agree to its humane and animal health guidelines. The American Veal Association, P.O. Box 306, North Manchester, IN 46962, claims that the veal industry raises 3.2 million calves each year, but the figure is believed to be exaggerated.

23. Interview with a veal producer, Connecticut, September 1974.

24. Ibid.

25. *Agricultural Statistics 1978* (Washington, D.C.: U.S. Government Printing Office, 1978), Table 454, p. 306. Cattle on grain or other concentrates on January 1, 1973, numbered 4.5 million.

26. Bill Miller, "Concentration Continues: NCA's Task Force Gives Its Report," *Beef Today* (a *Farm Journal* publication), March 1989.

27. Raymond C. Loehr, "Changing Practices: Livestock Production," in *Pollution Control for Agriculture,* 2d ed. (Orlando: Academic Press, 1984).

28. John Dawson, "Sheep Come Back," *Confinement,* March 1978, p. 9.

29. S. D. Lukefahr, D. D. Caveny, P. R. Cheeke, and N. M. Patton, "Rearing Weanling Rabbits in Large Cages," *Journal of Applied Rabbit Research* 3, no. 1 (1980): 20–21.

30. P. R. Cheeke, "The Potential Role of the Rabbit in Meeting World Food Needs," *Journal of Applied Rabbit Research* 3, (1980): 3–4.

Chapter 2

1. M. Kiley, "The Behavioural Problems That Interfere with Production in Animals under Intensive Husbandry," *Proceedings of the III World Conference on Animal Production,* R. L. Reid, ed. (Sydney: Sydney University Press, 1975), p. 431.

2. Remarks by Stanley E. Curtis, Ph.D., in a presentation entitled "Technical Overview of Disease Control in Animals," at the conference *Biotechnology and Sustainable Agriculture: Policy Alternatives,* Iowa State University, Ames, Iowa, May 22, 1989.

3. Ibid.

4. Stanley E. Curtis, "What Is 'Environmental Stress'?" *Confinement,* June 1976.

5. "Tail-Biting Is Really 'Anti-Comfort Syndrome,' " *Hog Farm Management,* March 1976, p. 94.

6. Neal Black, "Production Drops If Sows Confined," *National Hog Farmer,* Swine Information Service Bulletin no. E-13.

7. Kiley, "Behavioural Problems."

8. M. C. Appleby, A. B. Lawrence, and A. W. Illius, "Influence of Neighbors on Stereotypic Behaviour of Tethered Gilts," *Applied Animal Behaviour Science,* —— (1990): ——.

9. Ibid.; A. B. Lawrence, M. C. Appleby, and H. A. Macleod, "Measuring Hunger in the Pig Using Operant Conditioning: The Effect of Food Restriction," *Animal Production* 47 (1988): 131–137; and M. C. Appleby and A. B. Lawrence, "Food Restriction as a Cause of Stereotypic Behaviour in Tethered Gilts," *Animal Production* 45 (1987): 103–110.

10. *Feedstuffs,* January 7, 1985.

11. *Feedstuffs,* December 31, 1984.

12. Tom Brodus, "The Air They Breathe: How Good or Bad Is It?" *Pork '87,* February 1987.

13. Tony J. Cunha, "Efficiency, Efficiency: The Key to the Future," *Feedstuffs,* January 30, 1989, pp. 50, 52.

14. A good overview of the disease problems in the various types of confinement systems is presented by veterinarian and ethologist Dr. Michael W. Fox in his book *Farm Animals*, cited in the notes in chapter 1 above. See also Brodus, "The Air They Breathe," p. 25.

For information re a decade ago, see "A Status Report on the Six Most Deadly Hog Diseases," *Successful Farming*, October 1976.

In the 1970s operators of large pig farms were surveyed and asked to list the advantages and disadvantages of their systems. The most often cited (23 percent of respondents) disadvantage was "disease problems." The farms surveyed used a variety of systems, but 57.2 percent reported using some type of confinement facilities. "Disease Major Limiting Factor," *Hog Farm Management*, May 1976. See also G. W. Meyerholz, "Disease Management in Large Herds," *Confinement*, June 1976.

15. "Keep Those Dairy Calves Alive!" *Successful Farming*, p. 11.

16. Our calculations are roughly in line with USDA data, which show a 14.3 percent loss for the year 1987. Nearly 36.5 million layer hens succumbed to "death and other losses." See *Agricultural Statistics 1988*, Table 505, p. 353.

17. Stanley N. Gaunt and Roger M. Harrington, eds., *Raising Veal Calves* (n.p.: The Massachusetts Cooperative Extension Service, n.d.), no. 106, p. 4.

18. Interview with a veal producer, Connecticut, September 1973.

19. Eldon W. Kienholz, "Vitamin Deficiencies in Chickens and Turkeys," *Poultry Digest*, April 1976.

20. John B. Herrick, "Liver Abscesses Are Costly Problem in Most Feedlots," *Beef*, September 1976.

21. Gene Johnston, "Boars: Keeping Them on Their Feet," *Successful Farming*, October 1977; and Robert D. Fritschen, "Floors and Their Effects on Feet and Leg Problems in Swine," *Confinement*, June 1976.

22. Richard Wall, "Caged Layer Fatigue," *Poultry Digest*, January 1976.

23. Milton Y. Dendy, "Broiler 'Flip-over' Syndrome Still a Mystery," *Poultry Digest*, September 1976, p. 380.

24. Interview with a broiler producer, North Carolina, December 1978.

25. J. D. Simmons and B. D. Lott, "Natural and Forced Ventilation of Broiler Houses for Summertime Heat Removal," PSA and SPSS Abstracts, *Poultry Science*, Supplement 1, January 1989.

Chapter 3

1. "Highlights of Poultry Science Papers," *Poultry Digest*, October 1976, p. 422.

2. Paul Siegel and Bernie Gross, "We're Learning How to Let Bird Defend Itself," *Broiler Industry*, August 1977, p. 42.

3. Alex Hogg, "Swine Diseases," *Feedstuffs, 1988 Reference Issue,* July 27, 1988.

4. F. D. Thornberry, W. O. Crawley, and W. F. Krueger, "Debeaking Laying Stock to Control Cannibalism," *Poultry Digest,* May 1975, pp. 205–7.

5. Ibid., and "Best Age for Debeaking Is 6 Days," *Poultry Digest,* July 1976, p. 283.

6. R.W.R. Brambell, *Report of the Technical Committee to Enquire into the Welfare of Animals Kept Under Intensive Livestock Husbandry Systems,* Command Paper 2836 (London: Her Majesty's Stationery Office, 1965), par. 97, p. 26.

7. Rocky J. Terry, "How to Use Antibiotics Effectively," *Poultry Digest,* November 1975, p. 440.

8. Committee on Government Operations, U.S. House of Representatives, *Human Food Safety and the Regulation of Animal Drugs* (Washington, D.C.: U.S. Government Printing Office, 1985).

9. Robert Reinhold, "Beef Industry Reduces Use of Disputed Drugs in Feed," *The New York Times,* February 16, 1985, p. 8.

10. "Has the Egg Changed?" *Poultry Digest,* November 1977, p. 522.

11. Vernon G. Pursel et al., "Genetic Engineering of Livestock," *Science,* June 16, 1989, p. 1281.

12. Ibid., p. 1284.

13. "Naked Chick Gets Serious Attention," *Broiler Industry,* January 1979, p. 98.

14. ABC News Closeup, "Food: Green Grow the Profits," Friday, December 21, 1973.

15. "Tests Show Stress-prone Gilts Are Late Breeders," *National Hog Farmer,* October 1976, p. 98.

16. "Farm Animals of the Future," *Agricultural Research,* April 1989.

17. Ibid., and "Farm Animals of the Future," *Agricultural Research,* May 1989.

18. Thayne Cozart, "AI Cuts Costs, Forces Better Management," *National Hog Farmer,* January 1976, p. 86.

19. "Antibiotics in Animal Feeds Risk Assessment," *FDA Veterinarian,* May/June 1989.

20. U.S. Senate Committee on Agriculture, Nutrition and Forestry, *Food Safety and Quality, Use of Antibiotics in Animal Feed* (Washington, D.C.: U.S. Government Printing Office, 1977), Statement of Dr. Richard P. Novick, p. 108.

21. John B. Herrick, "Cattle Disease Guide," *Feedstuffs, 1988 Reference Issue,* July 27, 1988, Table 11, p. 116.

22. "What Tells Cattle to Stop Eating?" *Beef,* November 1976, p. 33.

23. Peter Watson, "Boss Cows and Sleepy Sheep," *Psychology Today,* December 1975, pp. 93–4.

24. James L. Kerwin, "Well, Son, Cows Eat Old Boxes, Give Milk," *The Detroit News,* April 19, 1976.

25. Orville Schell, *Modern Meat* (New York: Random House, 1984).

26. Remarks by Gerald B. Guest, D.V.M., Director of FDA's Center for Veterinary Medicine, at the FDA Pesticide Coordination Team Conference, February 1989, reported in "CVM Looks at Pesticide Residues," *FDA Veterinarian,* May/June 1989, p. 8.

27. Alfred Milbert, Ph.D., "Feed Grade Fats and Oils," in "Animal Feed Safety," *FDA Veterinarian,* July/August 1988, p. 3.

28. Ibid.

29. "My Dry Sows Go 90 Days Without Feed," *Hog Farm Management,* April 1978, p. 36.

30. Ibid.

31. Mack O. North, "Startling Changes Ahead in Production Practices," *Broiler Industry,* July 1976, pp. 81, 85.

32. Ibid.

33. Mack O. North, "Some Tips on Floor Space and Profits," *Broiler Industry,* December 1975, p. 24.

34. Veryl Sanderson and Bell Eftink, "Their Dream House Nearly Drove Them to the Poor House," *Successful Farming,* August 1978, pp. B-6, B-7.

35. Ibid.

36. C. E. Ostrander and R. J. Young, "Effects of Density on Caged Layers," *New York Food and Life Sciences,* July–September 1970, pp. 5–6.

37. Fox, *Farm Animals,* p. x.

Chapter 4

1. William J. Stadelman, "Lower Quality with Yolk Color Increase," *Egg Industry,* December 1975, p. 24.

2. Roger J. Williams et al., "The 'Trophic' Value of Foods," *Proceedings of the National Academy of Science, U.S.A.,* 70:3 (March 1973), 710–13; A. Tolan et al., "The Chemical Composition of Eggs Produced under Battery, Deep Litter and Free Range Conditions," *British Journal of Nutrition,* 30:181 (March 1974), p. 185.

3. M. A. Crawford, "A Re-evaluation of the Nutrient Role of Animal Products,"

Proceedings of the III World Conference on Animal Production, R. L. Reid, ed. (Sydney: Sydney University Press, 1975), p. 24.

4. Ibid., p. 26.

5. Jon Bennett, *The Hunger Machine: The Politics of Food* (Cambridge, U.K.: Polity Press, 1987).

6. Roy Gyles, "Technological Options for Improving the Nutritional Value of Poultry Products," in National Research Council, *Designing Foods: Animal Products Options in the Marketplace* (Washington, D.C.: National Academy Press, 1988), pp. 297, 299.

7. Ibid.

8. "Policies Affecting the Marketplace," in National Research Council, *Designing Foods,* p. 100.

9. Ibid.

10. William J. Stadelman, "Old-time Flavor: New Injectables Possible," *Broiler Industry,* April 1975, p. 79.

11. Gregory Leonardos, "Brand Life May Depend on Unique Flavors," *Broiler Industry,* October 1976, p. 33.

12. Ibid.

13. See note 19 to chapter 3.

14. National Research Council, *Human Health Risks with the Subtherapeutic Use of Penicillin or Tetracycline in Animal Feed* (Washington, D.C.: National Academy Press, 1989).

15. Bill Lawren, "Kinky Lambs," *Omni,* May 1988, p. 33.

16. "New Treatment Boosts Pigs Per Litter," *Farm Journal,* March 1976, p. Hog-2.

17. U.S. House of Representatives, Committee on Government Operations, *Human Food Safety and the Regulation of Animal Drugs* (Washington, D.C.: U.S. Government Printing Office, 1985), p. 4.

18. David Morris, "EC Meat-Hormone Stance May Be the Right One," *Agweek,* February 6, 1989, p. 8.

19. Monroe Babcock, "Shrinking Egg Market Is Our Own Fault," *Egg Industry,* January 1976, pp. 29–30.

20. Gale Kirking, "Dairyland's Milk Doesn't Match Ad Image," *Agri-view,* February 11, 1988.

21. "Fresh Chicken: It's a Long Way from Farmer Jones to Frank Perdue," *Consumer Reports,* May 1978, p. 255.

22. Earl Ainsworth, "Now a U.S. Ham That Will Cut into Competition," *Farm Journal,* September 1976, p. Hog-8.

23. Kathleen M. Dutro, "Swine Operations Need to Cut Variations in Carcass," *Illinois Agri-News,* Livestock, September 16, 1988, p. C-1.

24. Nita Effertz, "Can NCA Manage the Media?" *Beef Today* (a *Farm Journal* publication), January 1989, p. 11.

25. Ibid.

26. U.S. Department of Agriculture, Economics, Statistics and Cooperative Service, *Economic Effects of a Prohibition on the Use of Selected Animal Drugs,* Agricultural Economic Report No. 414 (Washington, D.C.: U.S. Department of Agriculture, November 1978), p. 4; and see note 19 to chapter 3.

27. "PBB: Michigan Contamination Continues," *Guardian,* May 4, 1977, p. 2.

28. Daniel Spitzer, "Is the Poisoning of Michigan Just the Start?" *Mother Jones,* May 1977, p. 18.

29. "Chlordane Residues in Broilers," *FDA Veterinarian,* March/April 1989, p. 12.

30. Charles W. Flora, "Heptachlor Contaminates Arkansas Poultry," *Feedstuffs,* January 30, 1989, p. 5.

31. Comptroller General of the United States, *Problems in Preventing the Marketing of Raw Meat and Poultry Containing Potentially Harmful Residues* (Washington, D.C.: General Accounting Office, April 17, 1979), p. i.

32. P. F. McGargle, "The Slaughterhouse Scandal," *World Magazine,* June 25, 1977, p. M-5.

33. Raghubir P. Sharma and Joseph C. Street, "Public Health Aspects of Toxic Metals in Animal Feeds," *American Veterinary Medical Association Journal,* July 15, 1980, p. 149.

34. "Hormones Used in Meat Are Safe," *FDA Veterinarian,* March/April 1989, p. 1.

35. National Research Council, *Regulating Pesticides in Food: The Delaney Paradox* (Washington D.C.: National Academy Press, 1987), Table 3-21, p. 79.

36. Ibid., Table 3-22, p. 80.

37. Remarks by Gerald B. Guest, D.V.M., Director of FDA's Center for Veterinary Medicine, at the FDA Pesticide Coordination Team Conference, February 1989, reported in "CVM Looks at Pesticide Residues," *FDA Veterinarian,* May/June 1989, pp. 7–8.

38. Ibid., p. 8.

39. Remarks by John C. Matheson III, Chief of Environmental Sciences of FDA's Center for Veterinary Medicine, at the symposium, *Environmental Studies Related to the Approval of New Animal Health Drugs,* Kalamazoo, Michigan, May 26, 1988, reported

in "Environmental Studies and the Approval of New Animal Drugs," *FDA Veterinarian,* September/October 1988, pp. 1–2.

40. U.S. House of Representatives, Committee on Government Operations, *Human Food Safety and Animal Drugs,* pp. 2–5.

41. "Sulfamethazine Update," *FDA Veterinarian,* May/June 1988.

42. Nancy King, "CVM Looks at Safety of Nation's Dairy Products," *FDA Veterinarian,* January/February 1989.

43. " 'Not for Use in Dairy Cattle' Label Required for Sulfa Drugs," *FDA Veterinarian,* March/April 1989, p. 5.

44. U.S. House of Representatives, Committee on Government Operations, *Human Food Safety and Animal Drugs,* p. 37.

45. Ibid., p. 38.

46. William K. Stevens, "Officials Call Microbes Most Urgent Food Threat," *The New York Times, Science Times,* March 28, 1989, p. B-5.

47. Ibid.

48. National Research Council, *Human Health Risks Penicillin Feed.* Tom Devine of Washington, D.C.'s Government Accountability Project estimates 9,000 deaths per year; see Tom Devine, "The Fox Guarding the Hen House," *Southern Exposure,* Summer 1989, p. 39.

49. "Egg-related Salmonellosis Stimulates Response," *Journal of the American Veterinary Medical Association,* March 1, 1989.

50. Jon F. Scheid, "Se-in-Egg Problem Divides Poultry Industry; Solutions Unclear," *Feedstuffs,* January 30, 1989.

51. Nancy King, "Salmonella Reported in Northeast," *FDA Veterinarian,* July/August 1988.

52. "Study Reveals Increasing Rate of Salmonella Excretion," *Journal of the American Medical Association,* July 1, 1989, p. 36.

53. Anthony Phelps, "Poultry Byproducts to No Longer Be Used in U.K. Poultry Feeds," *Feedstuffs,* January 1989, p. 8.

54. Marissa Miller, D.V.M., "Update on Human Foodborne Disease," *FDA Veterinarian,* November/December 1988, p. 7.

55. Ibid.

56. Daniel P. Puzo, "U.S. Finds Listeria in Raw Beef," *Los Angeles Times,* March 10, 1988.

57. "Listeria May Be Present in Hot Dogs," *Journal of the American Veterinary Medical Association,* March 1, 1989, p. 626.

58. "FSIS Takes Action to Combat *E. Coli* in Ground Beef," *Journal of the American Veterinary Medical Association,* March 1, 1989, p. 627.

59. Ibid.

60. "Chicken Soup: This Stuff Could Make You Sick—and Mad," *Arizona Daily Star,* Comment, Monday, July 10, 1989, p. A-10.

61. Schell, *Modern Meat,* pp. 324–5.

62. Remarks by Gerald B. Guest, Director of CVM, at the American Veterinary Distributors' Winter Conference, January 13, 1989, reported in "Need for Food Safety to Affect Animal Drug Problems," *Feedstuffs,* Viewpoints, February 13, 1989, p. 8.

63. "Feeder Pig Spokesman Asks Shipping, Starting Research," *National Hog Farmer,* May 1976, pp. 10–11.

64. An independent compilation of data from field investigations by both federal and state officials showed that failure to observe withdrawal times was the dominant cause of drug residues. In most cases, the farmer claimed he/she did not know the correct withdrawal time; in a minority of cases, the withdrawal time was known and disregarded. See W. R. Van Dresser, D.V.M., and J. R. Wilcke, D.V.M., "Drug Residues in Food Animals," *Journal of the American Medical Association,* June 15, 1989, p. 1700.

65. Ralph D. Wennblom, "Government Holds Firm on Sulfa Drugs," *Farm Journal,* mid-February 1978, p. Hog-13.

66. J. P. Kunesh, "Alternatives to Sulfamethazine in Swine Feeds and Therapeutics," *Large Animal Veterinarian,* November/December 1988.

67. D. L. Collins-Thompson et al., "Detection of Antibiotic Residues in Consumer Milk Supplies in North America Using the Charm Test II Procedure," *Journal of Food Protection,* August 1988, p. 632.

68. "FDA Studies Sulfamethazine in Milk," *FDA Veterinarian,* July/August 1989, p. 3.

69. "No Drugs Approved for Veal Calves, CVM Tells Producers," *Food Chemical News,* May 29, 1989, p. 41.

70. U.S. House of Representatives, Committee on Government Operations, *Human Food Safety and Animal Drugs,* pp. 24, 30.

71. Remarks of Richard H. Teske, D.V.M., Deputy Director, CVM, at the American Farm Bureau Federation Beef Cattle and Dairy Advisory Committee, reported in "Current Issues," *FDA Veterinarian,* May/June 1988, p. 12.

72. John Byrnes, "Let Them Eat Waste," *Hog Farm Management,* June 1978, p. 50.

73. Lester Crawford, then Director, CVM, quoted in *Feedstuffs,* March 12, 1984; "FDA Reports Illegal Sales of Animal Drugs," *Feedstuffs,* June 13, 1988.

74. U.S. House of Representatives, Committee on Government Operations, *Human Food Safety and Animal Drugs,* p. 5.

75. "Veterinary Drug Control Program Reported," *FDA Veterinarian,* March/April 1988, p. 8.

76. Ibid.

77. "USDA Planning Extended Sampling for Chloramphenicol, Neomycin," *Food Chemical News,* July 20, 1987.

78. "Availability of Compliance Policy Guide: Chloramphenicol as an Unapproved New Animal Drug," *FDA Veterinarian,* July/August 1988, p. 13.

79. Ibid.

80. "Survey Indicates Chloramphenicol Ban Successful," *FDA Veterinarian,* November/ December 1988, p. 11.

81. Ibid.

82. "Bulk Distributors Plead Guilty," *FDA Veterinarian,* July/August 1989, p. 11.

83. "Permanent Injunction Granted," *FDA Veterinarian,* November/December 1988, p. 12.

84. Ibid., p. 13.

85. Scott Holmberg, M.D., et al., "Drug Resistant Salmonella from Animals Fed Antimicrobials," *New England Journal of Medicine,* September 6, 1984.

86. A. Karim Ahmed, Ph.D., Sarah Chasis, and Bruce McBarnette, NRDC, to Hon. Margaret M. Heckler, Secretary of Health and Human Services, November 20, 1984, *Petition Requesting Immediate Suspension of Approval of the Subtherapeutic Use of Penicillin and Tetracycline in Animal Feeds,* Natural Resources Defense Council, 122 East 42d Street, New York, NY 10168.

87. E. R. Shipp, "Illinois Dairy Ceases Work in Outbreak of Salmonella," *The New York Times,* April 11, 1985.

88. John S. Spika, M.D., et al., "Chloramphenicol-Resistant *Salmonella newport* Traced Through Hamburger to Dairy Farms," *New England Journal of Medicine,* March 5, 1987.

89. M. S. Brady and S. E. Katz, "Antibiotic/Antimicrobial Residues in Milk," *Journal of Food Protection,* January 1988; H. Michael Wehr, "The Incidence of Antibiotics Other Than Penicillin in Producer Raw and Finished Milk Products," paper presented at the Annual Meeting of the International Association of Milk, Food and Environmental Sanitarians, held August 2–6, 1987 at Anaheim, California. (Not published.)

90. Mitchell L. Cohen and Robert V. Tauxe, "Drug-Resistant *Salmonella* in the United States: An Epidemiological Perspective," *Science,* November 21, 1986.

91. John K. Augsburg, D.V.M., Special Assistant to the Director, CVM, to Jim Mason,

August 8, 1989 (enclosing document entitled: "Recommendations of the Committee on Government Operations").

92. Ibid.

93. Ibid.

94. U.S. Department of Health and Human Services, U.S. Public Health Service, *Report of the Assistant Secretary for Health's Special Committee's Scientific Review of Concerns About the Animal Drug Evaluation Process Center for Veterinary Medicine, FDA,* April 1987.

95. Ibid.

96. Ibid.

97. U.S. House of Representatives, Committee on Government Operations, *Human Food Safety and Animal Drugs,* p. 8.

98. Van Dresser and Wilcke, *Drug Residues in Food Animals,* p. 1709.

99. U.S. House of Representatives, Committee on Government Operations, *Human Food Safety and Animal Drugs,* p. 27.

100. "Inspection—A Refreshing Challenge!" *Broiler Industry,* November 1975, p. 50.

101. National Research Council, *Meat and Poultry Inspection: The Scientific Basis of the Nation's Program* (Washington, D.C.: National Academy Press, 1985).

102. U.S. Congress, Office of Technology Assessment, *Pesticide Residues in Food: Technologies for Protection,* OTA-F-398 (Washington, D.C.: U.S. Government Printing Office, October 1988), p. 13.

103. Ibid., p. 88.

104. U.S. Department of Agriculture, Office of the Inspector General, Food Safety and Inspection Service, *Monitoring and Controlling Pesticide Residues in Domestic Meat and Poultry Products,* Audit Report No. 38609–1-At (Atlanta: U.S. Department of Agriculture, Office of the Inspector General, November 1988), p. 9.

105. Ibid., p. 1.

106. Ibid., p. 23.

107. Ibid., p. 28.

108. Bruce Ingersoll, "Slicing It Thin: Meat Inspection Cuts Proposed by Reagan Are Hot Issue for Bush; Consumerists Say Plan to End Daily Checks Comes Just as Food Poisoning Rises," *The Wall Street Journal,* February 2, 1989, p. 1.

109. Ibid., p. A12.

110. Nita Effertz, "Safe and Sorry: Beef Doesn't Escape the Flak over Tainted Food," *Beef Today* (a *Farm Journal* publication), May 1989, p. 11.

111. Ibid.

112. Daniel Hays, "Meat Packers Admit Bribes," *The Daily News* (New York), May 24, 1977; Peter Schuck, "The Curious Case of the Indicted Meat Inspectors," *Harper's,* September 1972, p. 81. The problems of industry influence and corruption of meat inspectors have been investigated and reported by a team of workers under Ralph Nader. Their report, written by Harrison Wellford, was published as *Sowing the Wind* (New York: Grossman Publishers, 1972).

113. "Grade A Whitewash," *The Progressive,* September 1985, p. 18.

114. "Angelotti Resigns as Head of Food Inspection Service," *Poultry Digest,* September 1978, p. 488; "Embattled USDA Chief Resigns," *National Hog Farmer,* September 1978, p. 106.

115. Animal Health Institute, *The Animal Health Institute Annual Report 1975* (Washington, D.C.: Animal Health Institute, 1975), p. 17.

116. Neal Black, "Prescription for High Costs, Less Drug Help," *National Hog Farmer,* September 1976, p. 36.

117. Gary L. Cromwell, "Antibiotic Feed Additive Benefits Documented," *National Hog Farmer,* April 1978, pp. 42, 46; and "Antibiotics," *NCA Digest* (National Cattlemen's Association, August 1978), I:9, p. 3.

118. John Russel, "Antibiotics in Feed: The First Punch Has Been Thrown," *Farm Journal,* June/July 1977, p. Hog-20; and Roland C. Hartman, "Will Antibiotics Use Survive?" *Poultry Digest,* October 1976, p. 395.

119. U.S. Department of Agriculture, Economics, Statistics and Cooperatives Service, National Economic Analysis Division, *Economic Effects of a Prohibition on the Use of Selected Animal Drugs,* Agricultural Economic Report No. 414 (Washington, D.C.: USDA, November 1978), p. ii; and John McClung, "Washington Report: USDA Reported Drug Ban Beneficial," *Hog Farm Management,* December 1978, p. 6.

120. Ibid.

121. Steve Frazier and Steve Weiner, "Many Cattlemen Ignored the Federal Ban on Use of DES to Speed Animals' Growth," *The Wall Street Journal,* July 15, 1980.

122. "DES Found in Veal Calves," *The New York Times,* March 16, 1984.

123. Samuel S. Epstein, M.D., "Potential Public Health Hazards of Biosynthetic Milk Hormones," *The Ecologist,* September 1989. See also: David S. Kronfeld, D.V.M., "Biologic and Economic Risks Associated with Use of Bovine Somatotropin," *Journal of the American Veterinary Medical Association,* June 15, 1989; and David S. Kronfeld, D.V.M., "BST Milk Safety," *Journal of the American Veterinary Medical Association,* Letters, August 1, 1989.

124. Committee on Government Operations, *Human Food Safety and Animal Drugs,* p. 6.

125. Ibid.

126. Ibid.

127. Comptroller General of the United States, Resources, Community and Economic Development Division, *Program to Address Problem Meat and Poultry Plants Needs Improvement* (Washington, D.C.: General Accounting Office, March 1989), p. 1.

128. Ibid.

129. Ibid.

Chapter 5

1. *Agricultural Statistics 1988,* Table 40, p. 31; Table 49, p. 39; Table 57, p. 44; Table 66, p. 51; Table 168, p. 125.

2. Frances Moore Lappé, *Diet for a Small Planet,* rev. ed. (New York: Ballentine Books, 1975).

3. "Eleven Thousand Dead Pigs on 26 Farms," *Successful Farming,* January 1977.

4. See generally, **Diseases in the Factory,** chapter 2.

5. Tony J. Cunha, "Productivity Must Be Increased," *Hog Farm Management,* February 1979.

6. D. G. Fox and F. R. Black, "New Tool Pulls It All Together: Systems Analysis," *Confinement,* May 1976.

7. Joy Collins, secretary to W. E. Huff, Agricultural Research Service, U.S. Department of Agriculture, to Jim Mason, August 25, 1989, with enclosure entitled "Animal Disease Research Priorities," Council of Deans, Association of American Veterinary Medical Colleges. The report's figures are based on 1976 information, however, so we may assume that current figures would be even higher.

8. *Agricultural Statistics 1988,* Table 581, p. 409. Total income to farmers from livestock and poultry production in 1987 was $74 billion.

9. B. H. Ashby and T. F. Webb, *Needs for Improving Livestock Transportation and Handling Facilities* (Beltsville, MD: U.S. Department of Agriculture, 1974).

10. John R. Dawson, "Death Enroute to Market," *Confinement,* June 1977, p. 14.

11. *Agricultural Statistics 1988,* Table 514, p. 359. Calculated by dividing pounds condemned antemortem by average live weight. Average live weight calculated by dividing pounds inspected by number inspected.

12. Ibid.

13. *Agricultural Statistics 1988,* Table 461, p. 312.

14. John B. Herrick, "Liver Abscesses Are Costly Problem in Most Feedlots," *Beef,* September 1976.

15. Temple Grandin, "Cutting PSE Takes Producer-Packer Commitment," *Hog Farm Management,* August 1983.

16. Ibid.

17. Ibid.

18. Harrison Wellford, *Sowing the Wind* (New York: Grossman Publishers, 1972).

19. J. T. Reid, "Comparative Efficiency of Animals in the Conversion of Feedstuffs to Human Foods," *Confinement,* April 1976.

20. "Oxidation Ditches Save Money," *Farm Journal,* October 1976.

21. W. L. Roller, H. M. Keener, and R. D. Kline, "Energy Costs of Intensive Livestock Production" (St. Joseph, MI: American Society of Agricultural Engineers, June 1975), paper no. 75-4042, Table 7, p. 14.

22. Ibid.

23. Ibid.

24. Ibid., p. 6.

25. Frances Moore Lappé, *Diet for a Small Planet,* Tenth Anniversary Edition (New York: Ballantine Books, 1982), p. 66.

Chapter 6

1. Raymond C. Loehr, *Pollution Control for Agriculture,* 2d ed. (Orlando, FL: Academic Press, Harcourt Brace Jovanovich, 1984).

2. Raymond C. Loehr, *Pollution Implications of Animals Wastes—A Forward-Oriented Review,* Water Pollution Control Research Series (Washington, D.C.: Office of Research and Monitoring, U.S. Environmental Protection Agency, 1968), p. 26 and Table 7, p. 27. A hen in confinement produces about 0.39 pounds of manure per day; 60,000 hens produce 163,800 pounds of manure per week, or 81.9 tons. One pig produces about 17.36 pounds of mixed manure and urine each day, or 121.52 pounds each week.

3. Ibid.

4. Loehr, *Pollution Control,* p. 72; and H. A. Jasiorowski, "Intensive Systems of Animal Production," *Proceedings of the III World Conference on Animal Production,* ed. R. L. Reid (Sydney: Sydney University Press, 1975), pp. 369, 384.

5. Loehr, *Pollution Implications*, pp. 22–3.

6. Sue Armstrong, "Marooned in a Mountain of Manure," *New Scientist*, November 26, 1988.

7. Ibid., pp. 51, 53.

8. Ibid.

9. "Products for Odor Control Fail Tests," *National Hog Farmer*, February 1979, p. 24.

10. Letter in "Hoginformation Please," *National Hog Farmer*, December 1975, p. 36.

11. "Feedlot Leaves Trail of Debt and Ill Feelings," *Lawrence County Record* (Mt. Vernon, MO), September 28, 1978.

12. Ralph Watkins, "Pollution Issue Used to Block Large Unit," *National Hog Farmer*, July 1978.

13. Ralph Watkins, "Odor Complaints Force Custom Feedlot Shutdown," *National Hog Farmer*, April 1978.

14. *Vegetarian Times*, News Digest, June 1989.

15. Andy Parker, "Virginians Raise Stink over Hog Farms," *Washington Business*, July 18, 1988.

16. Ibid.

17. Bradley Flory, " 'Them Fumes' Revolted Parma Neighbors," *The Jackson Citizen Patriot*, June 25, 1989.

18. Veronica Fowler, "Blocked in Iowa, Hog Operation Tries Missouri," *Des Moines Register*, April 27, 1989.

19. Patrick Beach, "State Actions Doom Hog Lot Next to Park," *Des Moines Register*, February 11, 1989, p. 1.

20. Ibid.

21. "Handling Waste Disposal Problems," *Hog Farm Management*, April 1978, pp. 16, 18.

22. Ibid., p. 17.

23. *Epidemiological Aspects of Some of the Zoonoses*, DHEW Publication no. CDC 75-8182 (Atlanta: U.S. Department of Health, Education and Welfare, Center for Disease Control, Office of Veterinary Public Health Services, November 1973); W. T. Hubbert, W. F. McCullough, and P. R. Schnurrenberger, *Diseases Transmitted from Animals to Man* (Springfield, IL: Charles C. Thomas, 1975).

24. Vivian Wiser, *Protecting American Agriculture: Inspection and Quarantine of Im-*

ported Plants and Animals, Agricultural Economic Report no. 266 (Washington, D.C.: U.S. Department of Agriculture, Veterinary Services, Animal and Plant Health Inspection Services, July 1975), p. 2.

25. Bill Miller, "Brucellosis," *Successful Farming,* August 1978, p. B-18.

26. John A. Rohlf, "We Have Tools to Eradicate Brucellosis," *Farm Journal,* March 1976, p. Beef-14; and "Showdown on Brucellosis," *Farm Journal,* January 1976, p. Beef-9.

27. Animal and Plant Inspection Service, *Hog Cholera and Its Eradication: A Review of the U.S. Experience,* APHIS 91-55 (Washington, D.C.: U.S. Department of Agriculture, September 1981).

28. Animal and Plant Inspection Service, *Eradication of Exotic Newcastle Disease in Southern California 1971–1974,* APHIS 91-34 (Washington, D.C.: U.S. Department of Agriculture, February 1978).

29. "Pseudorabies Eradication Plan Drafted," *National Hog Farmer,* March 1977, p. 136.

30. John Byrnes, "Demand Grows for PRV Vaccine," *Hog Farm Management,* May 1977, pp. 18, 20.

31. "Area Depopulation Plan Suggested for Dominican," *National Hog Farmer,* December 1978, p. 34.

32. *Agricultural Statistics 1988,* Table 628, p. 450.

33. Ibid.

34. According to the Federal Election Commission, three dairy cooperatives contributed a total of $1.5 million to campaigns for federal offices in 1987–88.

35. *Agricultural Statistics 1988,* Table 625, p. 450.

36. "SBA and FmHA Loan Programs Violate 1977 Farm Bill," Center for Rural Affairs Newsletter (Walthill, NE), August 1979.

37. Marty Strange, *Family Farming: A New Economic Vision* (San Francisco: Institute for Food and Development Policy, 1988), p. 156.

38. "Poultry Scientists Receive Awards," *Broiler Industry,* September 1976, p. 68.

39. Strange, *Family Farming,* p. 217.

Chapter 7

1. U.S. Congress, Office of Technology Assessment, *Technology, Public Policy and the Changing Structure of American Agriculture,* OTA-F-285 (Washington, D.C.: U.S. Government Printing Office, March 1986), p. 91.

2. Ibid.

3. Ibid.

4. Ibid.

5. Ibid.

6. Ibid.

7. Ibid.

8. David W. Wilson, "Hear Me. . . . Why Farmers Get Big," *Farm Journal,* September 1976, p. 14.

9. Strange, *Family Farming,* p. 127.

10. James T. Bonnen, "The Distribution of Benefits from Selected U.S. Farm Programs," *Rural Poverty in the United States: A Report by the President's National Advisory Commission on Rural Poverty* (Washington, D. C.: U.S. Government Printing Office, 1968), cited in Strange, *Family Farming,* p. 128.

11. The figures for 1987 are according to the Center for Rural Affairs, Walthill, NE. See also: OTA, *Technology, Public Policy;* "Making Farmers Disappear," *The Progressive,* November 1976, p. 9; and Peter M. Emerson et al., *Public Policy and the Changing Structure of American Agriculture* (Washington, D.C.: U.S. Government Printing Office, August 1975).

12. Strange, *Family Farming,* p. 130.

13. Don Paarlberg, "Land Prices Are Running a Fever," *Farm Journal,* April 1977, p. 17.

14. Robert L. Lam, "Beef Checkoff Problems," *Iowa Farmer Today,* Letters to the Editor, April 30, 1988, p. 2.

15. Neal Black, "Let's Give USDA to Do-Gooders, Gardeners," *National Hog Farmer,* August 1976, p. 26.

16. "New 'Food Policy' Report Overlooks Past Experiences," *Beef,* April 1977, p. 12.

17. Debra Switzky, "Seedstock, Confinement Trends Forecast," *National Hog Farmer,* February 1977, pp. 103–4.

18. From "The Industrial Farm as a Multinational Business," by Stephen Singular, copyright © 1975 by News Group Publications, Inc., Reprinted with the permission of *New York* magazine.

19. "Egg Business Roundup: The Big Boys Are Doing the Expansion," *Poultry Tribune,* February 1975, p. 8.

20. Ibid.

21. Robert H. Brown, "As Number of Flocks Drops, Industry Seeks Ways to Stem Loss of Producers," *Feedstuffs,* Special Emphasis, January 30, 1989.

22. Comptroller General of the United States, *Regulation of the Poultry Industry Under the Packers and Stockyards Act* (Washington, D.C.: U.S. General Accounting Office, April 13, 1984).

23. Ibid.; and *Agricultural Statistics 1988,* Table 508, p. 356.

24. Tom Devine, "The Fox Guarding the Hen House," *Southern Exposure,* Summer 1989.

25. Bob Hall, "Chicken Empires," *Southern Exposure,* Summer 1989.

26. Barry Yeoman, "Don't Count Your Chickens," *Southern Exposure,* Summer 1989.

27. Ibid., p. 22.

28. Hall, "Chicken Empires," *Southern Exposure.*

29. Edward H. Covell, "Enough Is Enough," *Broiler Industry,* June 1976.

30. "Automation Can Halve Plant Labor in 3 Years," *Broiler Industry,* January 1977.

31. Eldon Kreisel, Rocheport, Missouri, hog producer, quoted in Glenn Grimes, "Role of Large Hog Units Is Uncertain," *Hog Farm Management,* August 1977, p. 56.

32. Bob Tuten, "Hogs, Territory Expansion in Pennfield's Growth Plan," *Broiler Industry,* December 1975, pp. 22, 23.

33. Ken Haggerty, "Big Boys Smell Profits in Pork: That's Why Giants Like Tyson Are Pushing to Boost the Number of Poultry-Style Pork Production Outfits," *Agweek,* September 4, 1989, p. 17.

34. Ibid.

35. John Byrnes, "Rating Your Worst Nightmare," *Hogs Today* (A *Farm Journal* publication), May/June 1989, p. 36.

36. Haggerty, "Big Boys Smell Profits."

37. Joan M. McKee, "Corporate Farmer Cultivates New Agricultural Trends," *Missouri Alumnus,* Winter 1989, p. 80.

38. Ibid.

39. "Some Hogmen Quit—Others Keep Expanding," *Successful Farming,* 1976 Planning Issue, December 1975, p. H-12.

40. Ibid.

41. V. J. Rhodes and G. A. Grimes, "The Structure of Pork Production," *Confinement,* September 1976, p. 23.

42. John Russnogle, "Farm Countdown Continues," *Top Producer* (a *Farm Journal* publication), April 1989, p. 25.

43. John Byrnes, "In Surveys, Hogmen Nix Corporate Farms," *Hogs Today* (a *Farm Journal* publication), January 1989, p. 43.

44. Ibid.

45. "Pork Leader Sees Five Change Areas," *Hogs Today* (a *Farm Journal* publication), January 1989, p. 38.

46. Don Kendall, "Livestock Industry Grows Concentrated," *Tri-State Neighbor*, March 24, 1989.

47. William Robbins, "A Meat Packer Cartel Up Ahead?" *The New York Times*, May 29, 1988.

48. Ibid.

49. Charles Johnson, "A Herdsman at Heart," *Dairy Today* (a *Farm Journal* publication), May 1989, p. 26.

50. "$27 Million in Escrow to Kill Anti-trust Suit," *Broiler Industry*, September 1977, p. 24; and "Broiler Marketing Group Votes to Disband," *Poultry Digest*, September 1978, p. 488.

51. "EGGMAR Has 'Muscle' as It Starts Central Selling," *Egg Industry*, August 1976, p. 14; and "EGGMAR in Perspective," *Egg Industry*, October 1976, p. 38.

52. Joe Belden and Gregg Forte, *Toward a National Food Policy* (Washington, D.C.: Exploratory Project for Economic Alternatives, 1976), p. 80; Linda Kravitz, *Who's Minding the Co-op?* (Washington, D.C.: Agribusiness Accountability Project, March 1974).

53. Ibid.

54. Bob Doerschuk, "America's Last Monopoly: Milk Monoliths Examined," *Nutrition Action*, January 1976.

55. Kravitz, *Who's Minding the Co-op?*

56. "Beeferendum Effort," *Confinement*, October 1978.

57. "Beef Producers Face Off Over Checkoff," *The Farmer*, April 16, 1988.

58. "Egg Board Budgets $6.3 Million for 1979," *Poultry Digest*, September 1978.

59. "UDIA Working Hard to Promote Dairy Products," *Successful Farming*, March 1976.

60. "Swift to Push Chicken Brand," *Broiler Industry*, September 1976, p. 58.

61. Stanley E. Curtis, "Getting the Story Told," *Confinement*, May 1978, p. 18.

62. J. M. Lewis et al., "More on Sheep Flooring," *Confinement,* July–August 1977, p. 6.

63. John A. Rohlf, "Your Beef Business," *Farm Journal,* December 1978, p. Beef-20.

64. Roland C. Harman, "Countering with Facts," *Poultry Digest,* March 1978, p. 114.

65. Bayard Webster, "6 Scientists Quit Panel in Dispute over Livestock Drugs," *The New York Times,* January 23, 1979, p. C-2; "Scientists Quit Antibiotics Panel at CAST," *Science,* February 23, 1979, p. 732.

Chapter 8

1. *Agricultural Statistics 1988,* Table 680, p. 494.

2. Bernice K. Watt and Annabel L. Merrill, "Nutrients in the Edible Portion of One Pound of Food as Purchased," *Composition of Foods,* Agriculture Handbook No. 8 (Washington, D.C.: U.S. Department of Agriculture, October 1975), Table 2, pp. 68–121.
    The table lists the number of grams of protein in one pound of each of the various kinds of meat, eggs, and dairy products. For example, one pound of chicken (ready to cook) contains 57.4 grams of protein; one pound of whole eggs, 52.1 grams, one pound of whole fluid milk, 15.9 grams of protein, and so on. To calculate the grams of protein from animal products consumed by the average American, we multiplied each of these figures by the corresponding number of pounds of each animal product consumed per year (per capita consumption from Fig. 8-1). After totaling these, we find that per capita intake of protein from animal products is 23,373.19 grams each year, or 69.5 grams per day.

3. Boyce Rensberger, "For Most, Beef Is the Staple," *The New York Times,* May 24, 1978, p. C-1.

4. Belden and Forte, *Toward a National Food Policy.*

5. Nathaniel Altman, "Revising the 'Basic Four,'" *Vegetarian Times,* September/October 1977.

6. F. J. Schling and M. C. Phillips, *Meat Three Times a Day* (New York: Richard R. Smith, 1946), p. 54.

7. Frances Moore Lappé and Joseph Collins, *Food First: Beyond the Myth of Scarcity* (Boston: Houghton Mifflin Co., 1977).

8. Frances Moore Lappé, *Diet for a Small Planet,* rev. ed., (New York: Ballantine Books, 1975), p. xvii.

9. Ibid.

10. National Research Council, *Diet and Health: Implications for Reducing Chronic Disease Risk* (Washington, D.C.: National Academy Press, 1989), p. 7.

11. Ibid., p. 9.

12. *Beef,* January 1979, p. A-3.

13. "Climbing the Protein Ladder," *Farm Journal,* December 1978, p. 52.

14. Lappé and Collins, *Food First.*

15. Drew DeSilver, "Beefing Up Sales; Meat Industry Targets Japan," News Digest, *Vegetarian Times,* February 1988.

16. Wellford, *Sowing the Wind.*

17. Yeoman, *Southern Exposure.*

18. Warren Kester, "How Much Integration for the Pork Industry?" *Farm Journal,* October 1975, H-6.

19. OTA, *Technology, Public Policy;* and Emerson, *Public Policy.*

20. Gene Logsden, "Leave Us Alone and We'll Produce the Food," *Farm Journal,* June/July 1976, p. 16.

21. *Farm Journal,* August 1976, p. 12.

22. *An Enquiry into the Effects of Modern Livestock Production on the Total Environment* (London: The Farm and Food Society, 1972), p. 12.

23. A. J. Koltveit, D.V.M., of Elgin, IL, in *Confinement,* November/December 1976, p. 3.

24. Rod Smith, "Feed Official Asks Producers to Take Welfarists Seriously," *Feedstuffs,* July 11, 1988, p. 7.

25. Animal Industry Foundation, *Animal Agriculture: Myths and Facts* (no publisher, address, or date given).

26. Ibid., p. 10.

27. Ibid., p. 13.

28. Robert H. Brown, "UEP Developing Bird Welfare Guidelines for Family Farms," *Feedstuffs,* June 20, 1988.

29. Ibid.

30. John Russel, "Call Them Maternity Beds," Pigs and Pork, *Hogs Today* (a *Farm Journal* publication), March 1989, p. 4.

31. John Byrnes, "Rating Your Worst Nightmare," *Hogs Today* (a *Farm Journal* publication), May/June 1989.

32. Ralph Watkins, "Large Units Appear Inevitable," *Hogs Today* (a *Farm Journal* publication), July/August 1989, p. 11.

33. Gene Logsden, "Maybe the Animal Rights Movement Is Good for Us," *Farm Journal*, January 1989, p. 26-D.

34. Ibid.

35. Dan Murphy, "Achilles Heel on Veal," *Meat Processing*, February 1989, p. 4.

36. Page Smith and Charles Daniel, *The Chicken Book* (Boston and Toronto: Little, Brown and Company, 1975), p. 303.

Chapter 9

1. Frances Moore Lappé and Joseph Collins, *Food First: Beyond the Myth of Scarcity* (Boston: Houghton Mifflin Co., 1977), p. 403.

2. John Robbins, *Diet for a New America* (Walpole, New Hampshire: Stillpoint Publishing, 1987), p. xv.

3. "Vegetarianism Becoming More Popular, Menus Shifting to Match the Growing Demand," *Meat Board Reports* (Chicago: National Livestock and Meat Board), March 28, 1977, p. 4.

4. Private communication from the Roper Organization, December 1978; "A New Vegetarian Poll," *Vegetarian Times*, January/February 1979.

5. "How to Match Capital and Labor in the Hog Business," *Successful Farming*, January 1977.

6. John Dawson, "No Farrowing Crates, No Antibiotics, No Furnaces, No Fans . . . But the Pigs Come First," *Confinement*, June 1976.

7. "Planned Exposure Breaks SMEDI's Hold," *Successful Farming*, March 1976 (Nebraska); Vance Ehmke, "Farrowing Huts a Practical Way to Boost Volume," *Farm Journal*, December 1976 (Kansas); John Byrnes, "Slatted Floors Are Starting to Mix with Bedding," *Hog Farm Management*, November 1978 (Ohio); and Ron Brunoehler, "I'll Never Have Crates Again," *Successful Farming*, 1979 (Wisconsin).

8. Dale McKee, "Ten Years of Confinement Raises More Questions Than Answers," *Hog Farm Management*, March 1979, p. 124.

9. Ibid.

10. Ibid.

11. "Outside Pigs More Efficient," *National Hog Farmer*, January 1977.

12. Milton Y. Dendy, "Highlights of Poultry Science Meeting Reports: 20 More Eggs for Floor System," *Poultry Digest*, September 1976, p. 366; and G. A. Martin et al., "Layer Performance in Cage vs. Non-Cage Housing," paper presented by G. W. Morton, Jr., at 65th Annual Meeting of Poultry Science Association at Kansas State University, Manhattan, Kansas, August 2–6, 1976 (abstracted in *Poultry Science* 55:5 [1976], 2060).

13. National Research Council, *Alternative Agriculture* (Washington, D.C.: National Academy Press, 1989), pp. 167–8.

14. Ibid.

15. Ibid., p. 228.

16. Logsden, *Farm Journal.*

17. Ibid.

18. Swedish Ministry of Agriculture, press release #109 (Stockholm, December 2, 1987).

19. Keith Schneider, "Science Academy Says Chemicals Do Not Necessarily Increase Crops," *The New York Times,* September 8, 1989, p. A-1.

20. Karen Brown, "A Mobile Sow Is a Happy One," *Hog Farm Management,* March 1979, p. 18.

21. Ibid.

22. Ibid.

23. Robert C. Otte, "Farming in the City's Shadow: Urbanization of Land and Changes in Farm Output in Standard Metropolitan Statistical Areas, 1960–1970," Agricultural Economics Report no. 250 (Washington, D.C.: Economic Research Service, USDA, February 1974).

24. Terry Gips, "Silent Spring or Sustainable Agriculture?" An unpublished paper dated June 5, 1989. Gips is founder and director of the International Alliance for Sustainable Agriculture at the University of Minnesota, Minneapolis.

25. Marcia D. Lowe, "Low-Input Farming Holds High Promise," *Worldwatch,* November/December 1988.

26. National Research Council, *Designing Foods,* p. 298.

27. From an interview with Chuck Frazier, National Farmers Organization, April 20, 1979.

28. Lappé and Collins, *Food First;* Susan George, *How the Other Half Dies* (Montclair, New Jersey: Allanheld, Osmun and Company, 1977).

29. Ibid.

30. Joe Belden et al., eds., *New Directions in Farm, Land and Food Policies: A Time for State and Local Action* (Washington, D.C.: Conference on State and Local Policies, n.d.).

GENERAL REFERENCES

On Agriculture, Agribusiness, and Food Policy

Hassebrook, Chuck, and Hegyes, Gabriel. *Choices for the Heartland: Alternative Directions in Biotechnology and Implications for Family Farming, Rural Communities and the Environment*. Ames, Iowa: Iowa State University Research Foundation, 1989.

Hightower, Jim. *Eat Your Heart Out*. New York: Vintage Books, 1975.

Hur, Robin. *Food Reform: Our Desperate Need*. Austin, Texas: Heidelberg, 1975.

Lappé, Frances Moore, and Collins, Joseph. *Food First: Beyond the Myth of Scarcity*. Boston: Houghton Mifflin Company, 1977.

National Research Council. *Alternative Agriculture*. Washington, D.C.: National Academy Press, 1989.

Ray, Victor K. *The Corporate Invasion of American Agriculture*. Denver: The National Farmers Union, 1968.

Strange, Marty. *Family Farming: A New Economic Vision*. San Francisco: Institute for Food and Development Policy, 1988.

United States Congress, Office of Technology Assessment. *Technology, Public Policy, and the Changing Structure of American Agriculture*. Washington, D.C.: U.S. Government Printing Office, March 1986.

On Agriculture and Environment

Berry, Wendell. *A Continuous Harmony: Essays Cultural and Agricultural*. New York: Harcourt Brace Jovanovich (A Harvest Book), 1970.

Lappé, Frances Moore. *Diet for a Small Planet*, 2d rev. ed. New York: Ballantine Books, 1987.

National Research Council. *Alternative Agriculture*. Washington, D.C.: National Academy Press, 1989.

Regenstein, Lewis. *America the Poisoned*. Washington, D.C.: Acropolis Books, 1982.

On Intensive Animal Systems and Methods

Fox, Michael W. *Farm Animals: Husbandry, Behavior, and Veterinary Practice*. Baltimore: University Park Press, 1984.

Harrison, Ruth. *Animal Machines*. London: Vincent Stuart, Ltd., 1964.

Schell, Orville. *Modern Meat: Antibiotics, Hormones, and the Pharmaceutical Farm*. New York: Random House, 1984.

Singer, Peter. *Animal Liberation*, 2d ed. New York: New York Review of Books, 1990.

On Diet, Nutrition, and Living Without Animal Products

Boyd, Billy Ray. *For the Vegetarian in You*. San Francisco: Tater Hill Press, 1988.

Goldbeck, Nikki, and Goldbeck, David. *Nikki & David Goldbeck's American Wholefoods Cuisine*. New York: New American Library, 1984.

Langley, Gill. *Vegan Nutrition*. Oxford, U.K.: The Vegan Society, 1988.

Lappé, Frances Moore, *Diet for a Small Planet*, 2d rev. ed. New York: Ballantine Books, 1987.

McDougall, John A., and McDougall, Mary A., *The McDougall Plan*. Piscataway, New Jersey: New Century Publishers, 1983.

National Research Council. *Diet and Health: Implications for Reducing Chronic Disease Risk*. Washington, D.C.: National Academy Press, 1989.

Robbins, John. *Diet for a New America*. Walpole, New Hampshire: Stillpoint Publishing, 1987.

Robertson, Laurel, Flinders, Carol, and Ruppenthal, Brian. *The New Laurel's Kitchen*. Berkeley: Ten Speed Press, 1986.

Scharffenberg, John A., M.D. *Problems with Meat*. Santa Barbara, California: Woodbridge Press Publishing Company, 1979.

U.S. Department of Health, Education and Welfare, Public Health Service. *Healthy People: The Surgeon General's Report on Health Promotion and Disease Prevention*. Washington, D.C.: U.S. Government Printing Office, 1979.

Vegetarian Times. Monthly magazine. P.O. Box 570, Oak Park, Illinois, (708) 848-8100.

On Food Quality, Additives, and Consumer Concerns

National Research Council. *Designing Foods: Animal Product Options in the Marketplace*. Washington, D.C.: National Academy Press, 1988.

National Research Council. *Meat and Poultry Inspection: The Scientific Basis of the Nation's Program*. Washington, D.C.: National Academy Press, July 1985.

National Research Council. *Regulating Pesticides in Food: The Delaney Paradox*. Washington, D.C.: National Academy Press, 1987.

United States Congress, Office of Technology Assessment. *Pesticide Residues in Food: Technologies for Detection*. Washington, D.C.: U.S. Government Printing Office, October 1988.

United States House of Representatives, Committee on Government Operations. *Human Food Safety and the Regulation of Animal Drugs*. Washington, D.C.: U.S. Government Printing Office, 1985.

Organizations

Organizations with Actions and Publications on Agriculture and Food

Americans for Safe Food
1501 16th Street NW
Washington, DC 20036

Center for Rural Affairs
P.O. Box 405
Walthill, NE 68067

Institute for Food and Development Policy
2588 Mission Street
San Francisco, CA 94110

International Alliance for Sustainable Agriculture
Newman Center
1701 University Ave. SE
Minneapolis, MN 55414

Institute for Alternative Agriculture
9200 Edmonston Road
Suite 117
Greenbelt, MD 20770

National Save the Family Farm Coalition
Suite 714
80 F Street NW
Washington, DC 20001

Rural Advancement Fund
P.O. Box 1029
Pittsboro, NC 27312

Wisconsin Rural Development Center
P.O. Box 504
Black Earth, WI 53513

Organizations with Actions and Publications on Farm Animal Welfare

Animal Welfare Institute
P.O. Box 3650
Washington, DC 20007

Compassion in World Farming
20 Lavant Street
Petersfield, Hampshire GU32 3EW
United Kingdom

Farm Animal Reform Movement
P.O. Box 70123
Washington, DC 20088

Farm Animal Sanctuary
P.O. Box 150
Watkins Glen, NY 14891

Food Animal Concerns Trust
P.O. Box 14599
Chicago, IL 60614

Humane Farming Association
Suite 6
1550 California Street
San Francisco, CA 94109

Humane Sustainable Agriculture Program
The Humane Society of the United States
2100 L Street NW
Washington, DC 20037

INDEX

235